The Letchworth State Park Atlas

The Letchworth State Park Atlas

Exploring Its Nature, History, and Tourism through Maps

STEPHEN J. TULOWIECKI

EXCELSIOR EDITIONS

Cover image: Lower Falls, Upper Falls, and the Genesee Arch Bridge from Inspiration Point in autumn; cover image and all other photography by Keith Walters

Published by State University of New York Press, Albany

© 2022 State University of New York

Excelsior Editions is an imprint of State University of New York Press

For information, contact State University of New York Press, Albany, NY
www.sunypress.edu

Library of Congress Cataloging-in-Publication Data

Name: Tulowiecki, Stephen J., author.
Title: The Letchworth State Park atlas : exploring its nature, history, and
    tourism through maps / Stephen J. Tulowiecki.
Description: Albany : State University of New York Press, [2022] | Includes
    bibliographical references.
Identifiers: ISBN 9781438489513 (ebook) | ISBN 9781438489506 (pbk. : alk. paper)
Further information is available at the Library of Congress.

10 9 8 7 6 5 4 3 2 1

To my two best hiking partners:
Grace and Jonah, and to the one coming soon—
can't wait to get you on the trails

Contents

List of Maps

List of Photographs

Acknowledgments

This project would not have been possible without the help of many. I first thank those who assisted with data collection and the creation of maps. Thanks to the employees of Letchworth State Park and the New York State Office of Parks, Recreation, and Historic Preservation for providing datasets and access to their records, as well as early feedback on this project. These individuals are Douglas Kelly, Charles King, Karen Russell, Douglas Bassett, Brian Scriven, Elijah Kruger, and Sandra Wallace. I thank Thomas Cook of the Nunda Historical Society for his many helpful conversations and suggestions regarding the human history of the park. Cynthia Amrhein of the Wyoming County Historian's Office provided access to the original land survey "field notes" of the Cottringer Tract. Holly Watson of the Livingston County Historian's Office provided a transcription of the Cascade House guestbook. Nicole Manapol and Nina Puccini of the Letchworth Gateway Villages initiative provided results from their 2017 visitor survey. Thanks to the Sheriff's Offices of Livingston County and Wyoming County who provided data on 911 calls. Thank you to my research assistants during the spring of 2021, Katie Singleton and Emma Barrett, for assistance with creating some of the more challenging maps, including the original Glen Iris Estate and of the life journeys of Mary Jemison and William P. Letchworth.

Many individuals also assisted with improving and completing this atlas. Thanks to those who reviewed advanced drafts: Thomas Cook, Karen Russell, Dr. Richard Young, Dr. Paul Pacheco, Dr. Michael Oberg, Dr. D. Jeffrey Over, Thomas Breslin, and Charles King. Thanks to everyone at my publisher SUNY Press who helped me through the project. The Geneseo Foundation provided funding to hire an adjunct professor to grant me a course release for one semester to focus on this project, and provided funding to purchase rights to the photos that adorn this atlas. Thanks also to Keith Walters for capturing the beauty of the park through photos, and to my colleagues in the Department of Geography and Sustainability Studies for their various forms of support. Thank you to my wonderful wife Grace for her support and for reading early drafts of the atlas.

Preface

In 1899, Frank and Edith Hill of Mount Morris, New York, received a leather-bound photo album as a Christmas gift from Frank's brother Albert. Along with other photos of western New York locations—such as Niagara Falls, the Erie Canal, and the City of Rochester—the album contained photos of what would become Letchworth State Park. Taken in the 1890s, the photos showed the shale rock faces of the Mount Morris Highbanks and the grand waterfalls of the Genesee River within the Portage Glen. Another showed a railroad track at the top of a cliff hundreds of feet above the river downstream from Middle Falls. There were photos of rustic wooden fences bordering ponds on the country estate of Mr. Letchworth. Yet another captured the moment a train crossed the tall iron railroad bridge above Upper Falls. Another showed the ruins of a paper mill atop waterfalls on Silver Lake Outlet. In some of the photos, farms and houses dot the bottomlands of the valley upon lands that the Mount Morris Dam and Reservoir would flood six decades later.

I received this photo album after its previous owner passed away in 2004: my grandfather Howard Jr., grandson of Frank and great-nephew of the photographer Albert. Somehow these photos remained preserved. Like my great-grandfather Howard Sr.—son of Frank and who lived to the age of 106—the photos lived through the entire twentieth century.

Letchworth State Park has always been close to me both geographically and metaphorically. I grew up an hour west of the park. My first childhood visit to the cliffs at Great Bend remains fresh in my memory. I went to college at SUNY Geneseo ten minutes north of the park where I met my wife, and where I am now a professor in the Department of Geography and Sustainability Studies. For two decades I have visited the park to hike its trails, an activity that provided a respite during the pandemic in 2020 when I visited the park almost weekly—and a time when I first imagined this atlas. And here in the twenty-first century, I continue to photograph the same vistas of the park that Albert did in the 1890s.

The decision to create an atlas of Letchworth State Park was not only a professional decision as a researcher, but also a personal one. The project provided a reason for me to explore the park through texts, documents, articles, reports, maps, photos, and datasets. It addressed an absence of maps that explore the many facets of the park. It led me to visit places within the park that were new to me to learn more of its nature, history, and tourism. It was an opportunity to apply my writing, research, and cartography skills toward a project that could in turn enrich others' experiences within the park—to pay forward what the park had given me. Indirectly, my work enlivened and humanized those scenes shown in Albert's photos that were long a curiosity of mine. The project gave me the opportunity to answer questions I have long held about the park, questions motivated in part by Albert's photos: how such a spectacular landscape could exist within the otherwise modest terrain of western New York State, and how a landscape that today seems so pristine could have once been so heavily utilized by industry. And through the project, I realized just how intergenerational the park is to families, including my own: with my son Jonah's first trip in 2019 at the age of two months, he became at least the sixth generation in my family to visit the park.

I hope you enjoy this atlas as much as I enjoyed creating it, and as much as I enjoy the park itself. I also hope it allows you to rediscover and reimagine the park in many new ways.

Imperial to Metric Conversion
for this Atlas

Distance

1 inch = 2.54 centimeters

1 foot = 30.48 centimeters = 0.3048 meters

1 yard = 91.44 centimeters = 0.9144 meters

1 mile = 1,609 meters = 1.609 kilometers

Area

1 acre = 0.405 hectare

1 square mile = 259.0 hectares = 2.590 square kilometers

Volume

1 acre-foot = 1,233,482 liters = 1.233 megaliters

Temperature and temperature change

$$°C = \frac{5}{9} \ (°F - 32)$$

1° F increase = 0.6° C increase

Introduction

What Is the Scope of This Atlas?

The Letchworth State Park Atlas is a collection of thematic maps that provide a geographic perspective on the nature, human history, and tourism of Letchworth State Park. The atlas brings to light novel datasets and synthesizes existing data on the park in unique and meaningful ways. The atlas presents new maps on the park, rather than compiling existing maps; for those seeking historical and other maps, see the resources at the end of this introduction and in the bibliography. While this atlas attempts to provide a complete and well-rounded picture of the park, it supplements rather than repeats existing texts on Letchworth State Park. The atlas focuses on phenomena that vary across space within the park, yet many maps cover a wider geographic extent when more precise data are not available or when Letchworth State Park requires contextualization within a region. For example, Map 28 shows the number of rare species in New York state parks: precise locational data on these species are not publicly available nor shareable, and to manifest Letchworth State Park's relative value as a refuge for rare species the map compares the number of species in the park to other state parks.

This map atlas contains few "zoom-ins" (large-scale maps) of areas within the park. One reason is that much can change in the park at a fine scale in just a few years. More importantly, this atlas does not include detailed large-scale maps due to the archaeological and ecological sensitivity of the park. Including a detailed map of archaeological sites, such as former Native American camps or the former location of Gibsonville, might encourage individuals to explore those locations—in fact, some maps in this atlas intentionally move the locations of mapped phenomena to discourage such illegal activities. (If you should find an artifact, do not touch it: take a photo of it, record its location, and notify a park employee.)

What Are Some Characteristics of Maps in This Atlas?

The Letchworth State Park Atlas is a collection of thematic maps. A thematic map portrays a single topic or related topics within a single map. There are different types of thematic maps, many of which are found in this atlas. A *choropleth* map (e.g., Map 47) colors in geographical units such as towns or states to represent different numerical values associated with those units, typically with darker colors symbolizing higher values and lighter colors symbolizing lower values. Some maps use symbol sizes to represent a quantity: a *proportional symbol map* (e.g., Map 20) draws symbol sizes that are strictly proportional to the quantities they represent (larger symbol = higher amount), and a *graduated symbol map* (e.g., Map 28) draws larger symbols for higher amounts but using a finite number of symbol sizes. An *isopleth map* (e.g., Map 31) contains lines that connect locations with equal values, and then shades in areas between those lines. A *pie chart map* (e.g., Map 34), as the name suggests, superimposes pie charts at various locations on a map, and each chart represents different percentages of a whole as pie "slices" for its corresponding geographical unit—and sometimes the size of the "pie" is drawn proportional to a quantity. While other thematic map types exist, these five types are those that appear in this atlas. Despite the richness of the park's nature, history, and tourism, no comprehensive set of thematic maps existed prior to this atlas.

Maps in this atlas often depict roads and trails to help atlas users determine the relative locations of certain park features, if they choose to use this atlas during a park visit. For example, someone interested in the locations of historical events in the park could use Map 63 to find a road that provides access to view Civilian Conservation Corps projects. Or a person interested in waterfalls of the park can use Map 42 to find a trail that leads to one.

Many maps in this atlas also include a semi-transparent "hillshade," a technique that creates the illusion of a light source shining upon the terrain, and which creates a three-dimensional effect that helps readers see valleys, hills, gullies, and cliffs in a map. Hillshades often appear in maps given the importance of the complex terrain of Letchworth State Park on various phenomena mapped—and since the terrain can provide a reference to readers regarding the locations of mapped features. For example, a hillshade manifests how the terrain of the park dictated the placement of roads and buildings in the nineteenth century (Maps 46 and 54), and also helps convey the locations of ecological communities (Maps 26 and 27).

Readers should note other characteristics of maps in this atlas. The author strived to ensure that mapped features were as positionally accurate as possible—but minor positional errors do exist due to the impossibilities of in-the-field data collection for all maps, errors in datasets used for creating maps, and mapmaking decisions made to ensure the readability of maps. In maps where the park is spread over two or four pages, there is often just one legend to explain the symbols. Scale bars are rarely provided in maps, but readers should refer to early maps for a sense of the scale of Letchworth State Park. The author made the latter two decisions regarding legends and scale bars to save space and reduce redundancy.

Aside from a few pages, this map atlas does not provide extensive reference maps. As opposed to thematic maps, reference maps assist with navigation and simply show the locations of and spatial relationships among common features such as roads, populated places, and water bodies. However, the atlas contains some historical reference maps, such as Maps 46, 54, 58, 60, and 69. While readers could use the modern reference map in this atlas (Map 2) for navigation by road or by trail, those seeking up-to-date reference maps of Letchworth State Park should obtain one at an entrance station on their next visit to the park, or click on the "Maps" tab on the official Letchworth State Park Maps web page (https://parks.ny.gov/parks/letchworth).

What Is a Geographic Information System (GIS)?

The author of this atlas created maps using geographic information systems (GIS) software. A GIS is a computer-based system for collecting, organizing, analyzing, and presenting geographic data. GIS software was ideal for creating maps of the park, given the large amount of geographic data presented in this atlas. Users of GIS software create maps chiefly through the "layering" of different slices of data. For example, Map 64 on the locations of historical structures in the park contains five layers of data: historical structures, roads, water bodies, the park boundary, and a hillshade. For those interested in understanding the GIS-format sources of data for maps in this atlas, or the GIS software used for creating maps, please consult the bibliography.

Some Notes on Language

This atlas uses the imperial system of units (such as miles and acres) given that most readers of this atlas are more familiar with this system. However, given that a fair percentage of visitors to Letchworth State Park are international—especially Canadians—the text includes conversions to metric in parentheses wherever possible, as well as a conversion list (see "Imperial to Metric Conversion for This Atlas" preceding this Introduction).

When presenting the park's human history, this atlas uses the term "Native American" to describe cultures living in the present-day United States prior to the arrival of settlers of European descent. This atlas uses more familiar yet anglicized names of specific Native American groups, but still gives the group name as they refer to themselves in parentheses—for example, upon the arrival of European-American settlers, the Seneca (Onöndowa'ga:') lived along the Genesee River within and near the present park area.

This atlas frequently uses phrases such as the "present park area" or "within the present-day park boundary." These terms describe the portion of land that would eventually become the present-day Letchworth State Park of 14,427 acres (5,838 hectares) as of 2020. The atlas avoids using the term "park" by itself since that term may incorrectly suggest that the park existed at certain moments in time. Readers should keep in mind that the first 1,000 acres (405 hectares) of the park were formally established in 1906 and should use other context clues in the accompanying chapter text to establish whether the park existed at certain times for some maps and chapter sections.

Finally, for the sake of brevity, "New York" refers to New York *State* in this atlas rather than New York *City*.

How Can I Learn More about Letchworth State Park— and Where Can I Find More Maps?

This atlas contains a bibliography that lists texts, documents, articles, reports, maps, tabular data files, GIS-format datasets, and photographs used for creating the maps and writing each chapter's text. This atlas organizes the bibliography by chapter and chapter section to better allow readers to search for sources that provide specific pieces of data or information in this atlas. When maps were predominantly created from one or two key sources, they are listed on the map in its title or subtitle, or in credits at the bottom of the map. Note that this atlas does not present a detailed human history of the park. For those wishing to learn more, consult the many resources presented in the bibliography. Chapter 3, "Human History," relies on two sources in particular. Written and assembled by a historian and a former park manager, the first is Cook and Breslin's *Exploring Letchworth Park History* website, which is immensely valuable for its historical essays, primary documents, and historical photos. Second, the National Register of Historic Places Registration Form, written by the New York State Office of Parks, Recreation and Historic Preservation in 2003, contains a detailed narrative of the park's history and is available online. These two sources contain lengthy reference lists with additional historical resources on the park.

For those seeking more maps, online resources exist for viewing and downloading other high-resolution maps—both modern and historical—of Letchworth State Park and its surrounding region, many of which provided important data for maps in this atlas. The following is a list of suggested map resources:

- For reference and special-purpose maps of Letchworth State Park, simply pick up copies at an **entrance station** or **visitor center**, or click on the "Maps" tab on the official **Letchworth State Park web page** (https://parks.ny.gov/parks/letchworth/details.aspx).

- The **USGS TopoView website** (https://ngmdb.usgs.gov/topoview) provides access to United States Geological Survey maps for the Letchworth State Park area dating back to the early 1900s. The maps are available in various computer file formats as free high-resolution downloads. Topographic maps show buildings, roads, railroads, water bodies, terrain, and (starting in the 1940s) forest cover in high detail.

- The **Letchworth Park History website** contains excerpts of historical maps from throughout the history of the park (www.letchworthparkhistory.com/doc.html). Note that this website is not affiliated with the park nor other state entities.

- The **David Rumsey Map Collection website** (www.davidrumsey.com) provides a vast collection of historical maps scanned at high resolution, such as maps of counties comprising the future park area in 1829 and 1895.

- The **Library of Congress online map collection** (www.loc.gov/maps) contains important maps, such as the 1852 Livingston County and 1853 Wyoming County "from Actual Surveys" maps that show roads, some businesses, and property owner names.

- The New Century Atlases of 1902 show roads, property owners, some businesses, and property owner names. The Livingston County atlas is accessible via the Monroe County Library System (https://libraryweb.org), and both the Livingston County and Wyoming County atlases are available as previews or for purchase on the **Historic Map Works website** (www.historicmapworks.com). Various other atlases of the nineteenth and twentieth centuries are also available as previews or for purchase on this website.

- Those interested in Native American history should explore historical maps of Indian Reservations (i.e., Gardeau and Squawkie Hill) that overlapped the present-day border of the park on the **Iroquois Genealogy Society Map Gallery web page** (www.iroquois genealogysociety.org/map-gallery).

- More tech-savvy individuals interested in modern land use, land cover, infrastructure, and terrain in the park can explore the data layers available via **The National Map Viewer** (https://apps.nationalmap.gov/viewer).

Chapter 1

Overview of the Park

Photo 1. Sunrise over Great Bend.

Letchworth State Park is a 14,427-acre (5,838 hectare [ha]) park in Livingston and Wyoming Counties in New York, widely known for its scenic vistas of waterfalls, cliffs nearly 550 feet (168 m) in height, vibrant autumn foliage, and many outdoor recreational opportunities. First acquired by the State in 1906 from businessman and philanthropist William P. Letchworth, the area hosts some of the most spectacular scenery in the eastern United States, earning it the nickname "The Grand Canyon of the East." It accommodates many types of visitors, such as sightseers, photographers, campers, hikers, and history buffs. The park has hosted at least 13 million visitors since 2003. In 2005, the National Park Service added the park to the National Register of Historic Places, and in 2015 it gained national attention when it won the "Readers' Choice Best State Park" award from *USA Today* (the same year its "ice volcano" made national news). To help readers familiarize themselves with the basic layout of the park, Map 1 provides a high-resolution aerial view of the park along with roads, and Map 2 is a reference map showing various features including trails and important park locations.

Maps 3 through 7 give more context to the park's location on both a global and local scale. Located in western New York, Letchworth State Park is an hour's drive from the urban centers of Buffalo (2019 population: 255,284) and Rochester (2019 population: 205,695), and also from Lake Ontario and Lake Erie, two of the five Great Lakes. Though it is located in a sparsely populated rural region, the park is close to large populations (Map 4): approximately 3.4 million people live within 100 miles (including Toronto), 19.1 million live within 200 miles (including Cleveland and Pittsburgh), and 54.5 million live within 300 miles of the park (including Detroit, Ottawa, Montreal, Washington DC, Philadelphia, and New York City). The nearest notable natural attractions include Niagara Falls to the northwest (1.5 hours by car), the Finger Lakes to the east (20 minutes by car), and Allegany State Park to the southwest (1 hour by car). Map 7 shows driving times from major urban centers across the eastern United States and Canada.

The Towns of Leicester, Mount Morris, Castile, Genesee Falls, and Portage each contain a portion of the park. The Villages of Mount Morris, Perry, Castile, and Nunda are the main gateway villages within a five-minute drive of a park entrance (Maps 5 and 6). Communities surrounding the park are generally older, whiter, and possess other demographic characteristics representative of rural communities in upstate New York. An exception to this trend can be found with a ten-minute drive northeast, in the Village of Geneseo, a younger and more diverse town and home to the State University of New York (SUNY) at Geneseo. Recent additions to the fabric of communities in the park vicinity include the Amish: settling Livingston County in 2010, a small Amish community is located adjacent to the eastern side of the park.

Although it is the fifth largest state park in New York by geographic area, Letchworth State Park is small in comparison to other noteworthy parks. In addition to Map 8 showing driving times between park locations, Maps 9 and 10 convey the absolute and relative size of the park. The park is roughly fifteen miles by three miles at its widest, and it takes just over thirty minutes to drive the entire length of Park Road (the main access road) on its western side. As another means of comparison, both the size and shape of the park are similar to Manhattan in New York City. Grand Canyon National Park, Yellowstone National Park, and Adirondack Park (a collection of public and private lands in northern New York) are over 80 times, 150 times, and 400 times larger, respectively.

Map 2 shows the layout of the park: its major attractions, amenities, entrances, roads, and trails. Flowing from south to north is the Genesee River, which divides the park into west and east sides (Map 11 presents some vernacular terms for park locations such as "west side" and "east side"). Scenic vistas and tourism infrastructure are mostly concentrated at the northern and southern ends of the park on its west side. The southern end holds some of the most striking scenery—the tallest cliffs in the park at Great Bend along with Lower, Middle, and Upper Falls—and is the location of William P. Letchworth's original Glen Iris Estate and residence, which formed the original 1,000 acres (405 ha) of the park. The northern end also contains impressive cliff scenery along with the Highbanks Recreation Area and Mount Morris Dam, a major twentieth-century engineering project. The middle portion and much of the park's east side are its least developed and more remote areas explored primarily by hunters, hikers, and mountain bikers, and rarely explored by the crowds of first-time visitors and day-trippers. Many maps in this atlas echo this spatial pattern in scenery and development: everything from where historic events took place, to where noted architectural works are located, to where visitors most often take photos today, to park lodging options are both the cause and effect of this pattern.

Despites its relatively small size in comparison to other parks, Letchworth possesses great ecological, cultural, historical, and recreational significance, which this atlas expresses through the medium of the map. Its dramatic postglacial landscape, containing vertical cliffs and the winding Genesee River, is exceptional in the northeastern United States. Its continuous forest—with trees over 400 years old in places—is a sanctuary for numerous plant and animal species. It is home to endangered bird species and rare vegetation communities that cling to the sides of cliffs. It hosted Native American settlement for thousands of years, and two European-American villages during the nineteenth century that have since disappeared—Map 11 presents the names of select geographic features that the park's former residents bestowed upon the land. Famed nineteenth-century landscape painter Thomas Cole painted scenes from within the modern-day park area, including his "Portage Falls on the Genesee," valued at more than $18 million today. The efforts of Mr. Letchworth, who bequeathed his beloved Glen Iris Estate to the State of New York to form the original park, represent a unique and early land restoration and conservation story. The Civilian Conservation Corps, a program that employed citizens in conservation projects during the Great Depression, built many of the historic structures within the park that later provided a national model for building park infrastructure across the country. While mostly New York residents visit the park, a sizable percentage of visitors originate from out of state, and a fair number from other countries. Possessing its own unique history, the park also serves as a microcosm of land history in western New York—from Native American–white land transfers, to land development, to rural population trends, to deforestation and reforestation. This atlas covers these topics and more in the chapters that follow.

Map 1(a). Aerial view and roads, north end (2019)

Mount Morris Rd

Park Rd

Damsite Rd

Visitor Center Rd

Park Rd

Highbanks Camp Rd

River Rd

N

0   ¼   ½
mile

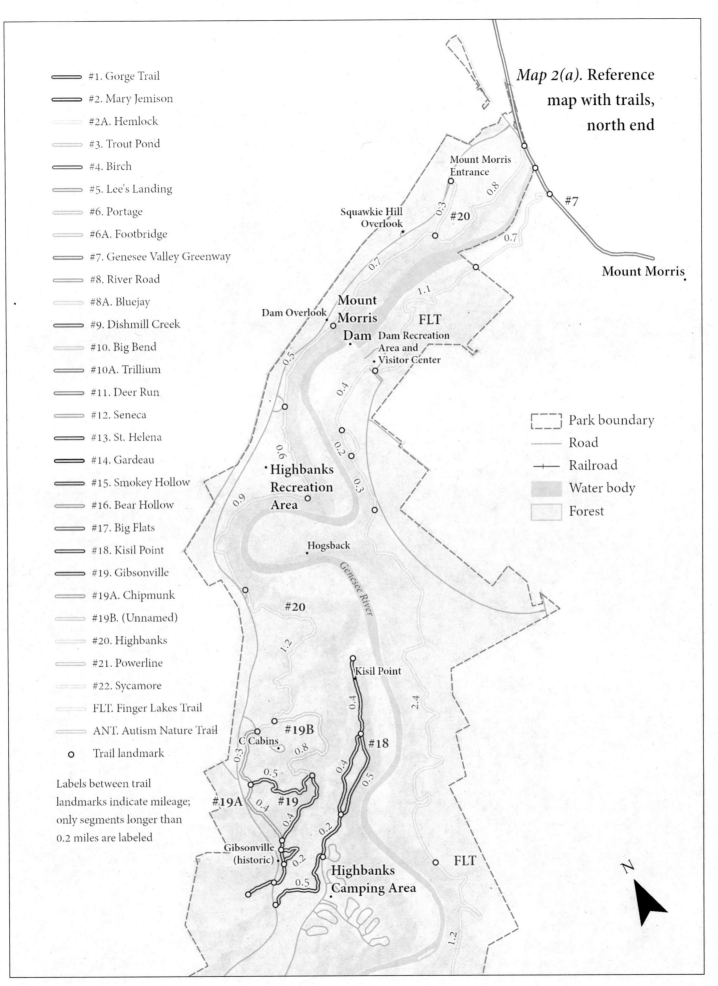

#1. Gorge Trail
#2. Mary Jemison
#2A. Hemlock
#3. Trout Pond
#4. Birch
#5. Lee's Landing
#6. Portage
#6A. Footbridge
#7. Genesee Valley Greenway
#8. River Road
#8A. Bluejay
#9. Dishmill Creek
#10. Big Bend
#10A. Trillium
#11. Deer Run
#12. Seneca
#13. St. Helena
#14. Gardeau
#15. Smokey Hollow
#16. Bear Hollow
#17. Big Flats
#18. Kisil Point
#19. Gibsonville
#19A. Chipmunk
#19B. (Unnamed)
#20. Highbanks
#21. Powerline
#22. Sycamore
FLT. Finger Lakes Trail
ANT. Autism Nature Trail
o Trail landmark

Labels between trail landmarks indicate mileage; only segments longer than 0.2 miles are labeled

Map 2(a). Reference map with trails, north end

Mount Morris Entrance

Squawkie Hill Overlook

#20

#7

0.3

0.8

0.7

Mount Morris

1.1

FLT

Dam Overlook

Mount Morris Dam

Dam Recreation Area and Visitor Center

0.5

0.4

Highbanks Recreation Area

0.6

0.2

0.9

0.3

Hogsback

Genesee River

#20

1.2

Kisil Point

0.4

2.4

C Cabins

#19B

0.8

#18

0.3

0.5

0.4

0.5

#19A

0.4

#19

0.4

0.2

Gibsonville (historic)

0.2

Highbanks Camping Area

0.5

FLT

1.2

Park boundary
Road
Railroad
Water body
Forest

N

11

Map 1(b). Aerial view and roads, north-central (2019)

Schenck Rd

Park Rd

Highbanks Camp Rd

River Rd

River Rd

Park Rd

N

0   ¼   ½
mile

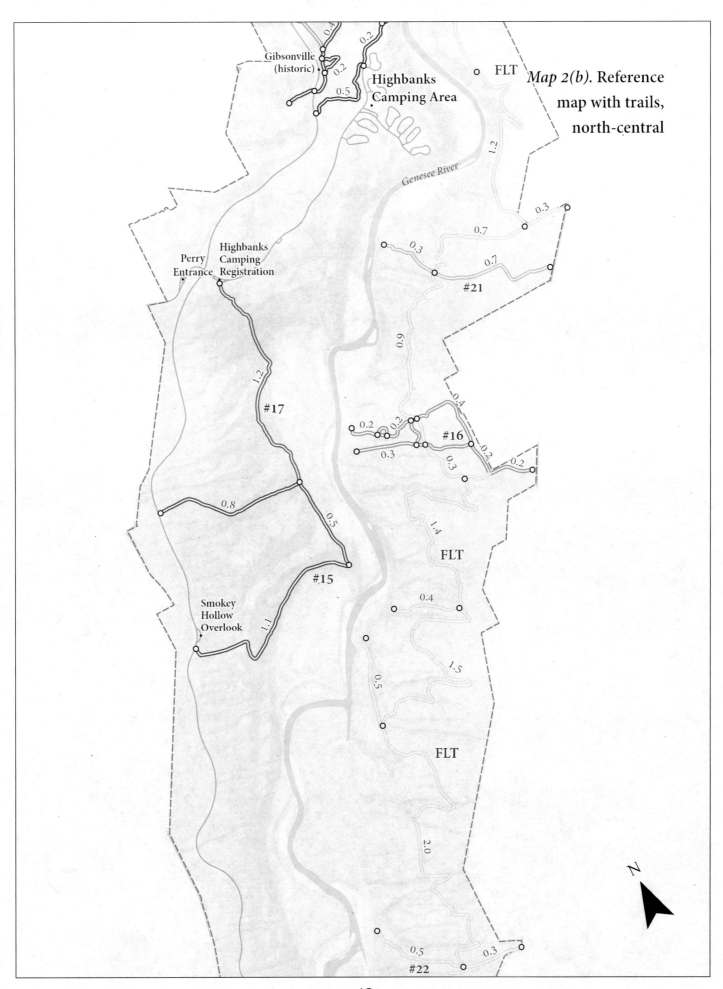

Gibsonville (historic)

0.4

0.2

0.2

0.5

Highbanks
Camping Area

Genesee River

FLT

Map 2(b). Reference
map with trails,
north-central

1.2

0.3

0.7

0.3

0.7

#21

Perry
Entrance

Highbanks
Camping
Registration

0.9

1.2

#17

0.4

0.2

0.2

0.2

0.3

#16

0.2

0.2

0.8

0.3

0.5

1.4

#15

FLT

Smokey
Hollow
Overlook

1.1

0.4

1.5

0.5

FLT

2.0

N

0.5

0.3

#22

13

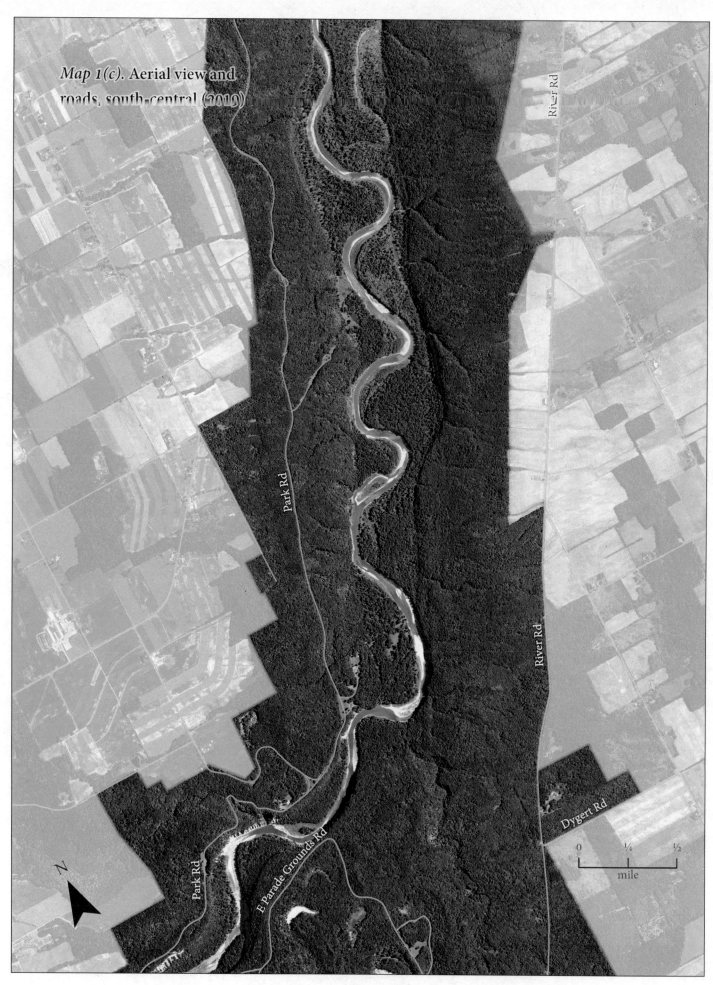

Map 1(c). Aerial view and roads, south-central (2019)

Park Rd

River Rd

River Rd

Dygert Rd

Park Rd

E Parade Grounds Rd

N

0   ¼   ½

mile

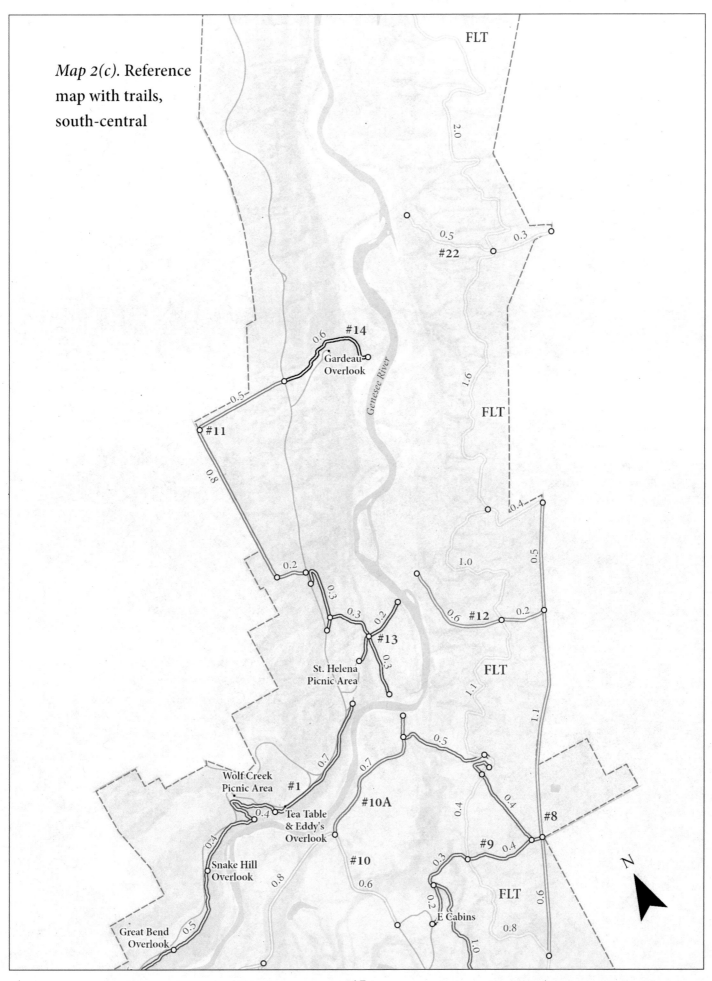

Map 2(c). Reference map with trails, south-central

FLT

2.0

0.5

#22

0.3

0.6 #14

Gardeau Overlook

Genesee River

0.5

#11

1.6

FLT

0.8

0.4

1.0

0.5

0.2

#12

0.6

0.2

0.3

0.3

0.2

#13

0.3

St. Helena
Picnic Area

FLT

1.1

1.1

0.5

0.7

Wolf Creek
Picnic Area

0.7

#10A

#1

0.4

Tea Table
& Eddy's
Overlook

0.4

0.4

#8

Snake Hill
Overlook

#10

0.4

#9

0.4

0.4

0.8

0.6

0.3

0.5

E Cabins

0.2

FLT

0.6

Great Bend
Overlook

0.8

1.0

N

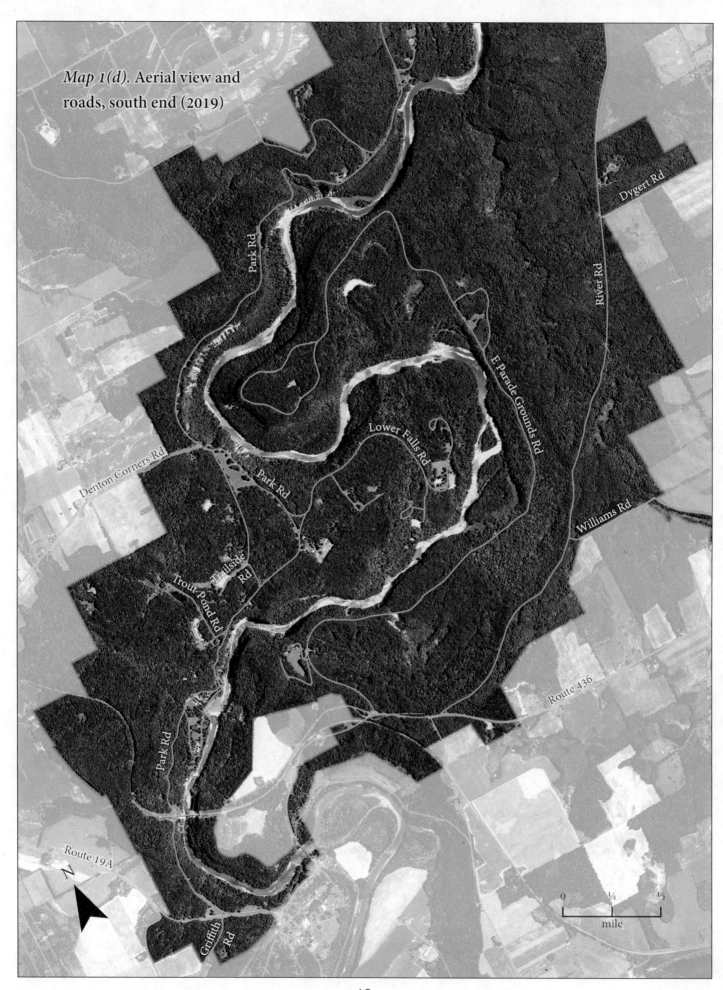

Map 1(d). Aerial view and roads, south end (2019)

Dygert Rd

Park Rd

River Rd

E Parade Grounds Rd

Lower Falls Rd

Denton Corners Rd

Park Rd

Williams Rd

Trailside Rd

Trout Pond Rd

Route 436

Park Rd

Route 19A

N

Griffith Rd

0   ¼   ½
mile

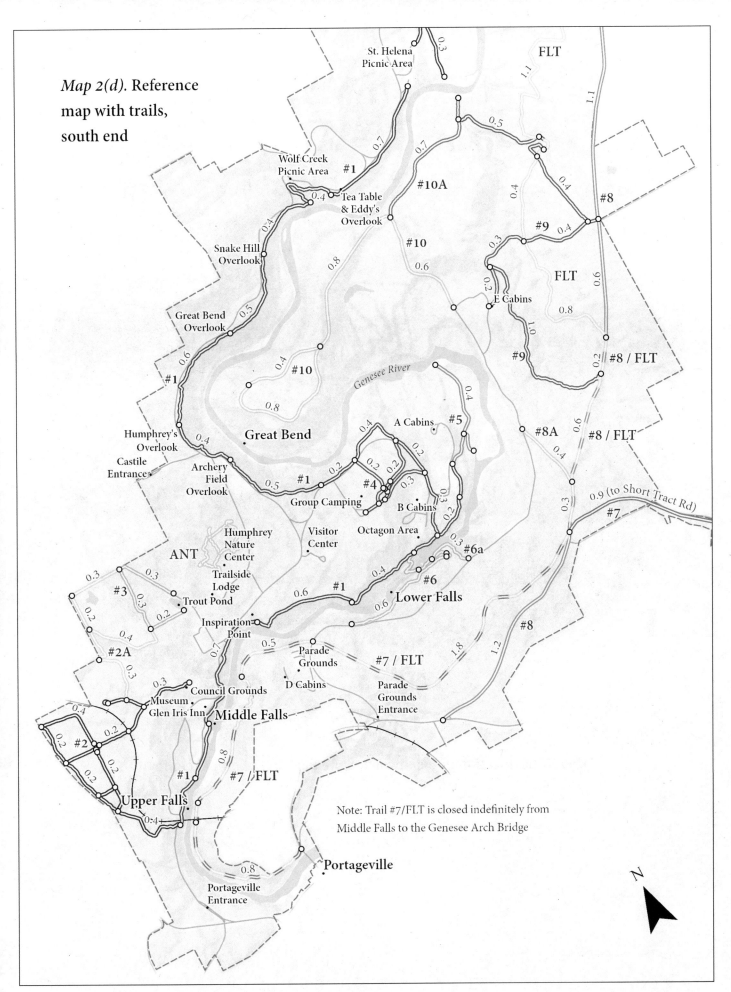

Map 2(d). Reference map with trails, south end

St. Helena
Picnic Area

FLT

1.1

1.1

0.3

0.7

0.5

0.7

Wolf Creek
Picnic Area   **#1**

#10A

0.4

0.4

Tea Table
& Eddy's
Overlook

0.4

0.4

0.5

#8

Snake Hill
Overlook

#10

0.3

#9

0.4

0.8

0.6

0.2

E Cabins

FLT

Great Bend
Overlook

0.5

0.8

1.0

#9

0.2   **#8 / FLT**

0.6

#1

0.6

0.4

Genesee River

Humphrey's
Overlook

0.4

#10

0.8

0.4

A Cabins   **#5**

#8A

#8 / FLT

0.6

Castile
Entrance

Archery
Field
Overlook

0.5   **#1**

0.2

0.2

0.2

0.2

0.3

0.4

0.4

0.9 (to Short Tract Rd)

Group Camping

#4

B Cabins

0.3

0.2

0.3

Octagon Area

0.3

#6a

0.3

#7

ANT

Humphrey
Nature
Center

Visitor
Center

0.4

0.3

Trailside
Lodge

0.3

0.3

#6

0.3

0.3

Trout Pond

0.2

#1

0.6

0.4

Lower Falls

#3

0.2

Inspiration
Point

0.6

0.7

0.5

Parade
Grounds

#7 / FLT

1.8

1.2

#8

0.4

#2A

0.3

0.3

Council Grounds

D Cabins

Parade
Grounds
Entrance

0.3

Museum

0.4

Glen Iris Inn   **Middle Falls**

0.8

0.2

#2

0.2

0.2

0.3

0.8

0.2

0.3

#1

#7 / FLT

Note: Trail #7/FLT is closed indefinitely from
Middle Falls to the Genesee Arch Bridge

Upper Falls

0.4

N

0.8

Portageville

Portageville
Entrance

17

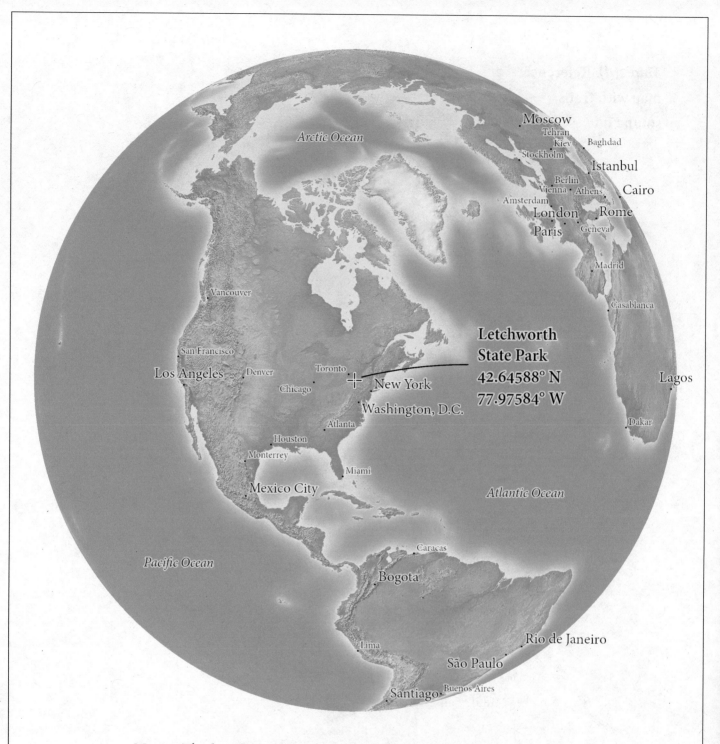

Arctic Ocean

Moscow
Tehran
Kiev   Baghdad
Stockholm
                    Istanbul
          Berlin   Cairo
Vienna   • Athens
Amsterdam   Rome
      London
    Paris   Geneva

Madrid

Vancouver   Casablanca

San Francisco   Letchworth
                    Toronto   State Park
Los Angeles   Denver   +   42.64588° N
          Chicago   New York   77.97584° W   Lagos
                    Washington, D.C.
            Atlanta   Dakar
      Houston
Monterrey   Miami

    Mexico City   Atlantic Ocean

                              Caracas
Pacific Ocean
                    Bogota

                                              Rio de Janeiro
            Lima   São Paulo
                  Santiago Buenos Aires

Map 3. The location of Letchworth State Park in the global context

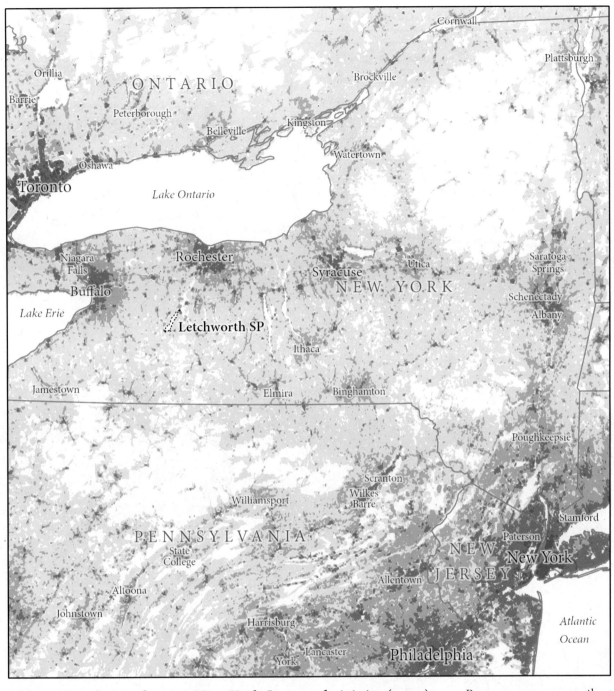

Map 4. Population density, New York State and vicinity (2015)

Persons per square mile

	0–10
	>10–100
	>100–1,000
	>1,000–10,000
	>10,000–100,000+

Data from CIESIN (2018)

Map 5. Populated places surrounding Letchworth State Park, 1:500,000 scale

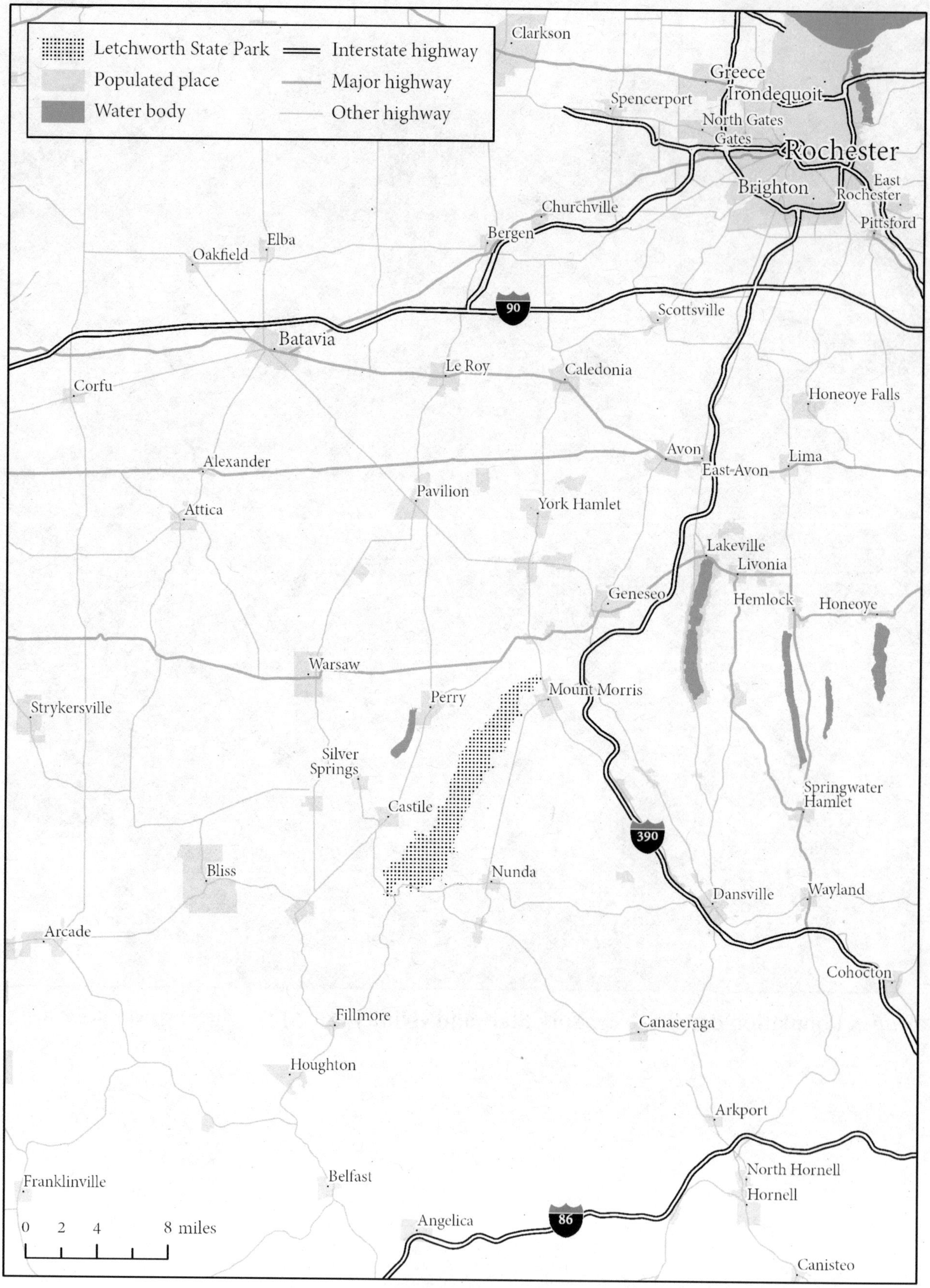

Legend:
- Letchworth State Park
- Populated place
- Water body
- Interstate highway
- Major highway
- Other highway

Clarkson

Greece
Irondequoit

Spencerport

North Gates
Gates

Rochester

Brighton

East Rochester

Pittsford

Churchville

Bergen

Oakfield

Elba

90

Scottsville

Batavia

Corfu

Le Roy

Caledonia

Honeoye Falls

Alexander

Avon

East Avon

Lima

Pavilion

York Hamlet

Attica

Lakeville
Livonia

Geneseo

Hemlock

Honeoye

Warsaw

Strykersville

Perry

Mount Morris

Silver Springs

Springwater Hamlet

Castile

390

Bliss

Nunda

Dansville

Wayland

Arcade

Cohocton

Fillmore

Canaseraga

Houghton

Arkport

Franklinville

Belfast

North Hornell
Hornell

Angelica

86

Canisteo

0   2   4   8 miles

Map 6. Populated places surrounding Letchworth State Park, 1:200,000 scale

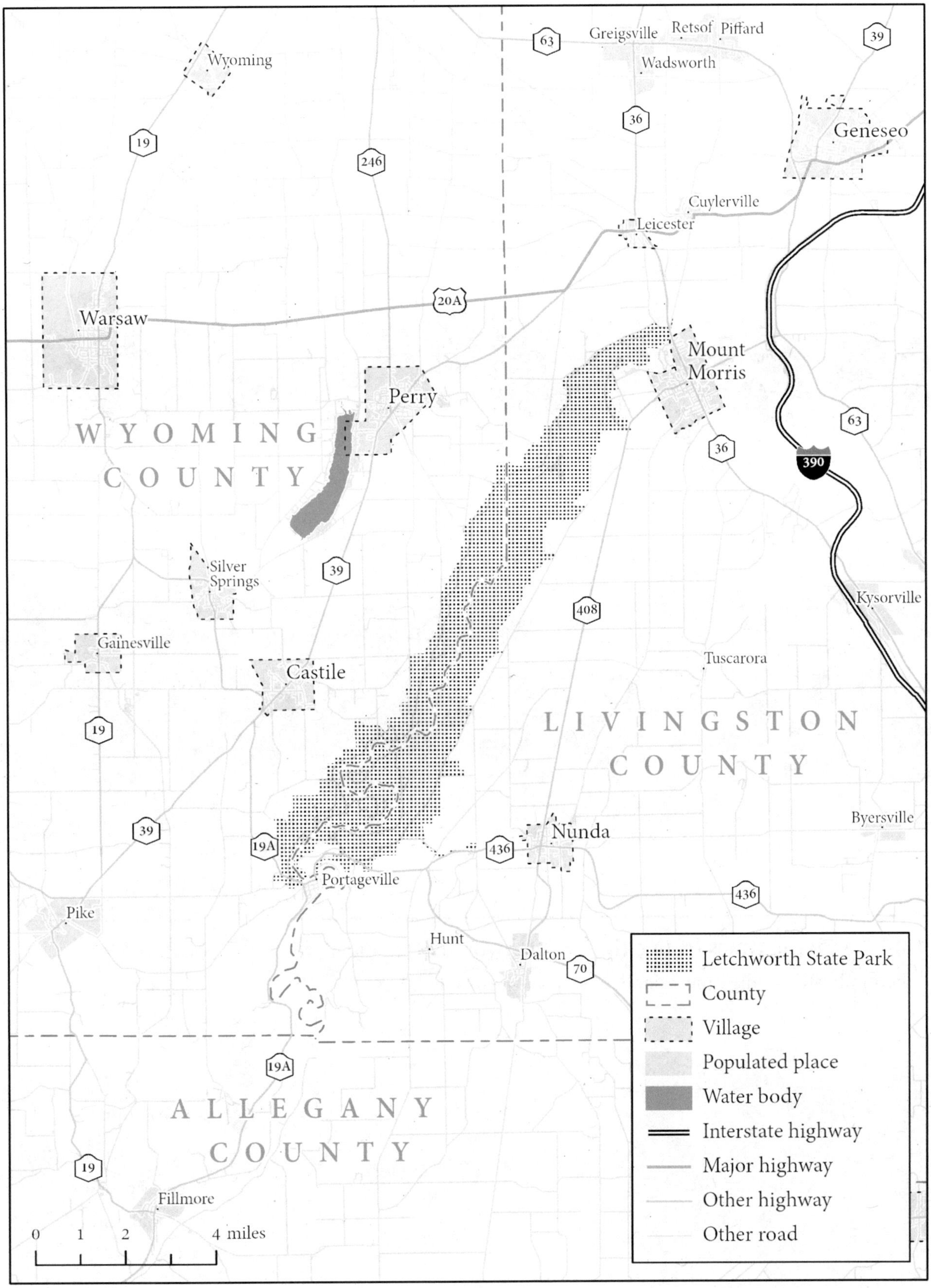

Greigsville Retsof Piffard

63

39

Wyoming

Wadsworth

36

19

Geneseo

246

Cuylerville

Leicester

20A

Warsaw

Mount
Morris

Perry

63

36

390

W Y O M I N G
C O U N T Y

39

Silver
Springs

Kysorville

Gainesville

408

Tuscarora

Castile

L I V I N G S T O N
C O U N T Y

19

Byersville

39

Nunda

19A

436

Portageville

436

Pike

Hunt

Dalton

70

19A

	Letchworth State Park
	County
	Village
	Populated place
	Water body
	Interstate highway
	Major highway
	Other highway
	Other road

A L L E G A N Y
C O U N T Y

19

Fillmore

0   1   2   4 miles

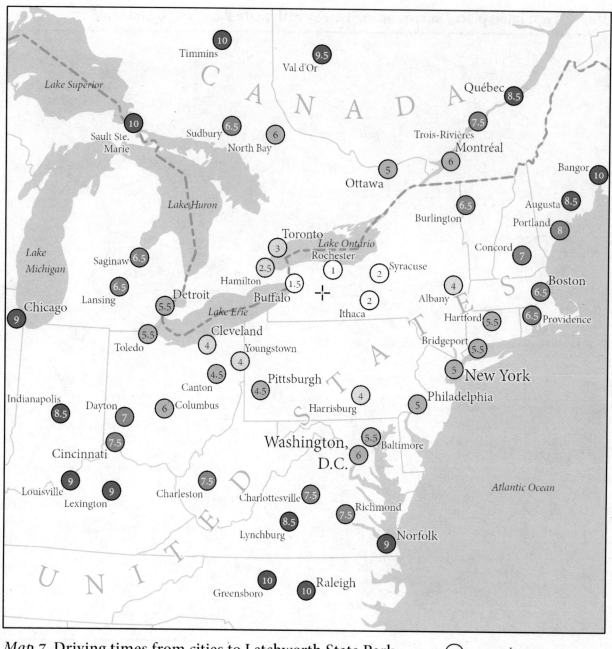

Map 7. Driving times from cities to Letchworth State Park

Labels indicate driving times rounded up to the nearest half hour

○	>0–2 hours
○	>2–4 hours
●	>4–6 hours
●	>6–8 hours
●	>8–10 hours
-|-	Letchworth State Park
☐	State or province
- - -	National border

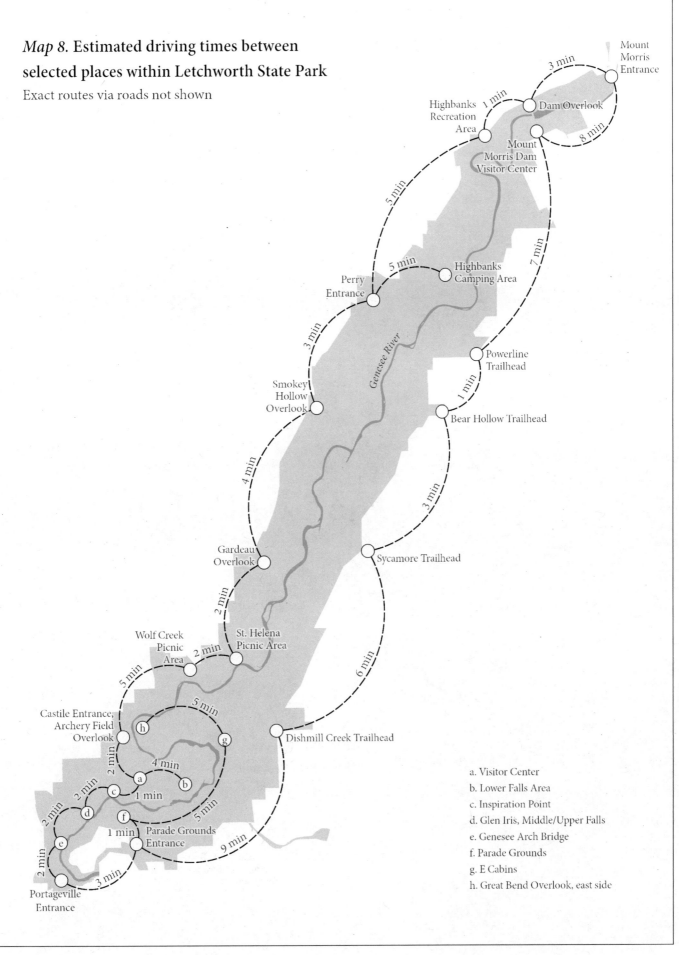

Map 8. **Estimated driving times between selected places within Letchworth State Park**

Exact routes via roads not shown

Mount Morris Entrance

3 min

Dam Overlook

Highbanks Recreation Area

1 min

Mount Morris Dam Visitor Center

8 min

7 min

5 min

Highbanks Camping Area

Perry Entrance

5 min

Powerline Trailhead

1 min

3 min

Smokey Hollow Overlook

Bear Hollow Trailhead

Genesee River

4 min

3 min

Gardeau Overlook

Sycamore Trailhead

2 min

6 min

Wolf Creek Picnic Area

St. Helena Picnic Area

2 min

Castile Entrance, Archery Field Overlook

5 min

5 min

h

g

Dishmill Creek Trailhead

2 min

4 min

a

b

2 min

c

1 min

d

f

5 min

2 min

e

1 min

Parade Grounds Entrance

2 min

9 min

3 min

Portageville Entrance

a. Visitor Center

b. Lower Falls Area

c. Inspiration Point

d. Glen Iris, Middle/Upper Falls

e. Genesee Arch Bridge

f. Parade Grounds

g. E Cabins

h. Great Bend Overlook, east side

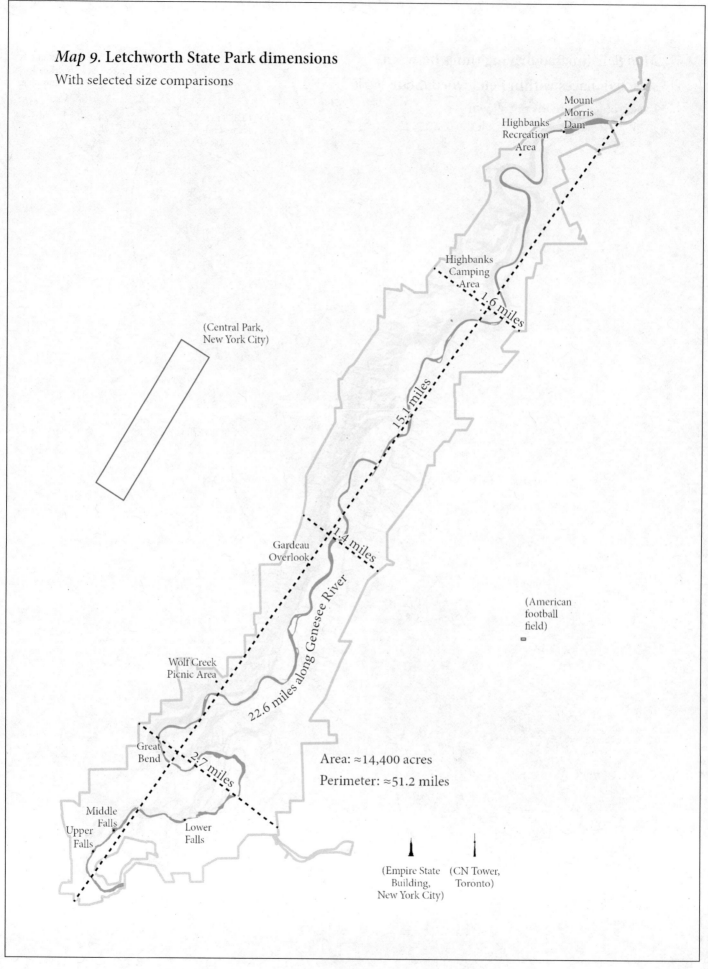

Map 9. Letchworth State Park dimensions
With selected size comparisons

(Central Park, New York City)

Mount Morris Dam

Highbanks Recreation Area

Highbanks Camping Area

1.6 miles

15.1 miles

(American football field)

Gardeau Overlook

1.4 miles

22.6 miles along Genesee River

Wolf Creek Picnic Area

Great Bend

2.7 miles

Area: ≈14,400 acres

Perimeter: ≈51.2 miles

Middle Falls

Upper Falls

Lower Falls

(Empire State Building, New York City)

(CN Tower, Toronto)

24

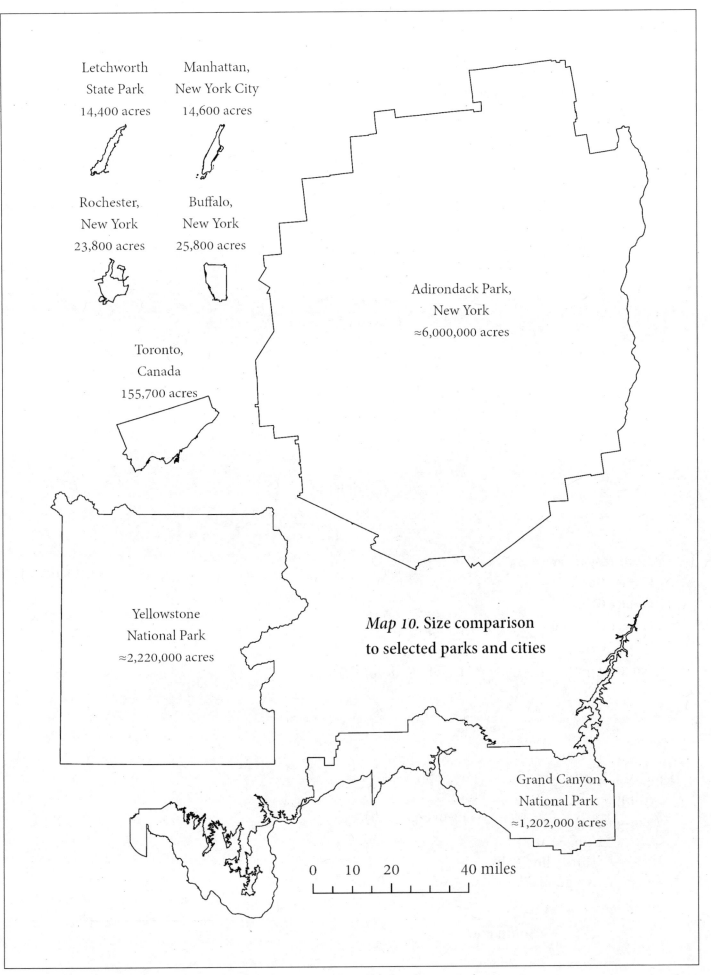

Letchworth
State Park
14,400 acres

Manhattan,
New York City
14,600 acres

Rochester,
New York
23,800 acres

Buffalo,
New York
25,800 acres

Adirondack Park,
New York
≈6,000,000 acres

Toronto,
Canada
155,700 acres

Yellowstone
National Park
≈2,220,000 acres

Map 10. Size comparison
to selected parks and cities

Grand Canyon
National Park
≈1,202,000 acres

0   10   20   40 miles

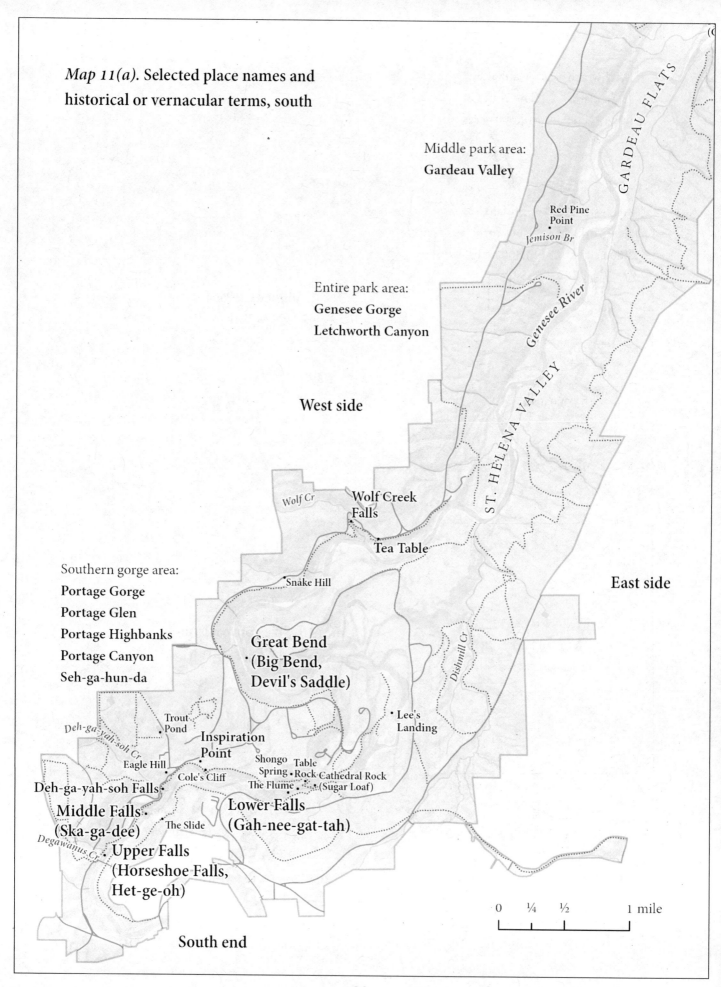

Map 11(a). Selected place names and historical or vernacular terms, south

GARDEAU FLATS

Middle park area:
Gardeau Valley

Red Pine
Point

Jemison Br

Genesee River

Entire park area:
Genesee Gorge
Letchworth Canyon

ST. HELENA VALLEY

West side

Wolf Cr   **Wolf Creek Falls**

Tea Table

East side

Southern gorge area:
Portage Gorge
Portage Glen
Portage Highbanks
Portage Canyon
Seh-ga-hun-da

Snake Hill

Dishmill Cr

Great Bend (Big Bend, Devil's Saddle)

Deh-ga-yah-soh Cr

Trout Pond

Lee's Landing

Inspiration Point

Eagle Hill

Shongo Spring   Table Rock   Cathedral Rock (Sugar Loaf)

Cole's Cliff

The Flume

Deh-ga-yah-soh Falls

Middle Falls (Ska-ga-dee)

The Slide

Lower Falls (Gah-nee-gat-tah)

Degawanus Cr

Upper Falls (Horseshoe Falls, Het-ge-oh)

0   ¼   ½   1 mile

South end

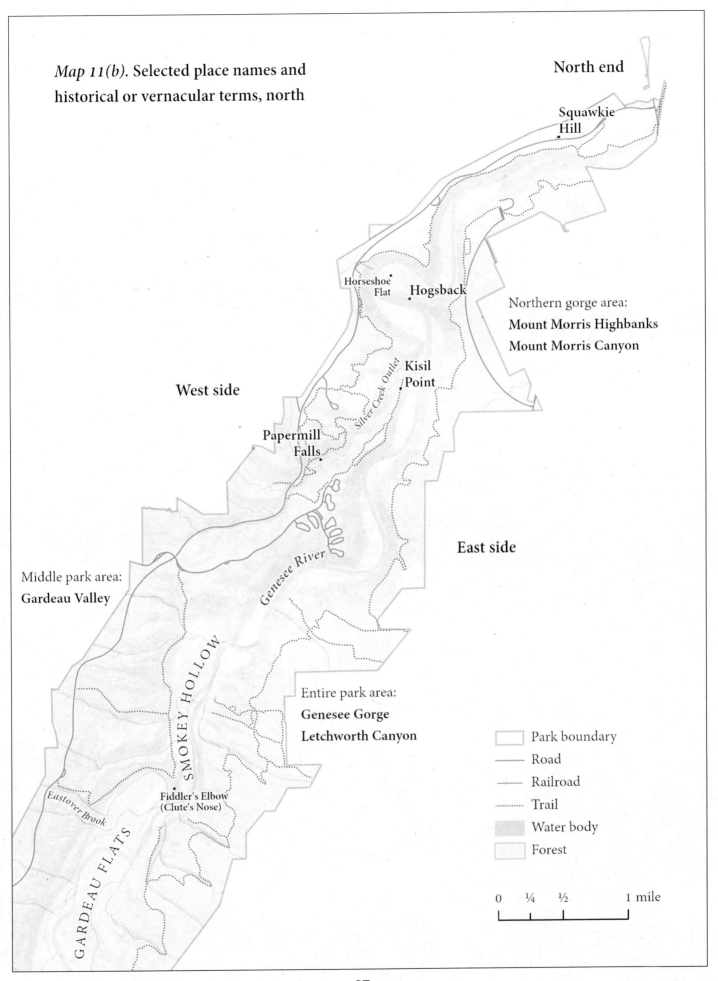

Map 11(b). Selected place names and historical or vernacular terms, north

North end

Squawkie Hill

Horseshoe Flat

Hogsback

Northern gorge area:
Mount Morris Highbanks
Mount Morris Canyon

West side

Kisil Point

Papermill Falls

Silver Creek Outlet

Genesee River

East side

Middle park area:
Gardeau Valley

SMOKEY HOLLOW

Entire park area:
Genesee Gorge
Letchworth Canyon

Eastover Brook

Fiddler's Elbow
(Clute's Nose)

GARDEAU FLATS

☐ Park boundary
— Road
—|— Railroad
······ Trail
▓ Water body
☐ Forest

0   ¼   ½   1 mile

Chapter 2
Physical Geography

Photo 2. Lower Falls in autumn.

The natural landscape of Letchworth State Park has long attracted people for a myriad of reasons. Native Americans farmed on the rich soils of its valley bottom and hunted on its valley slopes. European-American settlers and industrialists of the nineteenth century logged it for its timber, and cleared its forests to grow crops and raise cattle. Its geological wonders have attracted tourists who photograph it and geologists who study it. At present, the park

29

is a mostly forested landscape that provides habitat for several rare plant and animal species, but one with a complex history of land use under both Native American and white occupancy. Found in a temperate region of the world, the park seldom experiences severe weather, but occasionally a meteorological event affects the park and its nearby communities in significant ways. Beyond its impressive geological features and dense forests, perhaps the most dominant natural feature in the park is the Genesee River that, like the park's forest, has a complex history of human use and modification. This atlas now presents aspects of its physical geography: its geology, land history, ecological communities, weather and climate, and the Genesee River.

Geology

Letchworth State Park is located at the transition between two major geological provinces: the low-relief Lake Erie–Lake Ontario Lowlands to the north, and the hilly Allegheny Plateau to the south. Map 12 shows the elevation of the park: encompassing over 800 feet (244 m) of elevation change, it ranges from 579 feet (176 m) above sea level at its northern end, to 1,404 feet (428 m) above sea level in the south. Except for some upland areas and river terraces, the terrain of the park is rugged: much of the park is sloping, and in many places along the river there are vertical cliffs. The park generally becomes steeper as one moves toward the Genesee River, and the park is locally dissected by deep gullies formed by seasonal streams. The park's ruggedness, along with the barrier presented by the Genesee River itself, has directed most human travel in north–south directions, and less often in west–east directions except at a few strategically placed bridges and fords throughout its history (covered in subsequent sections).

Many geological processes can shape landscapes, but two main processes shaped the modern landscape of the park: the creation of its sedimentary bedrock, and their ongoing erosion to form its picturesque cliffs. The formation of the park's sedimentary rocks began over 360 million years ago during the Late Devonian Period. Devonian Earth looked dramatically different from today: the southern hemisphere contained most of the landmasses, and an ocean covered much of what is today North America. A tectonic collision between North America and the microcontinent Avalonia (now portions of New England) had formed the Acadian Mountains, a precursor to the Allegheny Mountains, in the millions of years preceding. Ancient rivers flowed off the western slopes of these relatively young mountains, depositing layers of sediment in a vast shallow ocean that covered modern-day western New York. The older rock formations found at lower elevations in the park are finer-grained "mudstones" and shales created as rivers deposited sediments in a deep ocean over

Photo 3. Cliffs below Inspiration Point viewed from the east side of the park.

what is present-day western New York. The relatively newer rock layers occurring at higher elevations in the park are siltstones and sandstones that formed as rivers deposited coarser sediments into a shallower ocean. This change from finer- to coarser-grained sedimentation was accomplished by several large river deltas located well east of the park, collectively called the Catskill Delta, which slowly "prograded" westward, filling in the subsiding ocean floor with sediments, and resulting in a shallowing of sediment deposition over time. Map 13 focuses on the time when rivers deposited sediments and uplift occurred, whereas Map 14 shows the general location of sedimentary bedrock formations in the park today.

After deposition of sediments and their subsequent slow conversion to rock, the North American continent was slowly uplifted until the ocean floor rose above sea level. An unknown thickness of younger bedrock formations was subsequently eroded from the western New York area prior to glaciation. Continuing geological processes cracked and shifted the bedrock, forming natural weak-

Photo 4. Cliffs downstream from Inspiration Point in autumn.

nesses known as "joints" along which water drained and erosion was concentrated. Over millions of years, the generally southward flow (following the natural dip of the bedrock) was reversed by glacial events and the modern south-to-north flow of the Genesee River eventually was established, but its several glacially disrupted channels have varied over time. At various times a more mature ancient drainage occupied portions of the park area. It was not until the catastrophic forces of continental ice sheets transformed New York and retreated several times that the modern-day canyon of the park formed, directing the Genesee River's flow into the present location of the park.

During the last 2.5 million years (known as the Pleistocene Epoch), vast continental ice sheets have advanced and retreated with the regular changes in global climate, scouring and shaping the landscape of northern North America. Ice sheets have advanced and retreated about twenty times, approximately every 100,000 years, as dictated by the Earth's orbital variations. As many as ten of these advances could have reached the Genesee River Valley. The process that most recently shaped the terrain of modern Letchworth State Park was the Wisconsin glacial Stage, beginning roughly 123,000 years ago. Massive amounts of snow and ice accumulated at two centers in Canada to form the Laurentide Ice Sheet, a giant continental ice cap that was three to four miles thick near its center and that advanced southward under the pressure of its own weight. This expanding ice sheet extended southward into Pennsylvania, covered the modern-day park area, and temporarily buried the Genesee River and other valleys throughout the region as the ice both eroded bedrock and deposited an assortment of glacial sediments.

During the Wisconsin Stage, the ice sheet experienced a shorter series of advances and retreats—"stadials and interstadials"—along its southern margin in response to hemispheric climatic changes that constantly reworked the landscape, often burying or erasing geological evidence of previous events. During minor retreats, glacial meltwater formed "proglacial" lakes along the southern margin of the ice sheet due to the increasing southward elevation of the terrain as the land rebounded after being depressed from the weight of the ice sheet. Importantly, the ice sheet deposited large volumes of till composed of sand and gravel along its occasionally stationary southern edges, called end moraines, which formed from the scraping of bedrock and complex transport of sedimentary debris. One of these deposits is called the Valley Heads moraine, which dammed the ancient Genesee River near the south end of the present-day park, blocking its flow about 13,000 years ago, and subsequently creating a series of lowering proglacial lakes as the ice receded northward to Lake Ontario.

As the massive ice sheet retreated with a warming climate around 12,000 years ago (Map 15) at the beginning of the modern postglacial Holocene Epoch, the river gradually carved a new path, producing the impressive postglacial gorge sections seen within portions of the park today as it eroded the newly exposed sedimentary rock (Map 16). For a time, a glacial Lake Hall formed from meltwater that covered much of the present-day park near an elevation of 1,000 feet (305 m). The Genesee River in the middle portion of the park flows through a wider valley that was part of an earlier and more mature course that existed prior to the most recent glaciation. The narrower gorges toward the park's northern and southern ends are sections where the river worked successfully in postglacial time to erode newly encountered bedrock while linking the older, preexisting valley segments. Map 16 shows the approximate location of the Valley Heads moraine, and also distinguishes between the few known ancient and current paths of the Genesee River. The ice sheets left behind other evidence: glacial tills of unstratified ground-up rock material from their advance, as well as finer lake sediments formed at the bottom of ancient proglacial lakes created from glacial meltwater during the ice sheet recession.

Aside from the gorges and their prominent cliffs, other reminders of Letchworth State Park's glacial past are evident. Anyone who has visited the southern portion of the park and paid attention to the soils has noticed two qualities: the rockiness of the soil ("channery" and "flaggy" soils in Map 17 are those with large flat rock fragments), and how well drained the soil is—some stretches of trail are free of mud after even heavy rainfalls. Many of these porous, rocky soils are the product of the complex erosive forces of the Laurentide Ice Sheet that churned up and pulverized the coarser-grained bedrock. Map 17 classifies soil by general type, and Map 18 classifies soil by drainage characteristics.

Geological forces are still at work within Letchworth State Park. Rockfalls and landslides, in addition to postglacial gully erosion, have occurred throughout the park along the steep cliffs (see Map 45 later for locations of some of these events). In the late 1990s, a massive rockfall occurred downstream from Inspiration Point that released rocks larger than buses, leveled nearby trees from its shockwave, and temporarily dammed the Genesee River. In 2005, unstable cliffs below Middle Falls and Pinewood Lodge were injected with concrete to reinforce them. And in 2010 a substantial rockfall occurred that is easily visible downstream from Table Rock near Lower Falls. Where fine glacial lake clays are found, landslides occur. The Genesee River continues to reshape the riverbed and undercut the bedrock cliffs. Some of the most notable changes to the park have occurred in the Lower Falls area, where erosion has caused portions of the falls to move upstream about 900 feet (274 m) in the last two centuries. Although not a tectonic hotspot, western New York does occasionally experience minor earthquakes. In 2021, a 2.4 magnitude earthquake occurred a few miles east of the park, shaking houses but not causing visible damage. A bedrock joint—a crack caused by the slow bending of bedrock over time—is visible near the northern end of the Lee's Landing trail in the bedrock cliff across the river, where an enlarged vertical crack interrupts the horizontal layers of sedimentary rock.

Photo 5. Middle Falls.

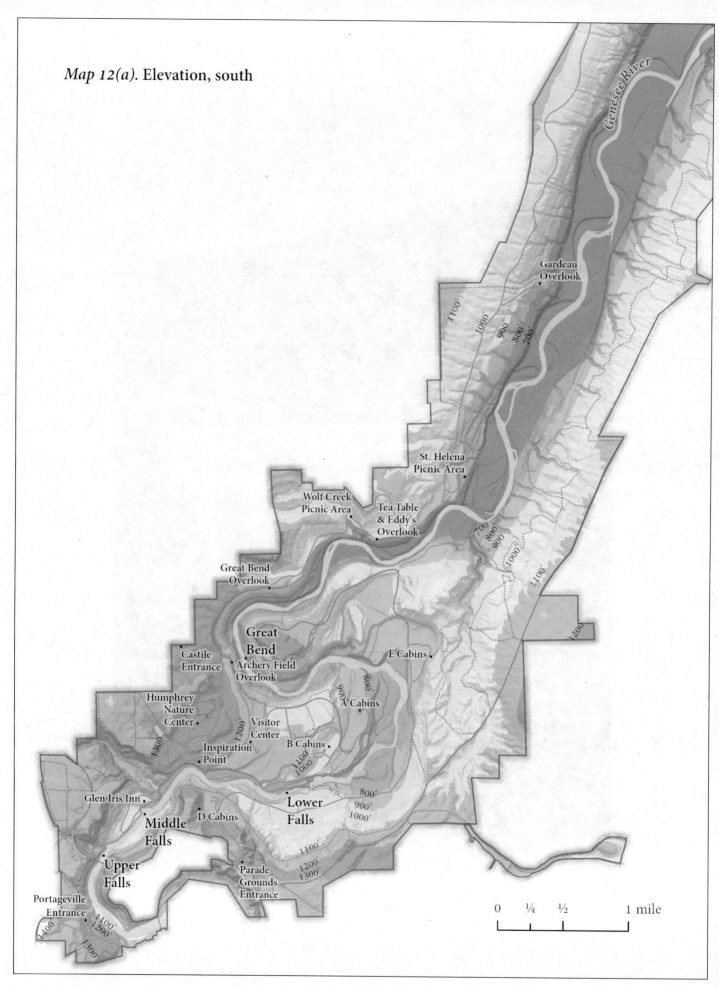

Map 12(a). Elevation, south

Genesee River

Gardeau
Overlook

1100'
1000'
900'
800'
700'

St. Helena
Picnic Area

Wolf Creek
Picnic Area

Tea Table
& Eddy's
Overlook

700'
800'
900'
1000'
1100'
1200'

Great Bend
Overlook

Great
Bend

Castile
Entrance

Archery Field
Overlook

E Cabins

Humphrey
Nature
Center

800'
900'

A Cabins

1300'

1200'

Visitor
Center

B Cabins

Inspiration
Point

1100'
1000'

Glen Iris Inn

Middle
Falls

D Cabins

Lower
Falls

800'
900'
1000'

Upper
Falls

1100'

1200'
1300'

Parade
Grounds
Entrance

Portageville
Entrance

1100'
1200'

1400'

1300'

0   ¼   ½   1 mile

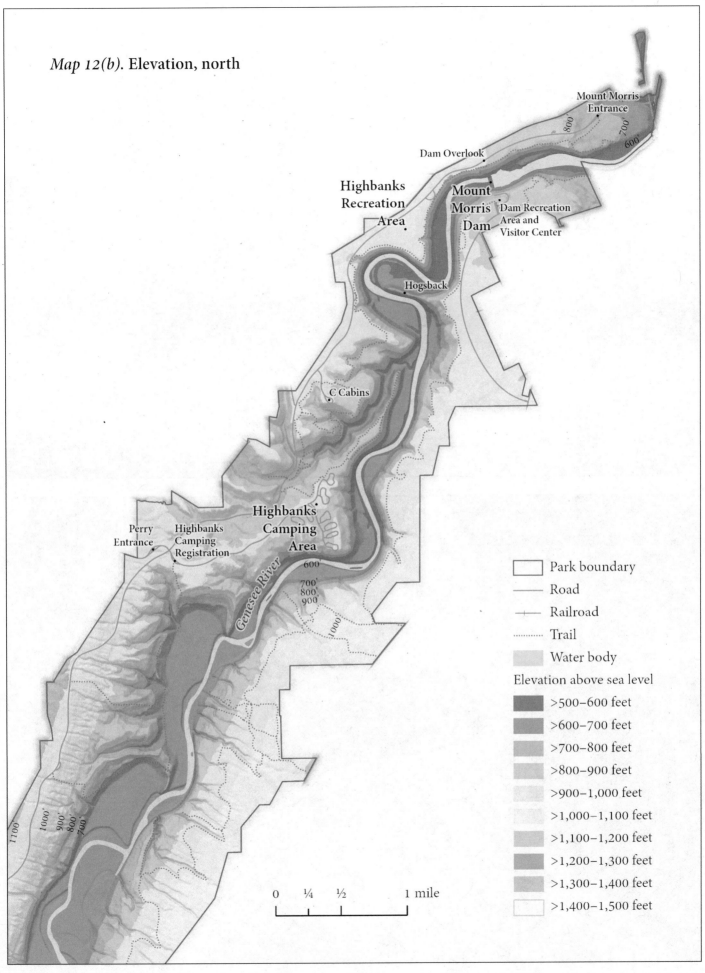

Map 12(b). Elevation, north

Mount Morris
Entrance

800
700
600

Dam Overlook

Highbanks
Recreation
Area

Mount
Morris
Dam

Dam Recreation
Area and
Visitor Center

Hogsback

C Cabins

Highbanks
Camping
Area

Perry
Entrance

Highbanks
Camping
Registration

Genesee River

600
700'
800'
900'

1000

1100
1000'
900'
800'
700'

Park boundary

Road

Railroad

Trail

Water body

Elevation above sea level

>500–600 feet

>600–700 feet

>700–800 feet

>800–900 feet

>900–1,000 feet

>1,000–1,100 feet

>1,100–1,200 feet

>1,200–1,300 feet

>1,300–1,400 feet

>1,400–1,500 feet

0   ¼   ½   1 mile

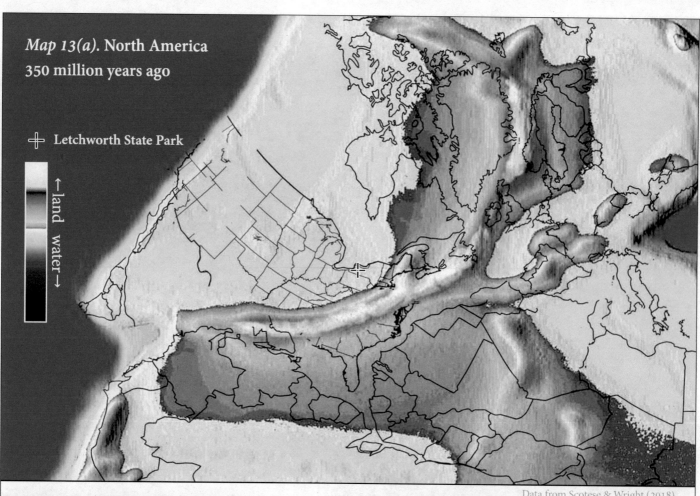

Map 13(a). North America
350 million years ago

⊹ Letchworth State Park

←land
water→

Data from Scotese & Wright (2018)

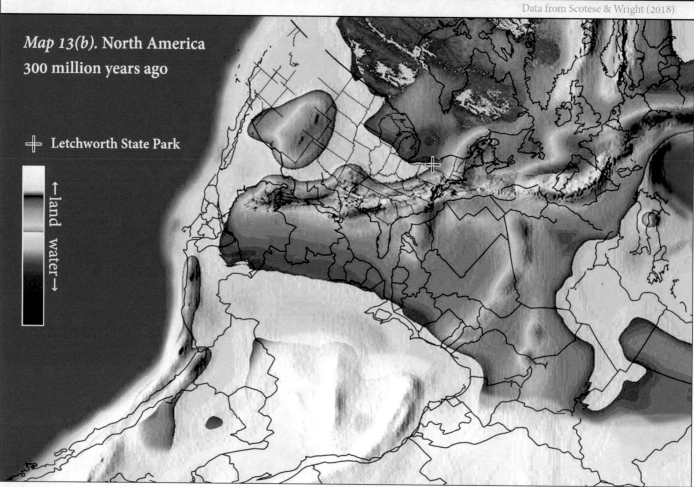

Map 13(b). North America
300 million years ago

⊹ Letchworth State Park

←land
water→

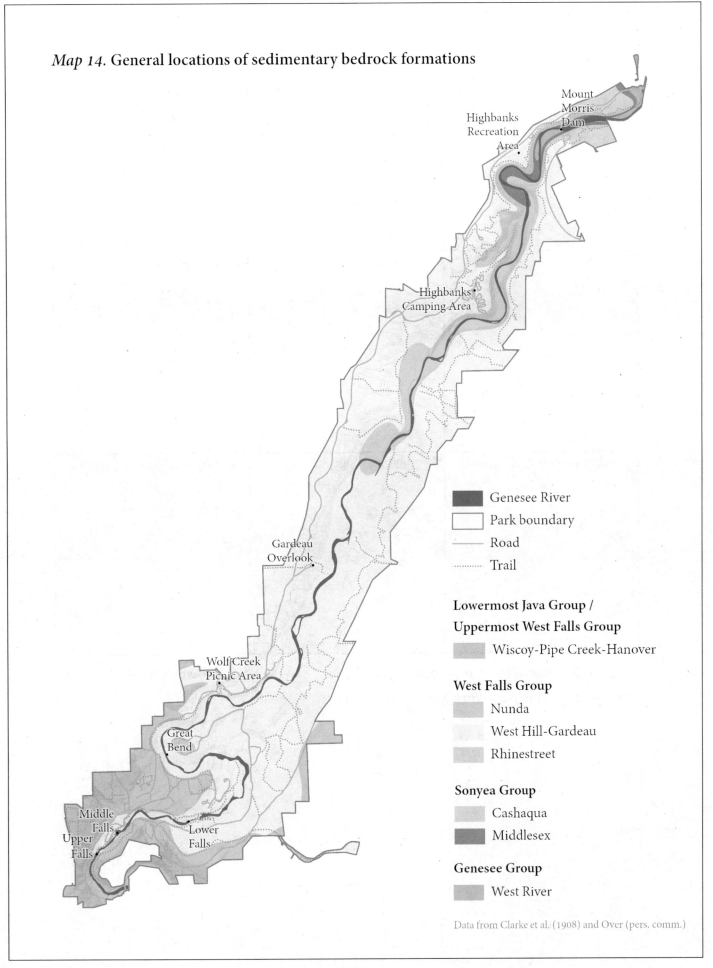

Map 14. General locations of sedimentary bedrock formations

Mount Morris Dam

Highbanks Recreation Area

Highbanks Camping Area

Gardeau Overlook

Wolf Creek Picnic Area

Great Bend

Middle Falls

Upper Falls

Lower Falls

Genesee River

Park boundary

Road

Trail

Lowermost Java Group /
Uppermost West Falls Group

Wiscoy-Pipe Creek-Hanover

West Falls Group

Nunda

West Hill-Gardeau

Rhinestreet

Sonyea Group

Cashaqua

Middlesex

Genesee Group

West River

Data from Clarke et al. (1908) and Over (pers. comm.)

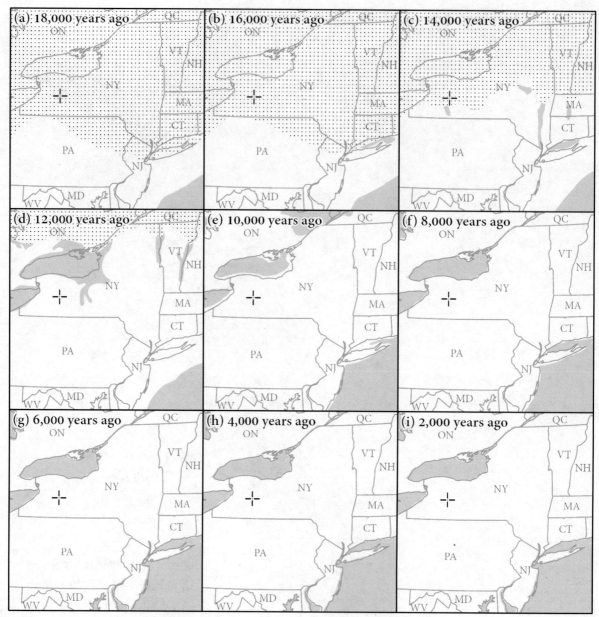

Map 15. Retreat of the Laurentide Ice Sheet
from present-day New York State and vicinity

::::::: Laurentide Ice Sheet

☐ Land

▨ Water

☐ Present-day state or province

-╀- Letchworth State Park

Data from Dyke et al. (2003)

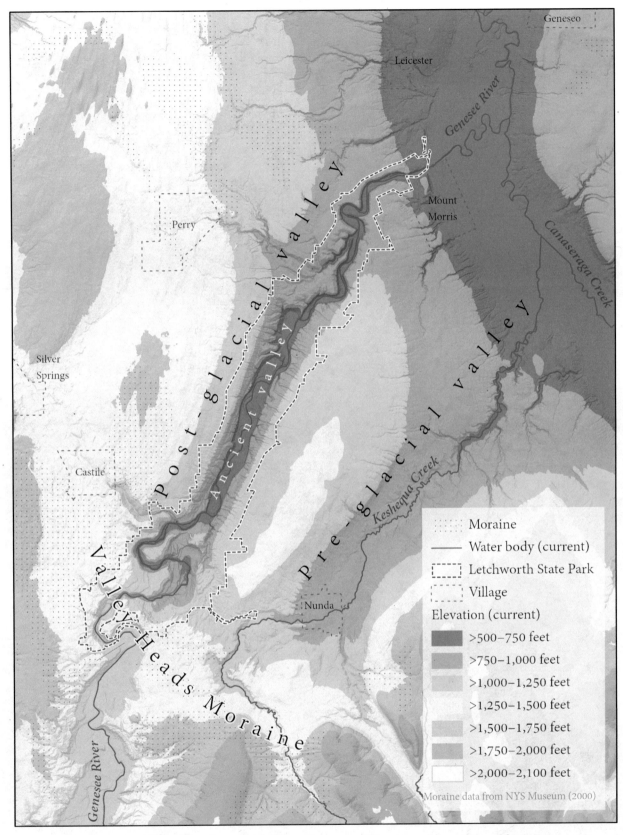

Map 16. Pre- and post-glacial paths of the Genesee River, and location of moraines

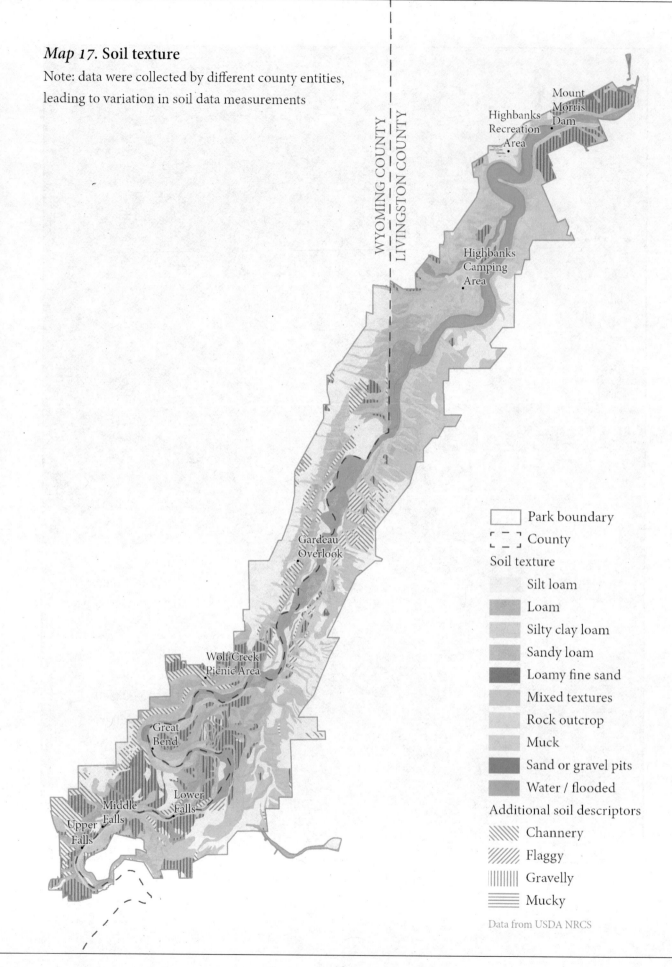

Map 17. Soil texture
Note: data were collected by different county entities,
leading to variation in soil data measurements

Mount
Morris
Dam

Highbanks
Recreation
Area

WYOMING COUNTY
LIVINGSTON COUNTY

Highbanks
Camping
Area

Gardeau
Overlook

Wolf Creek
Picnic Area

Great
Bend

Lower
Falls

Middle
Falls

Upper
Falls

Park boundary
County
Soil texture
Silt loam
Loam
Silty clay loam
Sandy loam
Loamy fine sand
Mixed textures
Rock outcrop
Muck
Sand or gravel pits
Water / flooded
Additional soil descriptors
Channery
Flaggy
Gravelly
Mucky

Data from USDA NRCS

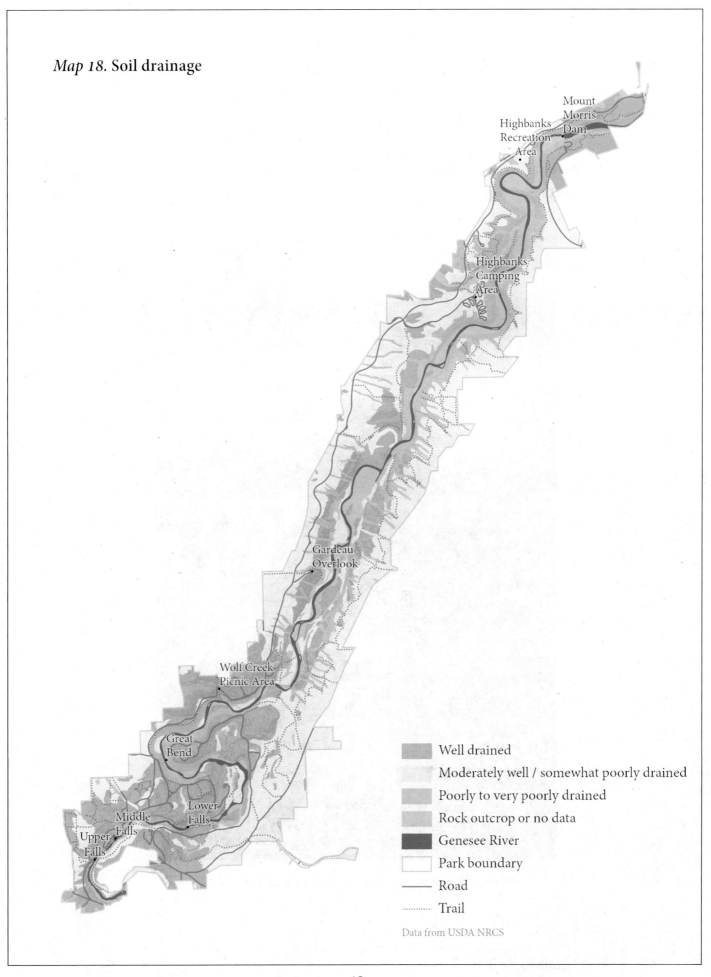

Map 18. Soil drainage

Well drained

Moderately well / somewhat poorly drained

Poorly to very poorly drained

Rock outcrop or no data

Genesee River

Park boundary

Road

Trail

Data from USDA NRCS

Mount
Morris
Dam

Highbanks
Recreation
Area

Highbanks
Camping
Area

Gardeau
Overlook

Wolf Creek
Picnic Area

Great
Bend

Lower
Falls

Middle
Falls

Upper
Falls

Land History and Ecological Communities

Left behind from the retreat of the Laurentide Ice Sheet was a landscape bare of soil and vegetation. A long process of soil development and ecological succession began. Following glaciation, the region around Letchworth State Park was a tundra-like environment, and then as the climate warmed and

Photo 6. A mature forest along the trail near Lower Falls.

more southerly tree species migrated northward a mixed forest resembling today's eventually developed. The forests of the area have always been in a state of flux during this time, as different plant species migrated northward at varying rates due to differences in seed dispersal strategies, and as individual plant species have responded to climatic changes and other environmental forces.

Prior to European-American settlement, the land that would become Letchworth State Park was predominantly forest. Providing an invaluable yet brief record of the landscape around the year 1800, land surveyors described forest conditions in and near the present-day park, as they measured lands into towns and lots that were later sold to settlers (Map 19). Toward the southern end of the park, forests were a mix of upland tree species composed of oak (*Quercus* spp.), pine (*Pinus strobus*), chestnut (*Castanea dentata*), and hemlock (*Tsuga canadensis*), with beech (*Fagus grandifolia*), maple (*Acer* spp.), hickory (*Carya* spp.), and ironwood (*Ostrya virginiana*) in smaller amounts. Toward the northern end, forests contained mainly oak and hickory. Wetlands, along with "swales" of moister land containing ash (*Fraxinus* spp.) and basswood (*Tilia americana*) and steep gullies containing pine

Photo 7. A footbridge crossing a stream through young forest in autumn near the former site of Gibsonville.

and hemlock, occasionally disrupted this pattern in the uplands. In the bottomland forests along the Genesee River, forests growing atop rich alluvial soils contained elm (*Ulmus americana*), sycamore (aka buttonwood, *Platanus occidentalis*), butternut (aka white walnut, *Juglans cinerea*), poplar (or "Balm of Gilead," *Populus* spp.), sugar maple (*Acer saccharum*), basswood, ash, and black walnut (*Juglans nigra*). Presenting a different and more generalized view of forest patterns around 1800, Map 20 estimates the relative abundance of trees in the area—the percentage of all trees that were of a given genus or species (a dataset also derived from land survey records). This map suggests that within the larger region embracing the park area, few tree types dominated the area: beech, maple, and oak, with other species present in lower abundances. Map 20 also suggests that the park was located at a transition zone regionally, between beech- and maple-dominated forests in the cooler and moister regions west, versus oak-dominated forests in the warmer and drier regions east. The original forests were home to many animals commonly found today, along with those that humans extirpated such as wolves (*Canis lupus*) and mountain lions (*Puma concolor*).

The landscape in and around the present-day park also contained considerable areas that Native Americans utilized during the eighteenth century and earlier. Native Americans—mainly Iroquois (Haudenosaunee) groups, including most importantly the Seneca (Onöndowa'ga:')—located towns

Photo 8. A forest of conifer trees in winter planted during the twentieth century.

along the Genesee River both within and outside the modern-day park boundary, connecting them by a network of well-established footpaths and canoe routes (chapter 3 covers Native American settlement in greater detail). Near towns were large clearings for agriculture, and in the uplands Native Americans burned forests to remove brush to create an open environment that facilitated travel and hunting. Surveyors observed evidence of Native American land use: described were occasional "open flats" along the Genesee River where Native Americans grew crops (Map 19). To the north, west, and south of the park's eventual location were descriptions of "thinly timbered" landscapes that suggest forests with widely spaced trees, thinned from surface burning and absent of brush and undergrowth. One surveyor even noted a "hunting ground . . . burnt over" between the park area and Silver Lake to the west. Just north in the current Town of Geneseo was an expansive agricultural area along the Genesee River known as the Genesee Flats. Together with other data, these survey records suggest that in 1800 the present-day Letchworth State Park was predominantly forested but also a mosaic of ecological communities, and a mixture of both natural and human landscapes.

Letchworth State Park embodies regional land-use trends over the last 200-plus years since white settlement began. Much like the rest of the northeastern United States, European-American settlement has initiated great change on the landscape within and around the park. Map 21 presents a coarse-resolution summary of land-cover change over the last three centuries. In 1700, western New York was heavily forested—"wild or remote woodlands" as symbolized in Map 21—except for those areas where Native Americans managed the land. By 1800, whites had sparsely settled the region (the "populated woodlands" in Map 21), mainly confined to areas along major travel routes. The region reached its peak deforestation just before the turn of the twentieth century: in 1900, western New York was largely agricultural and forest cover was patchy at both local and regional scales. By 2000, much of the former agricultural lands in the southern portion of western New York reforested, including within the present-day park.

While current visitors appreciate its forests, the park has historically been agricultural—in the generalized view of land cover in Map 21, the park's forest area is so comparatively small that the area is symbolized as farmland in 1900 and 2000 (later, Map 69 provides a detailed view of land use in the mid–twentieth century). Today the park forms a forest "island" amidst a heavily farmed region (Map 22), with approximately 70 percent of its perimeter directly adjacent to private farmland. The striking contrast between Letchworth State Park's forests and the surrounding area is perhaps best depicted in Map 23, which shows aerial imagery of the park and areas east (and which also shows the park during peak fall foliage).

The forested character of the park emerged only after twentieth-century park expansion via land acquisitions (shown later in Map 61) and subsequent reforestation. Based on early topographic

Photo 9. Forests in autumn at Great Bend.

maps and aerial photos, Map 24 shows areas that have reforested since 1940, versus those areas that were forested in 1940. In 1940, roughly half of the park was forested. Today, that number has increased to over 70 percent, yet this number excludes the flooded bottomland of the Mount Morris Reservoir that contains patches of younger floodplain forest that are variably classified as forest or shrubland among different datasets. Older forests are likely those that reforested in the nineteenth century after clearcutting, former woodlots that their owners selectively logged, or untouched forests in inaccessible locations like remote river terraces and steep ravines. As opposed to Map 24, Map 25 estimates the minimum age of forests within the original Glen Iris Estate area by showing which patches of current forest were also forested in 1880 or 1950, as determined from historical maps and aerial photos. While mature forests of the park typically started growing around 1890, tree-ring samples from fallen trees have provided evidence of ancient trees in the oldest forests in Map 25: one white oak (*Quercus alba*) south of Upper Falls was 375 years old, and an eastern redcedar (*Juniperus virginiana*) near Inspiration Point was 435 years old.

Even more so than the past, modern-day Letchworth State Park is a patchwork of land-cover types and forests of varying ages that has resulted from both the variability of environmental conditions and its history of human land use. Two general land covers dominate Letchworth State Park at present: forests cover the valley slopes and uplands, whereas shrublands and other areas routinely flooded by the Mount Morris Reservoir (covered later) are found throughout the valley bottom of the northern two-thirds of the park. In total, forests comprise approximately 72 percent of the park, according to a 2004 survey. As shown in Map 26, the most common types are older oak-hickory (23%) and hemlock-northern hardwood forests (23%), and younger (successional) northern hardwood forests (22%). Conifer (evergreen) plantations (16%) and older maple-basswood forests (14%) also make up sizeable portions of total forest cover, whereas floodplain forests (2%) found along the Genesee River are less common. Map 27 shows other ecological communities besides forests: cliffside plant communities and wetlands (such as marshes, swamps, and fens) are examples of minor but important parts of the park's natural ecosystem.

The above ecosystems host numerous plant, animal, and fungus species both common and rare within the northeastern United States. One biodiversity database containing records of species observations along with museum and herbarium specimens tallied around 1,150 species within the park that included roughly 220 species of arthropods (mostly insects), 200 species of birds, 30 species of fishes, 20 species of mammals, 20 species of amphibians, 10 species of reptiles, 370 species of plants, and 260 species of fungi. The actual number of species in the park is likely much higher. Some of the most visible and common animals in the park include white-tailed deer (*Odocoileus virginianus*) and turkey vultures (*Cathartes aura*), whereas some of the most notable but less-observed animals include the rare timber rattlesnake (*Crotalus horridus*) and the occasional black bear (*Ursus americanus*). This atlas does not provide maps of individual species locations since many species are distributed more or less evenly throughout the park. Later, Maps 87 through 90 present some of the notable animal life in the park as it relates to hunting and birdwatching.

Just how important is Letchworth State Park as a habitat and refuge for plant and animal species, and how does Letchworth State Park fit within the larger regional picture of land conservation? Compared to other state parks in New York, the park is one of the most important for protecting species of concern in the state. As shown in Map 28, the park ranks highly among state parks, according to a 2004 report: it ranks first in documented rare plants (18 total), tied for second in

Photo 10. An eastern redcedar tree (*Juniperus virginiana*) atop the cliffs near Highbanks Recreation Area.

documented imperiled animals (9 total), first in documented listed species combined (27 total), and tied for eleventh in documented significant natural communities (6 total). None of those species of concern are federally listed endangered species, but the park could still contain undiscovered rare species. Map 29 shows the "human footprint" in the region, a measure of human pressure on the natural environment due to development, population, land use, and transportation: according to this map, the park conserves lands nearly as wild as the Adirondack Park to the northeast and the Pennsylvania Wilds to the south. And, as shown in Map 30, the park is one of the few large tracts of protected land in western New York, where it is only smaller than Allegany State Park and Finger Lakes National Forest. Overall, Letchworth State Park is a valuable refuge for species and natural communities, and reversion to more natural land cover via reforestation is an emerging ecological success story. However, life within the park faces threats such as invasive species that outcompete natives and the growing threat of climate change—both of which could alter the composition, structure, and function of the park ecosystem.

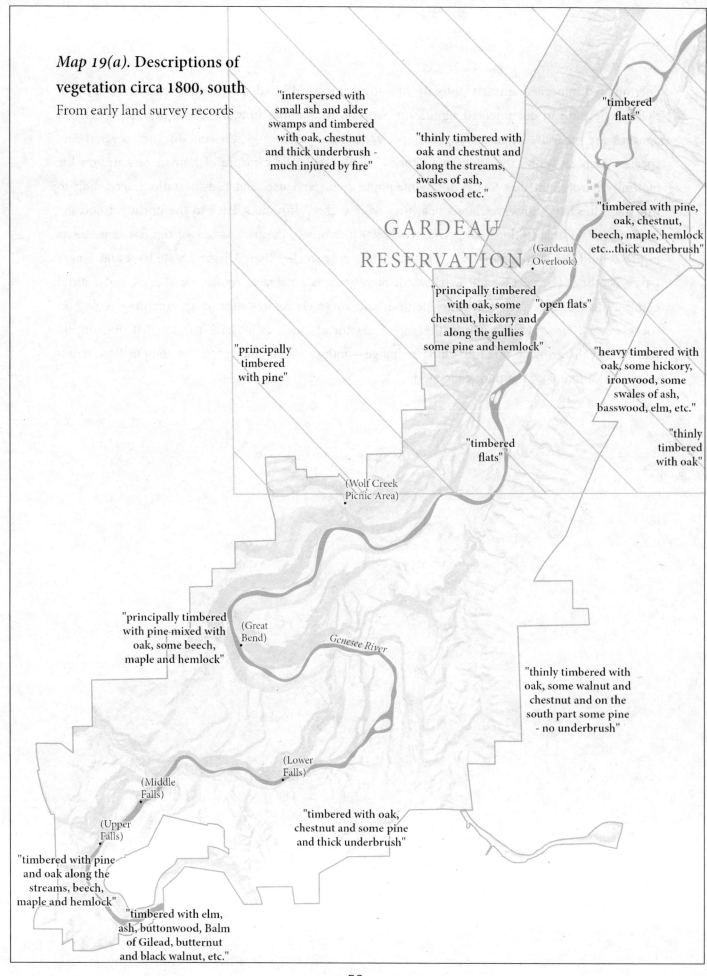

Map 19(a). **Descriptions of vegetation circa 1800, south**
From early land survey records

"interspersed with small ash and alder swamps and timbered with oak, chestnut and thick underbrush - much injured by fire"

"thinly timbered with oak and chestnut and along the streams, swales of ash, basswood etc."

"timbered flats"

"timbered with pine, oak, chestnut, beech, maple, hemlock etc...thick underbrush"

GARDEAU
RESERVATION

(Gardeau Overlook)

"principally timbered with oak, some chestnut, hickory and along the gullies some pine and hemlock"

"open flats"

"heavy timbered with oak, some hickory, ironwood, some swales of ash, basswood, elm, etc."

"principally timbered with pine"

"thinly timbered with oak"

"timbered flats"

(Wolf Creek Picnic Area)

"principally timbered with pine mixed with oak, some beech, maple and hemlock"

(Great Bend)

Genesee River

"thinly timbered with oak, some walnut and chestnut and on the south part some pine - no underbrush"

(Lower Falls)

(Middle Falls)

"timbered with oak, chestnut and some pine and thick underbrush"

(Upper Falls)

"timbered with pine and oak along the streams, beech, maple and hemlock"

"timbered with elm, ash, buttonwood, Balm of Gilead, butternut and black walnut, etc."

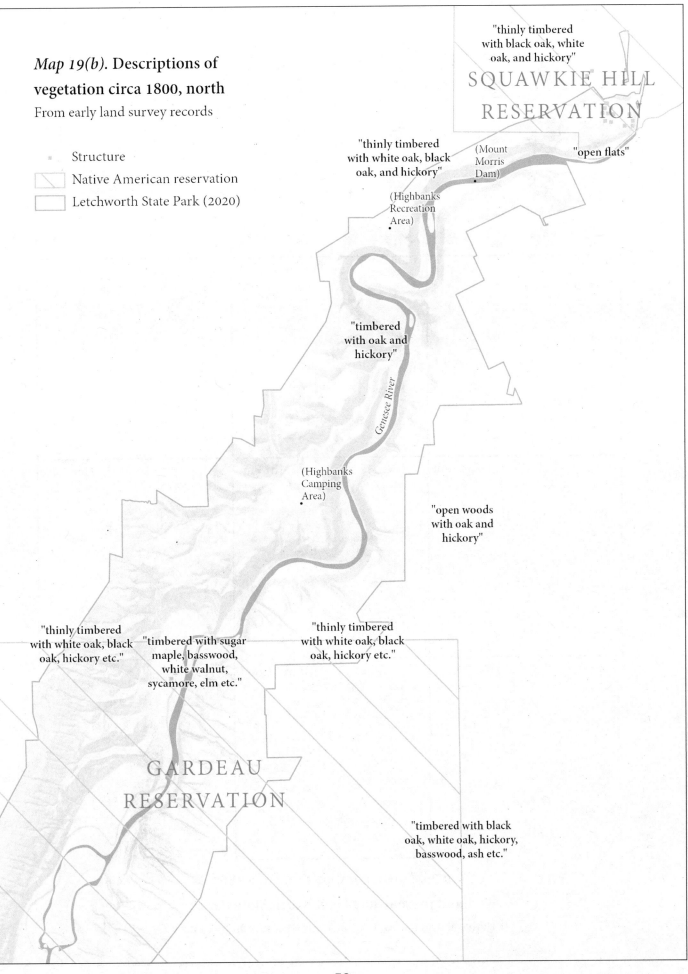

Map 19(b). Descriptions of vegetation circa 1800, north

From early land survey records

- Structure
- Native American reservation
- Letchworth State Park (2020)

"thinly timbered with black oak, white oak, and hickory"

SQUAWKIE HILL RESERVATION

"thinly timbered with white oak, black oak, and hickory"

(Mount Morris Dam)

(Highbanks Recreation Area)

"open flats"

"timbered with oak and hickory"

Genesee River

(Highbanks Camping Area)

"open woods with oak and hickory"

"thinly timbered with white oak, black oak, hickory etc."

"timbered with sugar maple, basswood, white walnut, sycamore, elm etc."

"thinly timbered with white oak, black oak, hickory etc."

GARDEAU RESERVATION

"timbered with black oak, white oak, hickory, basswood, ash etc."

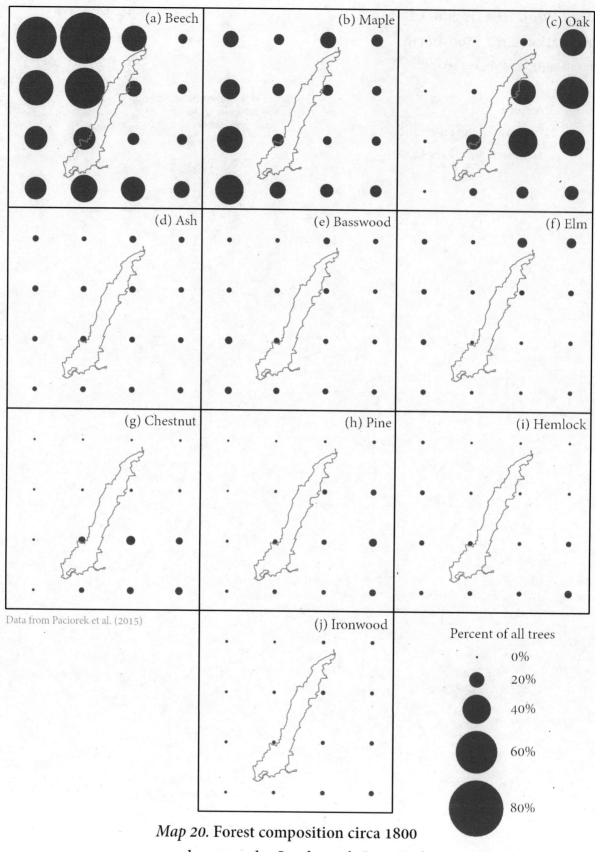

Map 20. Forest composition circa 1800 around present-day Letchworth State Park

Relative abundance of the top 10 most common tree taxa

Data from Paciorek et al. (2015)

Percent of all trees

0%
20%
40%
60%
80%

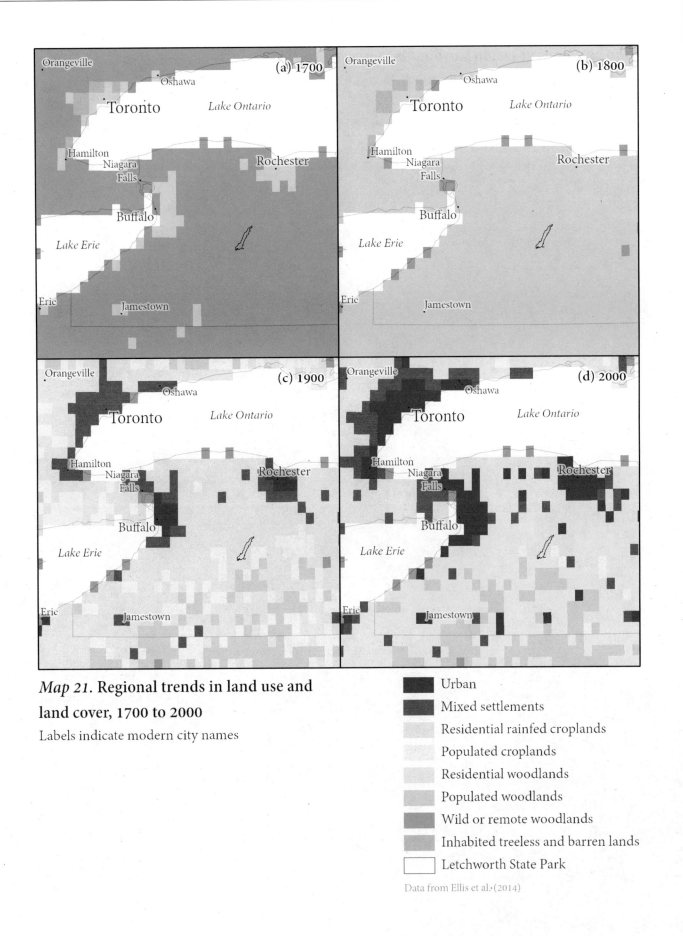

Map 21. Regional trends in land use and land cover, 1700 to 2000

Labels indicate modern city names

Urban
Mixed settlements
Residential rainfed croplands
Populated croplands
Residential woodlands
Populated woodlands
Wild or remote woodlands
Inhabited treeless and barren lands
Letchworth State Park

Data from Ellis et al. (2014)

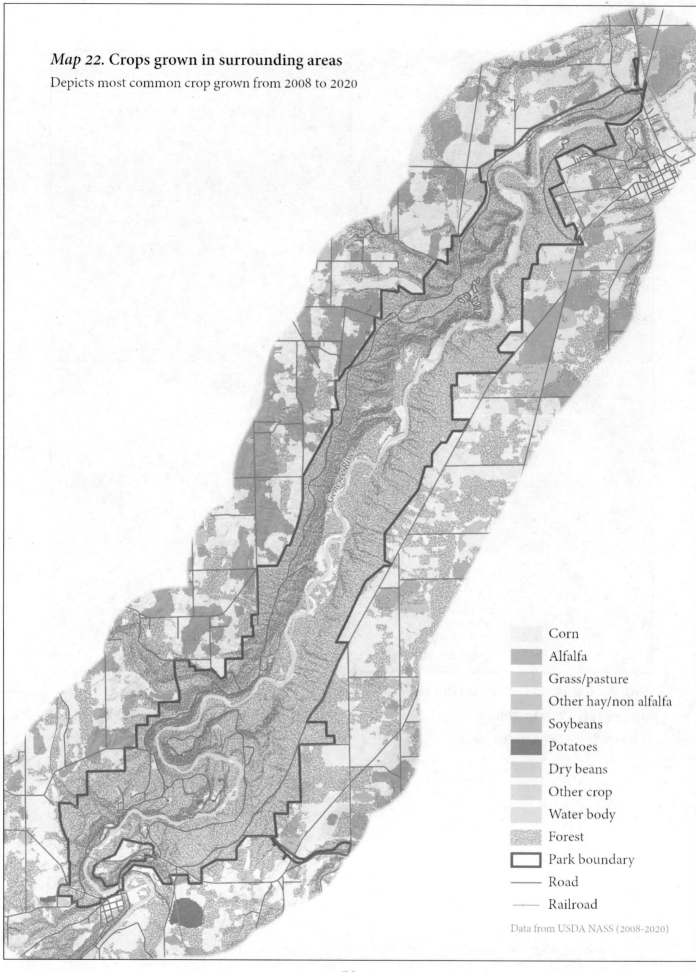

Map 22. Crops grown in surrounding areas

Depicts most common crop grown from 2008 to 2020

Genesee River

Corn
Alfalfa
Grass/pasture
Other hay/non alfalfa
Soybeans
Potatoes
Dry beans
Other crop
Water body
Forest
Park boundary
Road
Railroad

Data from USDA NASS (2008-2020)

Map 23. Satellite imagery of Letchworth State Park and western Finger Lakes during peak foliage
Landsat satellite imagery collected on October 24, 2014

Honeoye Lake

Canadice Lake

Hemlock Lake

Conesus Lake

Dansville

Geneseo

Mount Morris

Perry

Silver Lake

Letchworth State Park

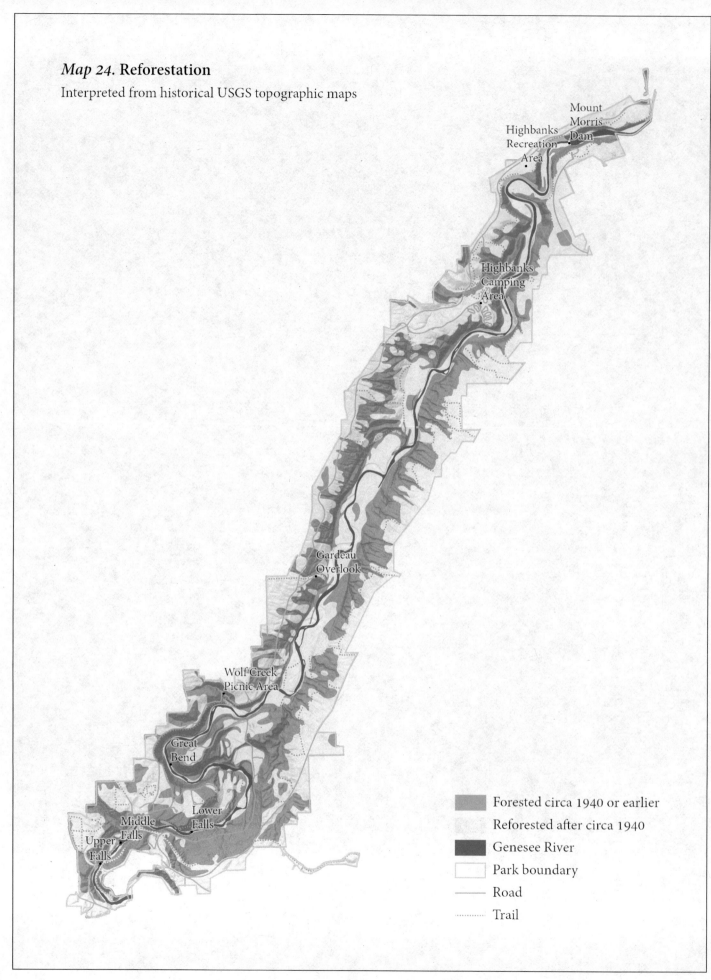

Map 24. Reforestation

Interpreted from historical USGS topographic maps

Mount
Morris
Dam

Highbanks
Recreation
Area

Highbanks
Camping
Area

Gardeau
Overlook

Wolf Creek
Picnic Area

Great
Bend

Lower
Falls

Middle
Falls

Upper
Falls

Forested circa 1940 or earlier

Reforested after circa 1940

Genesee River

Park boundary

Road

Trail

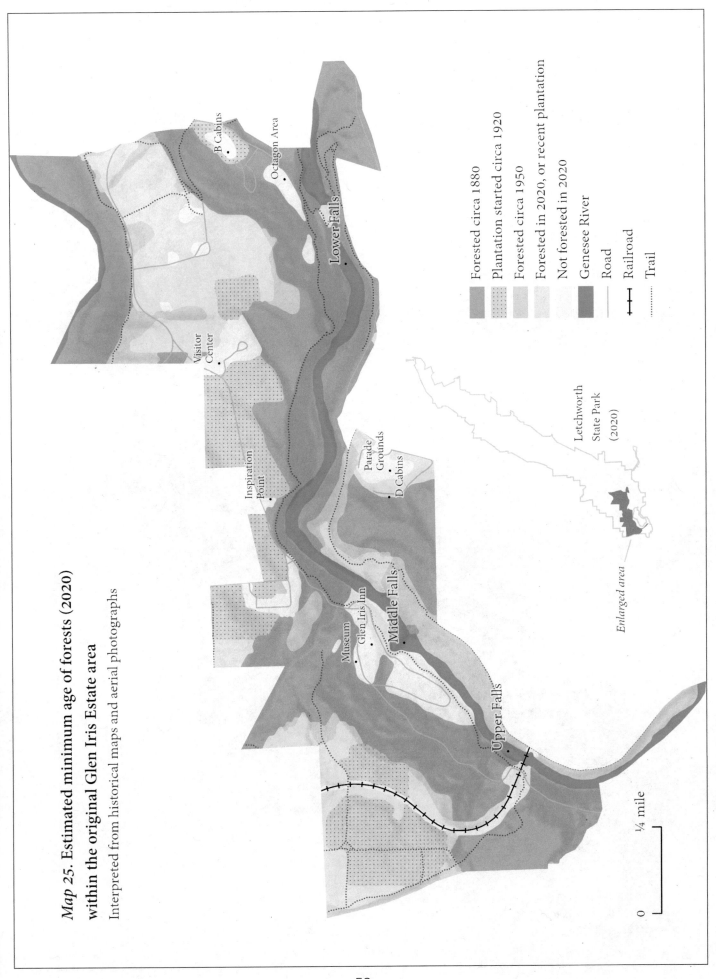

Map 25. **Estimated minimum age of forests (2020) within the original Glen Iris Estate area**
Interpreted from historical maps and aerial photographs

Forested circa 1880
Plantation started circa 1920
Forested circa 1950
Forested in 2020, or recent plantation
Not forested in 2020
Genesee River
Road
Railroad
Trail

B Cabins
Octagon Area
Lower Falls
Visitor Center
Inspiration Point
Parade Grounds
D Cabins
Museum
Glen Iris Inn
Middle Falls
Upper Falls

Letchworth State Park (2020)
Enlarged area

0   ¼ mile

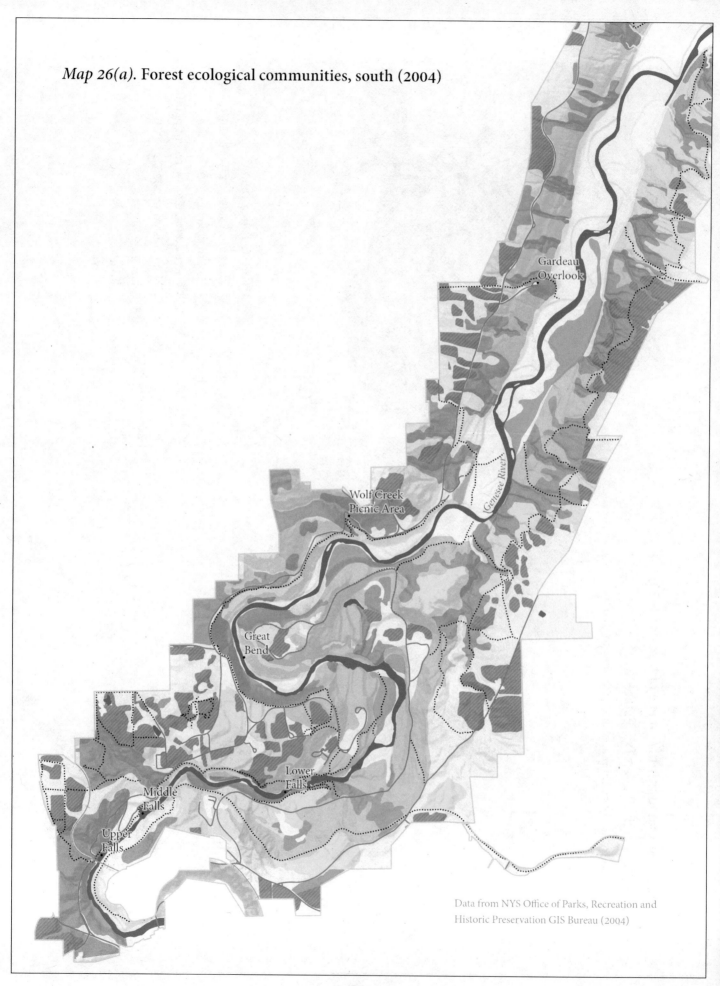

Map 26(a). Forest ecological communities, south (2004)

Gardeau
Overlook

Wolf Creek
Picnic Area

Genesee River

Great
Bend

Lower
Falls

Middle
Falls

Upper
Falls

Data from NYS Office of Parks, Recreation and
Historic Preservation GIS Bureau (2004)

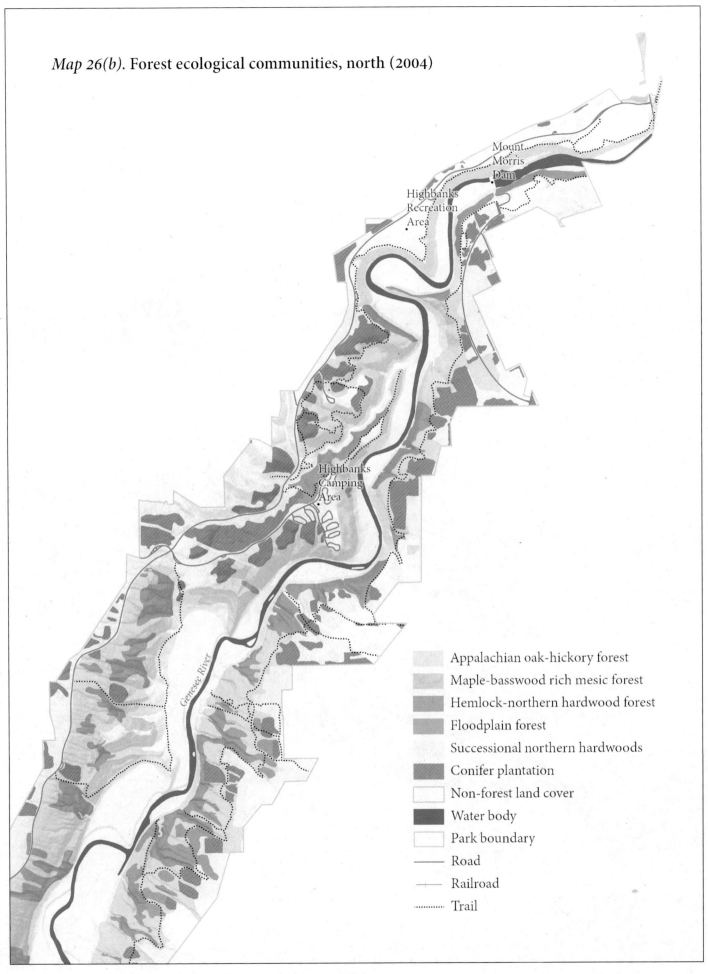

Map 26(b). Forest ecological communities, north (2004)

Mount Morris Dam

Highbanks Recreation Area

Highbanks Camping Area

Genesee River

Appalachian oak-hickory forest

Maple-basswood rich mesic forest

Hemlock-northern hardwood forest

Floodplain forest

Successional northern hardwoods

Conifer plantation

Non-forest land cover

Water body

Park boundary

— Road

— Railroad

······ Trail

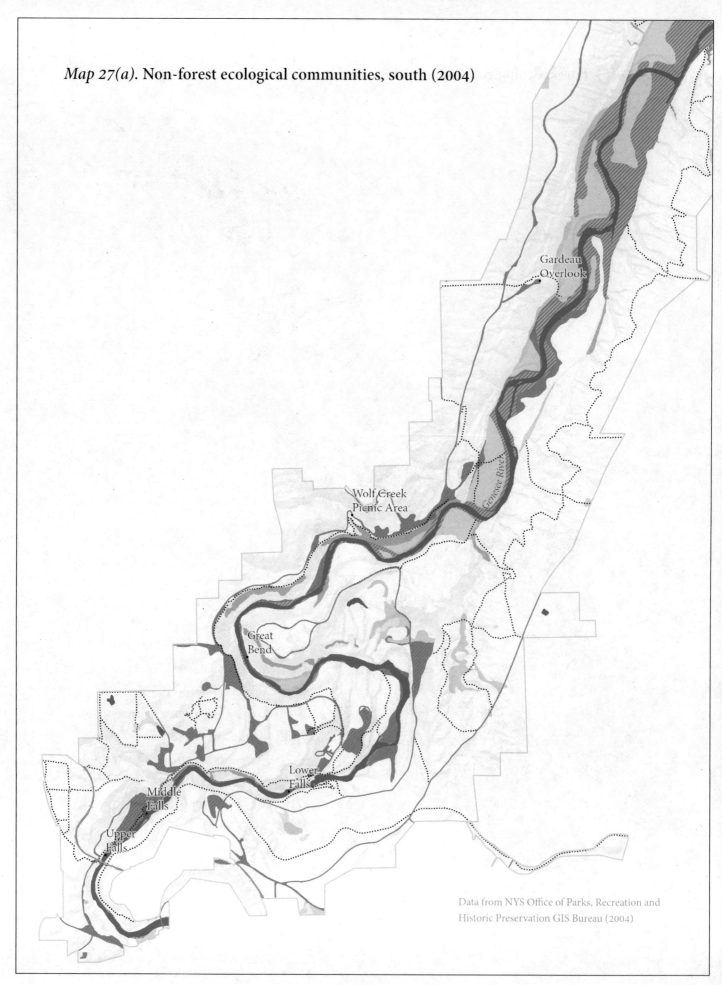

Map 27(a). Non-forest ecological communities, south (2004)

Gardeau
Overlook

Genesee River

Wolf Creek
Picnic Area

Great
Bend

Lower
Falls

Middle
Falls

Upper
Falls

Data from NYS Office of Parks, Recreation and
Historic Preservation GIS Bureau (2004)

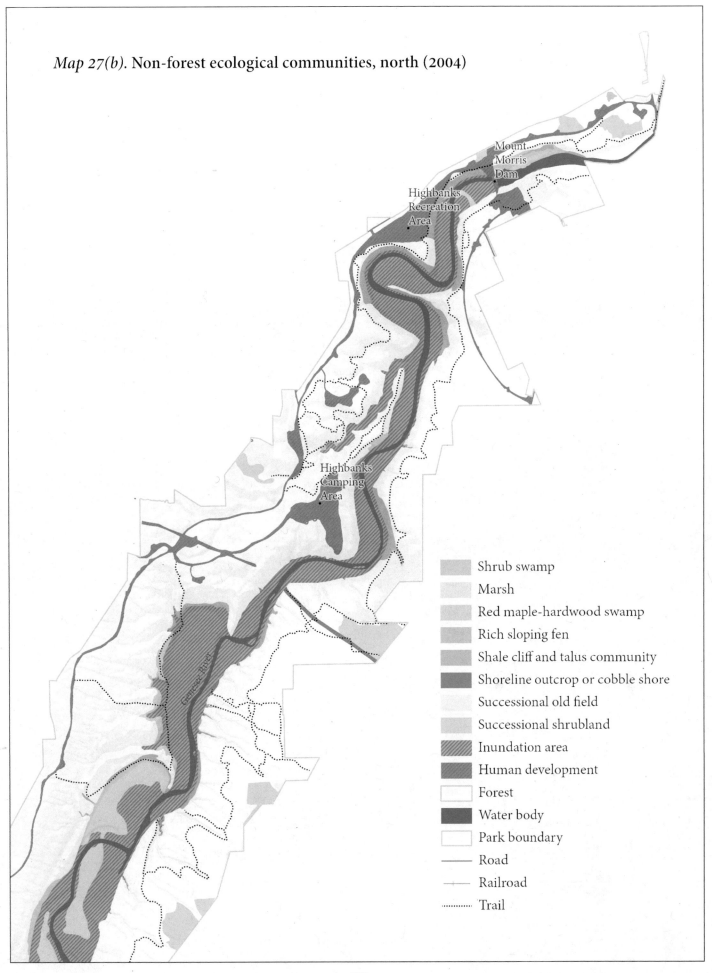

Map 27(b). Non-forest ecological communities, north (2004)

Mount
Mörris
Dam

Highbanks
Recreation
Area

Highbanks
Camping
Area

Genesee River

	Shrub swamp
	Marsh
	Red maple-hardwood swamp
	Rich sloping fen
	Shale cliff and talus community
	Shoreline outcrop or cobble shore
	Successional old field
	Successional shrubland
	Inundation area
	Human development
	Forest
	Water body
	Park boundary
——	Road
—+—	Railroad
·········	Trail

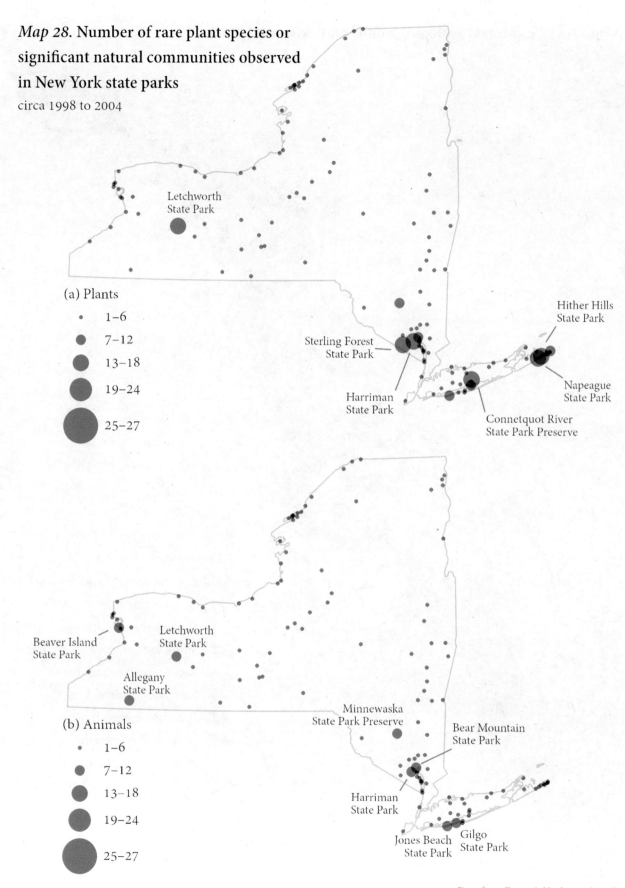

Map 28. Number of rare plant species or significant natural communities observed in New York state parks
circa 1998 to 2004

(a) Plants

- · 1–6
- ● 7–12
- ● 13–18
- ● 19–24
- ● 25–27

Letchworth State Park

Hither Hills State Park

Sterling Forest State Park

Harriman State Park

Connetquot River State Park Preserve

Napeague State Park

(b) Animals

- · 1–6
- ● 7–12
- ● 13–18
- ● 19–24
- ● 25–27

Beaver Island State Park

Letchworth State Park

Allegany State Park

Minnewaska State Park Preserve

Bear Mountain State Park

Harriman State Park

Jones Beach State Park

Gilgo State Park

Data from Evans & VanLuven (2007)

64

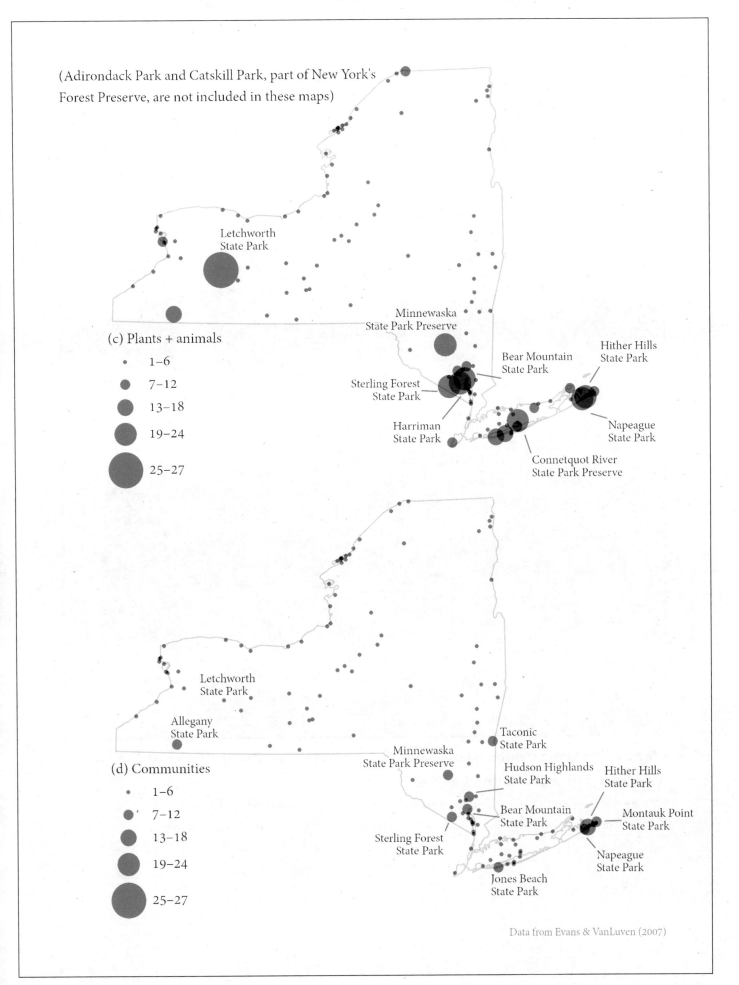

(Adirondack Park and Catskill Park, part of New York's Forest Preserve, are not included in these maps)

(c) Plants + animals

- 1–6
- 7–12
- 13–18
- 19–24
- 25–27

Letchworth State Park

Minnewaska State Park Preserve

Sterling Forest State Park

Harriman State Park

Bear Mountain State Park

Hither Hills State Park

Napeague State Park

Connetquot River State Park Preserve

(d) Communities

- 1–6
- 7–12
- 13–18
- 19–24
- 25–27

Letchworth State Park

Allegany State Park

Minnewaska State Park Preserve

Sterling Forest State Park

Taconic State Park

Hudson Highlands State Park

Bear Mountain State Park

Jones Beach State Park

Hither Hills State Park

Montauk Point State Park

Napeague State Park

Data from Evans & VanLuven (2007)

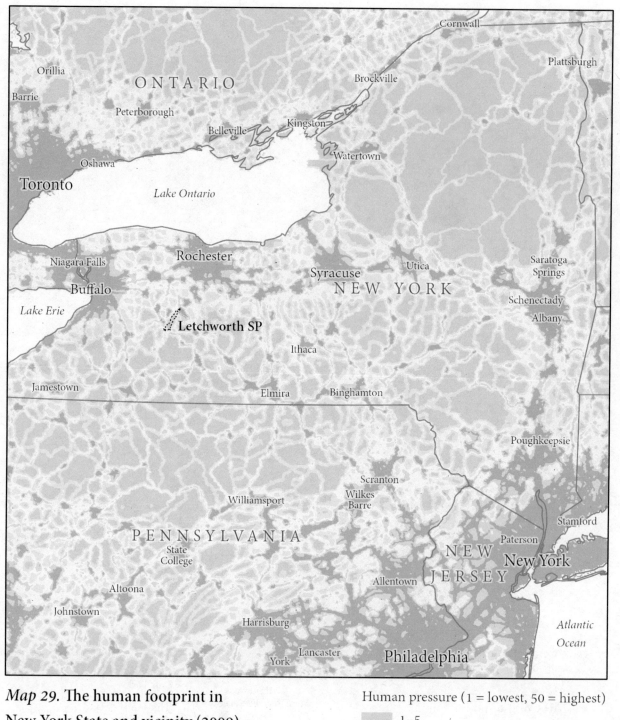

Map 29. The human footprint in
New York State and vicinity (2009)

Human pressure on the natural environment

Human pressure (1 = lowest, 50 = highest)

	1–5
	6–10
	11–20
	21–30
	31–50

Data from Venter et al. (2018)

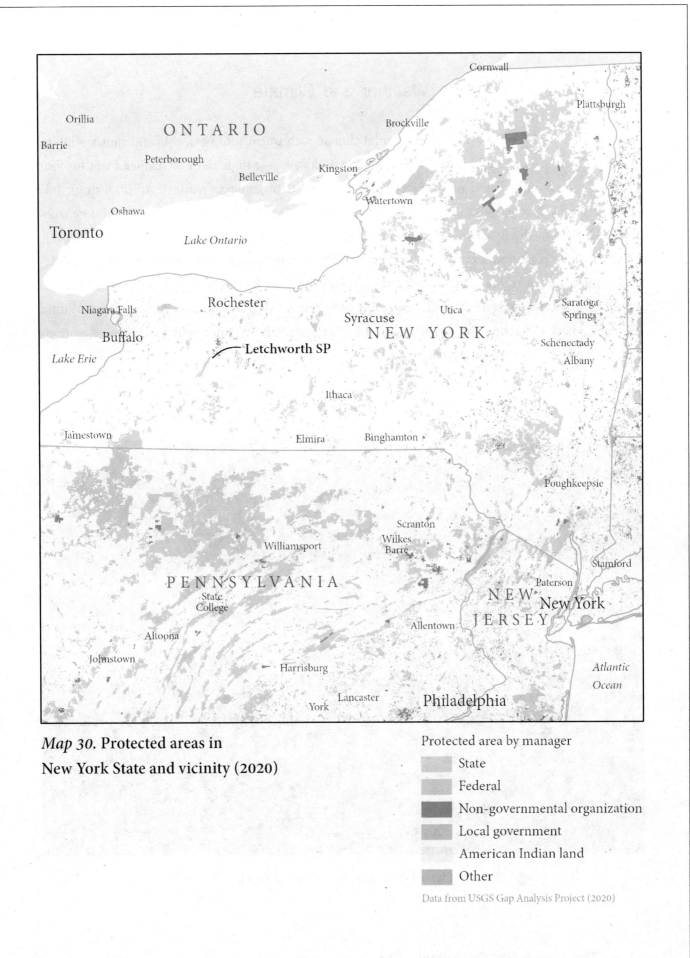

Map 30. Protected areas in
New York State and vicinity (2020)

Protected area by manager

- State
- Federal
- Non-governmental organization
- Local government
- American Indian land
- Other

Data from USGS Gap Analysis Project (2020)

Weather and Climate

Letchworth State Park has a humid continental climate with warm summers, cold and snowy winters, and precipitation year-round. Map 31 presents the park's average high and low temperatures for four representative months based on averages from 1981 to 2010: January (winter), April (spring), July (summer), and October (autumn). The park experiences average high temperatures that range from about 32 degrees (F) (0 C) in January to 81 degrees (F) (27 C) in July. Yet, for being a relatively small area, the park does experience some variability in temperatures due to its differences in elevation. Also shown in Map 31, average temperatures can vary by as much as 5 degrees (F) (2.8 C) across the park during some months, especially with respect to overnight low temperatures. Within the park, lower elevations and northerly locations are generally warmer, whereas higher elevations and southerly locations are generally cooler.

Photo 11. A rainbow over Great Bend.

Photo 12. Autumn foliage above the Genesee River downstream from Mount Morris Dam.

The park receives 34 inches (86 cm) of precipitation per year based on averages from 1981 to 2020, but that also varies: from drier in the lower and northerly locations, to moister in the higher and southerly areas (Map 32). Snowfall departs from these spatial patterns: averaging about 75 inches (191 cm) each winter, the west side of the park receives slightly more snowfall than the east side, since it is closer to a major lake-effect snowbelt west of the park (Map 33). Lake-effect snow occurs when relatively warm air blows across cold Lake Erie, affecting areas downwind from the Great Lakes. Despite being just 25 miles (40 km) apart, Warsaw to the northwest receives 142 inches (361 cm) per winter, and Dansville to the southeast receives just 40 inches (102 cm) per winter.

The park is fortunate to experience few severe weather events and natural disasters. Map 34 shows the number and types of recorded severe weather events in Wyoming, Livingston, and Allegany Counties from 1991 to 2020: note that severe weather events are recorded at the county level when they are more widespread, and at the town level when they are more localized. On average, five (Livingston County) to eight (Wyoming County) events are recorded at the county level each year. County-level events are most often snow related such as lake-effect snowstorms, large snowstorms associated with low-pressure systems, and blizzards. High winds are the second-most common event at the county-level. As for events recorded at the town level, the five towns containing the park average one event every two to ten years: by far the most common are strong winds associated with thunderstorms, followed by hail and flooding. Tornadoes are quite rare, but predating the data shown in Map 34 was the "centennial tornado"—a tornado that struck the hamlet of Portageville at the south end of the park on July 4, 1876, destroying property, injuring many, and killing one. Since 1955, Livingston and Wyoming Counties have received a FEMA disaster declaration once every two-and-a-half to three years, but most typically for snowstorms, floods, or other storms that do not have long-lasting or widespread impacts on life or property.

Every few years the park experiences wind and rain from tropical storms or depressions, which are weakened hurricanes that formed in the North Atlantic Ocean (Map 35). However, one hurricane—Hurricane Agnes of 1972—was uniquely destructive to Letchworth State Park as a tropical

Photo 13. A footbridge crossing Wolf Creek beneath hemlock trees (*Tsuga canadensis*) in winter.

storm and is given greater attention later in Maps 70 and 71. To summarize weather hazards in the park by considering both the frequency and types of events, typically severe weather produces downed tree limbs, localized flooding, or snowy road conditions once every few years.

With a warming planet due to human-caused carbon emissions that enhance Earth's greenhouse effect, global climate models are predicting major changes to Earth's climate, including that of Letchworth State Park. Maps 36 and 37 show predictions for average annual temperature and precipitation (respectively) in the years 2050 and 2080, for both low emissions and high emissions scenarios. If humankind follows a low emissions path, the park will still see increases in average annual temperature upward of 2 degrees (F) (1.1 C) by 2080, but the "business-as-usual" high emissions path would lead to warming as high as 5 degrees (F) (2.8 C). Average annual precipitation could be 2 inches (5 cm) higher. These maps obscure seasonal variability, meaning that temperature and precipitation changes may be more severe in certain seasons and less severe in others. Also predicted around the Letchworth State Park region are more days over 90 degrees (F) (32 C), fewer days under 32 degrees (F) (0 C), more and longer heat waves, more droughts, less snowfall, and more extreme weather events. Moreover, climate change may mute the park's renowned autumn foliage: in addition to climate-induced impacts upon the timing of color change and leaf drop, trees that turn vibrant colors (such as maple) could diminish and trees that turn duller colors (such as oak) could persist.

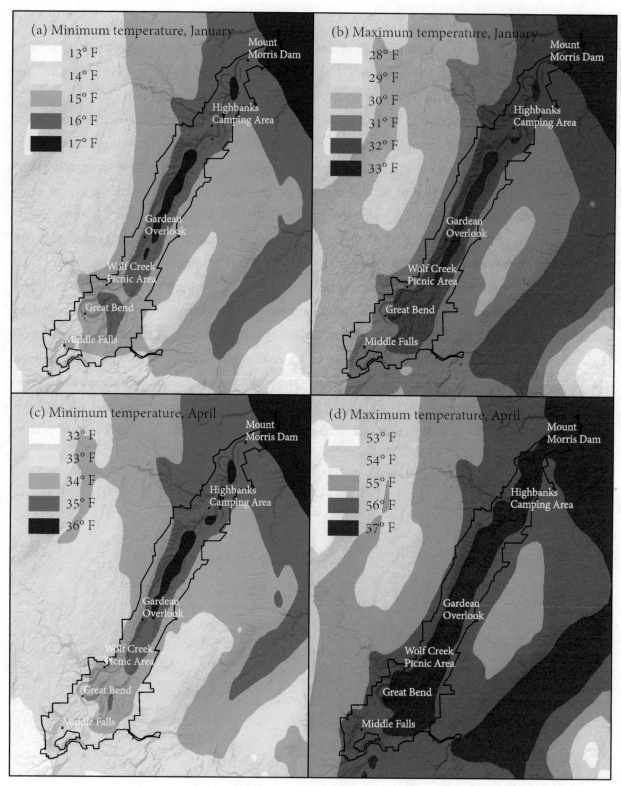

Map 31(a–d). Average minimum and maximum temperature in January and April, 1981 to 2010

Data from PRISM Climate Group (2012)

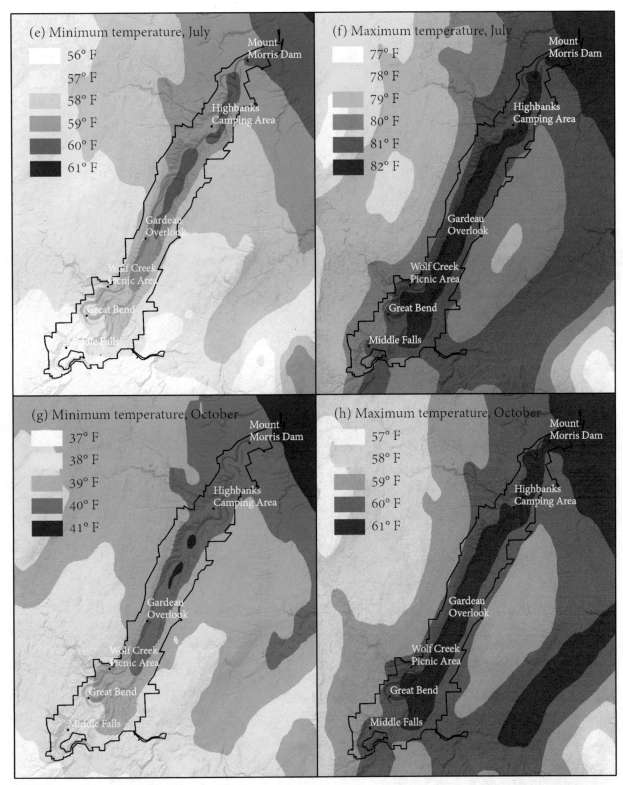

Map 31(e–h). Average minimum and maximum temperature in July and October, 1981 to 2010

Data from PRISM Climate Group (2012)

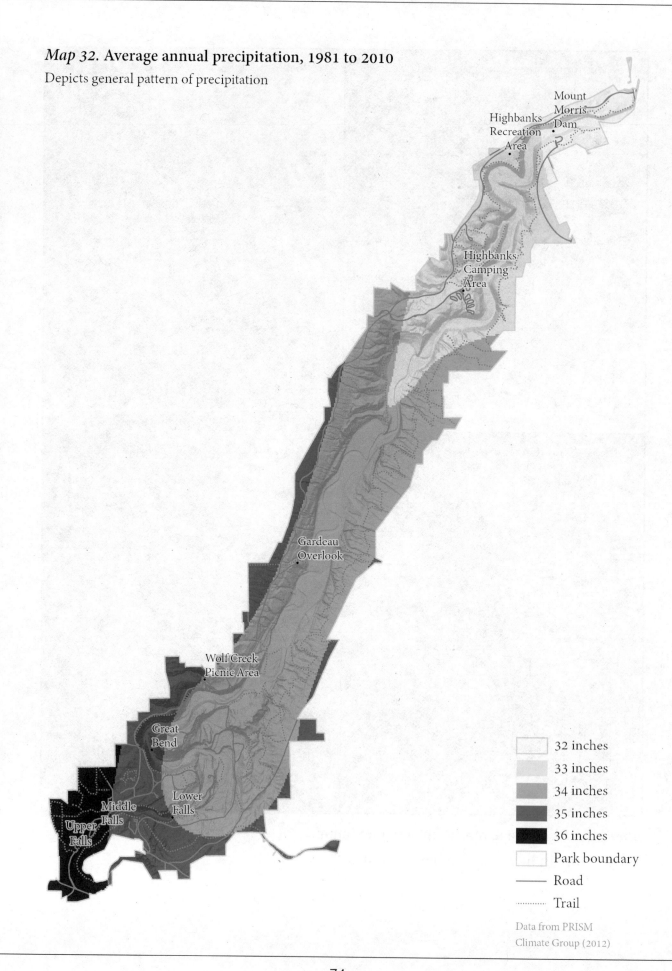

Map 32. **Average annual precipitation, 1981 to 2010**

Depicts general pattern of precipitation

Mount
Morris
Dam

Highbanks
Recreation
Area

Highbanks
Camping
Area

Gardeau
Overlook

Wolf Creek
Picnic Area

Great
Bend

Lower
Falls

Middle
Falls

Upper
Falls

32 inches
33 inches
34 inches
35 inches
36 inches
Park boundary
——— Road
·········· Trail

Data from PRISM
Climate Group (2012)

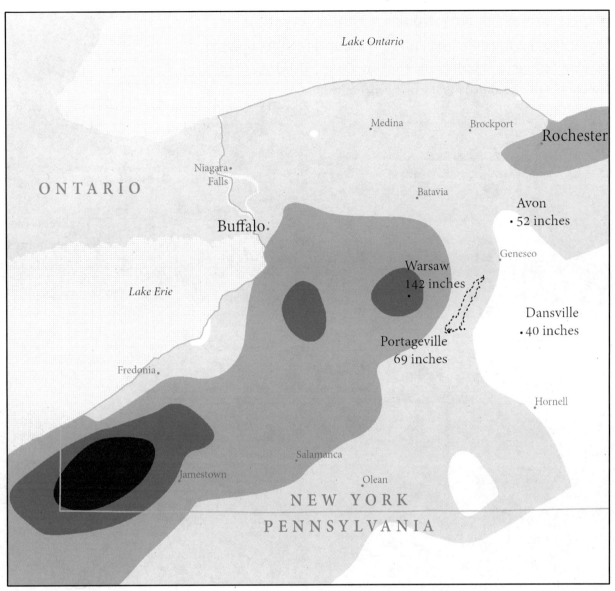

Lake Ontario

ONTARIO

Medina ·   Brockport ·

Rochester

Niagara ·
Falls

Batavia ·

Buffalo ·

Avon
· 52 inches

Lake Erie

Geneseo ·

Warsaw
142 inches
·

Dansville
· 40 inches

Portageville
69 inches

Fredonia ·

Hornell ·

Salamanca ·

Jamestown ·

Olean ·

NEW YORK

PENNSYLVANIA

Map 33. **Average snowfall in western New York State, 1981 to 2010**

Annual snowfall is labeled for four stations closest to Letchworth SP

60 inches and fewer

\>60–90 inches

\>90–120 inches

\>120–150 inches

\>150 inches

Letchworth SP

Water body

Data from NOAA NCDC (2011)

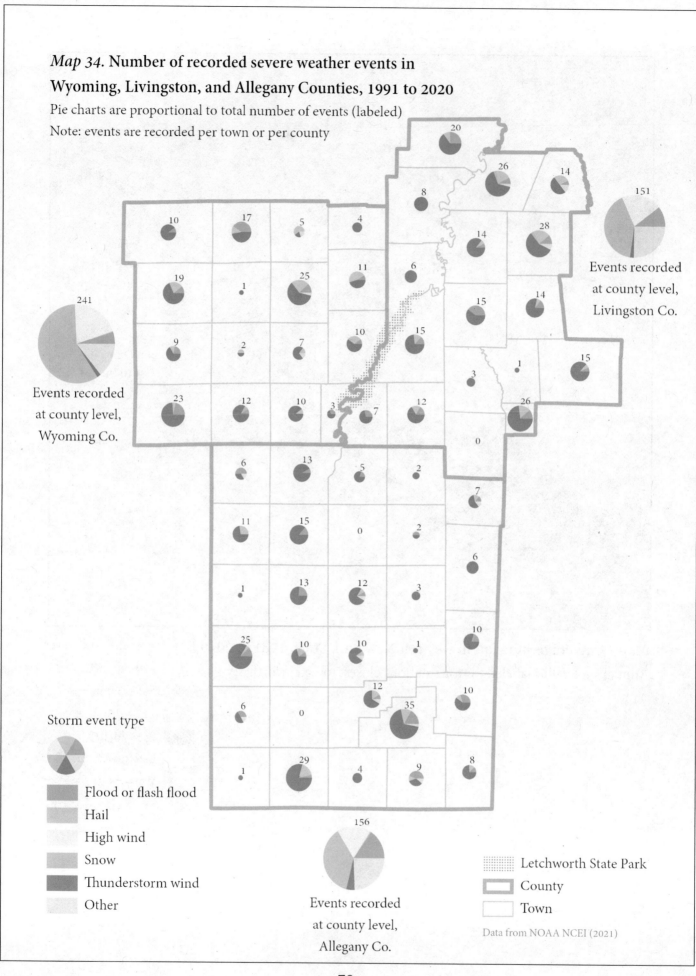

Map 34. Number of recorded severe weather events in Wyoming, Livingston, and Allegany Counties, 1991 to 2020

Pie charts are proportional to total number of events (labeled)

Note: events are recorded per town or per county

Events recorded at county level, Livingston Co.

Events recorded at county level, Wyoming Co.

Storm event type

Flood or flash flood
Hail
High wind
Snow
Thunderstorm wind
Other

Letchworth State Park
County
Town

Data from NOAA NCEI (2021)

Events recorded at county level, Allegany Co.

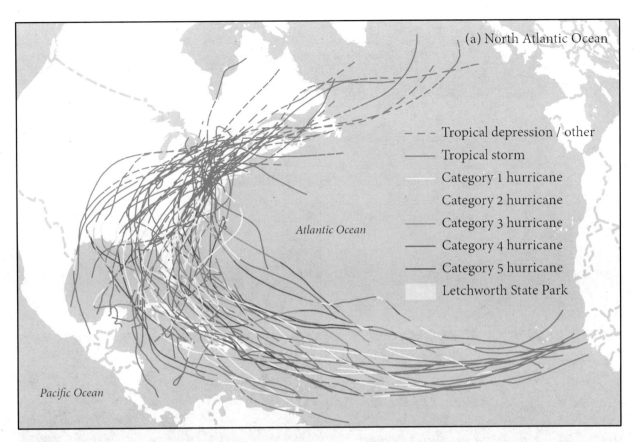

(a) North Atlantic Ocean

Atlantic Ocean

Pacific Ocean

- - - Tropical depression / other
——— Tropical storm
——— Category 1 hurricane
——— Category 2 hurricane
——— Category 3 hurricane
——— Category 4 hurricane
——— Category 5 hurricane
▓ Letchworth State Park

Map 35. **Tropical cyclones within 200 miles of Letchworth State Park, 1851 to 2020**

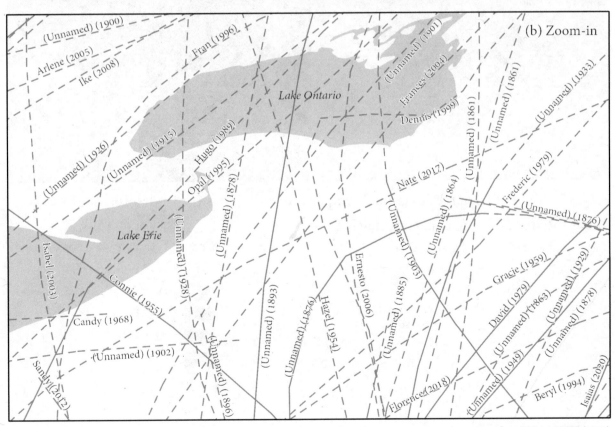

(b) Zoom-in

(Unnamed) (1900)
Arlene (2005)
Ike (2008)
Fran (1996)
(Unnamed) (1901)
Frances (2004)
(Unnamed) (1861)
(Unnamed) (1933)
Lake Ontario
Dennis (1999)
(Unnamed) (1861)
Frederic (1979)
(Unnamed) (1926)
(Unnamed) (1915)
Hugo (1989)
Opal (1995)
(Unnamed) (1878)
Nate (2017)
(Unnamed) (1864)
(Unnamed) (1876)
Isabel (2003)
Lake Erie
(Unnamed) (1928)
(Unnamed) (1893)
(Unnamed) (1876)
Hazel (1954)
Ernesto (2006)
(Unnamed) (1903)
(Unnamed) (1881)
Gracie (1959)
David (1979)
(Unnamed) (1863)
(Unnamed) (1929)
(Unnamed) (1878)
Connie (1955)
Candy (1968)
(Unnamed) (1902)
(Unnamed) (1896)
Sandy (2012)
Florence (2018)
(Unnamed) (1949)
Beryl (1994)
Isaias (2020)

Data from NOAA NCEI (2020)

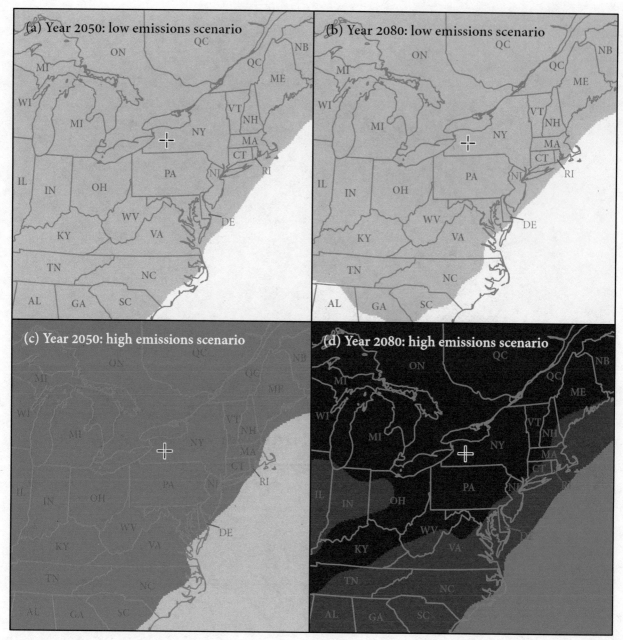

Map 36. Predicted changes in annual temperature under different climate change scenarios

Portions of eastern United States and Canada

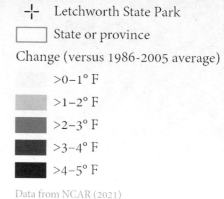

Letchworth State Park

State or province

Change (versus 1986-2005 average)

>0–1° F

>1–2° F

>2–3° F

>3–4° F

>4–5° F

Data from NCAR (2021)

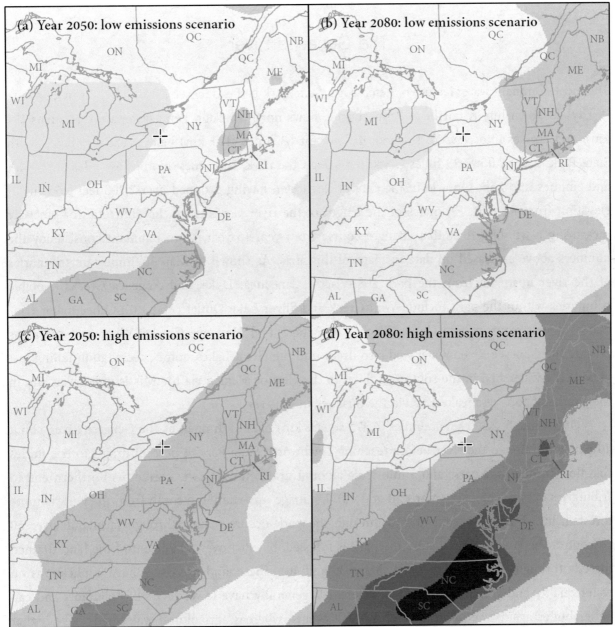

(a) Year 2050: low emissions scenario

(b) Year 2080: low emissions scenario

(c) Year 2050: high emissions scenario

(d) Year 2080: high emissions scenario

Map 37. Predicted changes in annual precipitation under different climate change scenarios

Portions of eastern United States and Canada

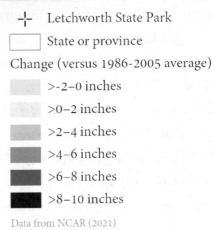

Letchworth State Park

State or province

Change (versus 1986-2005 average)

>-2–0 inches

>0–2 inches

>2–4 inches

>4–6 inches

>6–8 inches

>8–10 inches

Data from NCAR (2021)

The Genesee River

The most dominant water feature of Letchworth State Park is the Genesee River. It begins in a pasture in Ulysses Township in northern Pennsylvania, flows north through Pennsylvania for 13 miles (21 km), and crosses into New York where it flows for 63 miles (101 km) before reaching Letchworth State Park. It then flows 23 miles (37 km) through the park, continues another 69 miles (111 km), and empties into Lake Ontario in the City of Rochester, having dropped over 2,200 feet (671 m) in elevation from its start. Estimates of the length of the river vary due to the difficulties of precisely measuring a winding river that changes course from year to year, so to maintain consistency the numbers above are based on data in maps of this atlas. As shown in Map 38, important tributaries of the river upstream from the park are Wiscoy, Caneadea, Dyke, and Angelica Creeks. Notable tributaries within the park include Wolf Creek and Silver Lake Outlet (Map 40). Other major tributaries downstream include Oatka, Black, Canaseraga, and Honeoye Creeks. Whereas some areas outside the Genesee River Watershed also drain into the Great Lakes, some precipitation falling just outside the watershed in the southwest flows to the Gulf of Mexico via the Mississippi River, and in the southeast to Chesapeake Bay via the Susquehanna River.

Of the nearly 2,500 square miles (6,475 square km) of land drained by the Genesee River, about 40 percent drains to the river before reaching Letchworth State Park, 4 percent drains to tributaries that flow through the park, and a miniscule amount drains through the park at its northern end to tributaries outside the park (Maps 38 and 40). Drainage upstream and south from the park is more forested, but drainage via tributaries through the park occurs mainly through farmland: over 60 percent of the land drained before the park is forested, but just over 30 percent of the land drained directly through the park is forested (Maps 39 and 40). These land-use issues have implications on water quality and amount, as forested watersheds generally have lower levels of pollutants and can better buffer against floods from high rainfall events, whereas agricultural watersheds have higher levels of pollutants from agricultural practices and have less capacity to protect against floods.

The Genesee River drops over 500 feet (152 m) in elevation over its northerly course through Letchworth State Park, most dramatically at Upper, Middle, and Lower Falls. Map 41 shows the "gradient" of the Genesee River, a measure of elevation change over a distance. There is a clear difference between the flat water of the central and northern sections of the park, versus the rapids of the southern end. It is apparent in Map 41 why whitewater rafting occurs from Lee's Landing to St. Helena, where the river drops 75 feet over 5 miles (23 m over 8 km) while offering views of the cliffs of Great Bend from below—and also avoiding the three major waterfalls. Coincidentally, some key elevations correspond with major landmarks along the river: Middle Falls embraces elevations

Photo 14. The Genesee River at the Hogsback upstream from Highbanks Recreation Area in autumn.

of both 1,000 feet (305 m) and 900 feet (274 m) above sea level, Lower Falls is at 800 feet (244 m), and the river at Great Bend below the Castile Entrance is at 700 feet (231 m).

Letchworth State Park contains nearly thirty named waterfalls (Map 42). The most notable are those found on the Genesee River: Upper Falls (70 ft in height; 21 m), Middle Falls (107 ft; 33 m), and Lower Falls (70 ft; 21 m). Other notable waterfalls along important tributaries include multitiered falls such as Deh-ga-ya-soh Falls (150 ft; 46 m) and Wolf Creek Falls (225 ft; 69 m), and Papermill Falls (45 ft; 14 m) along Silver Lake Outlet in the northern end of the park. Another waterfall of note is Inspiration Falls near Inspiration Point, which is said to have the highest single drop of any waterfall in the park at 350 feet (107 m)—but which is visible as only a narrow ribbon of water after heavy rains. Most of the remaining waterfalls are located along small tributaries of the Genesee River and are often dry during the summer.

Humans have long altered the Genesee River's flow—the State dredged the river to deepen it from St. Helena within the park downstream to York Landing in the nineteenth century, for example—but the biggest alteration to its flow is the Mount Morris Dam. Constructed for flood control near the park's northern end, the dam regulates flow by impounding water in its reservoir and later releasing it at a rate downstream that does not cause flooding. Map 43 provides an aerial view of the dam and associated features, including a rope-and-timber "boom" that catches debris that might damage the dam (such as downed trees), and an empty reservoir bed for holding floodwaters. Map

Photo 15. The Mount Morris Dam in autumn.

44 shows trends in reservoir size from 1990 to 2019 in four months: January (winter), April (spring), July (summer), and October (autumn). To capture the variability in reservoir size in these months, the map shows the reservoir area as different percentiles: for example, a value of 25 percent means the reservoir is that size or smaller 25 percent of the time. The map also shows the maximum-recorded reservoir area for each of the four months over this thirty-year period.

The reservoir typically holds the most water in spring due to snowmelt and rains, and the least water in mid- and late summer when the river often flows unimpeded through the dam gates. During April when the reservoir is its highest, it is typically around 40 feet (12 m) deep at the dam,

Photo 16. Lower Falls at sunset.

impounding around 30,000 acre-feet in volume (37,000 ML), and over 800 acres (324 ha) in area. However, during the wettest Aprils these numbers swell to around 150 feet (46 m) deep, 300,000 acre-feet (370,000 ML), and over 2,800 acres (1,130 ha). Located at the extreme northern end of the park is another but much smaller dam operated by Rochester Gas and Electric for hydroelectric power, which impounds waters up to the Mount Morris Dam. The next chapter contains more details about the Mount Morris Dam, including its role during Hurricane Agnes (see especially Maps 70 and 71). To view the original path of the Genesee River in the 1930s and 1940s prior to dam construction, later see Maps 67 through 69.

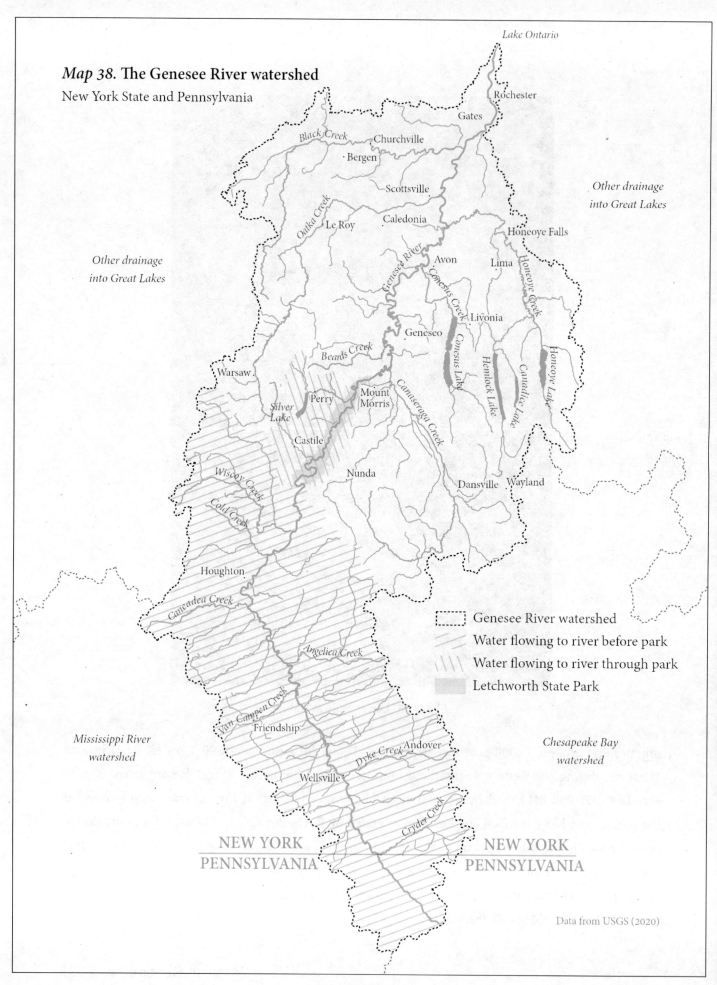

Map 38. The Genesee River watershed

New York State and Pennsylvania

Lake Ontario

Rochester

Gates

Churchville

Black Creek

Bergen

Scottsville

Other drainage
into Great Lakes

Oatka Creek

Le Roy

Caledonia

Honeoye Falls

Genesee River

Avon

Lima

Conesus Creek

Honeoye Creek

Livonia

Geneseo

Conesus Lake

Beards Creek

Warsaw

Hemlock Lake

Canaseraga Creek

Canadice Lake

Honeoye Lake

Perry

Mount
Morris

Silver
Lake

Castile

Nunda

Dansville

Wayland

Wiscoy Creek

Cold Creek

Houghton

Caneadea Creek

Angelica Creek

Van Campen Creek

Friendship

Dyke Creek

Andover

Mississippi River
watershed

Chesapeake Bay
watershed

Wellsville

Cryder Creek

NEW YORK

NEW YORK

PENNSYLVANIA

PENNSYLVANIA

Data from USGS (2020)

Other drainage
into Great Lakes

☐ Genesee River watershed

⫽ Water flowing to river before park

⫽ Water flowing to river through park

▨ Letchworth State Park

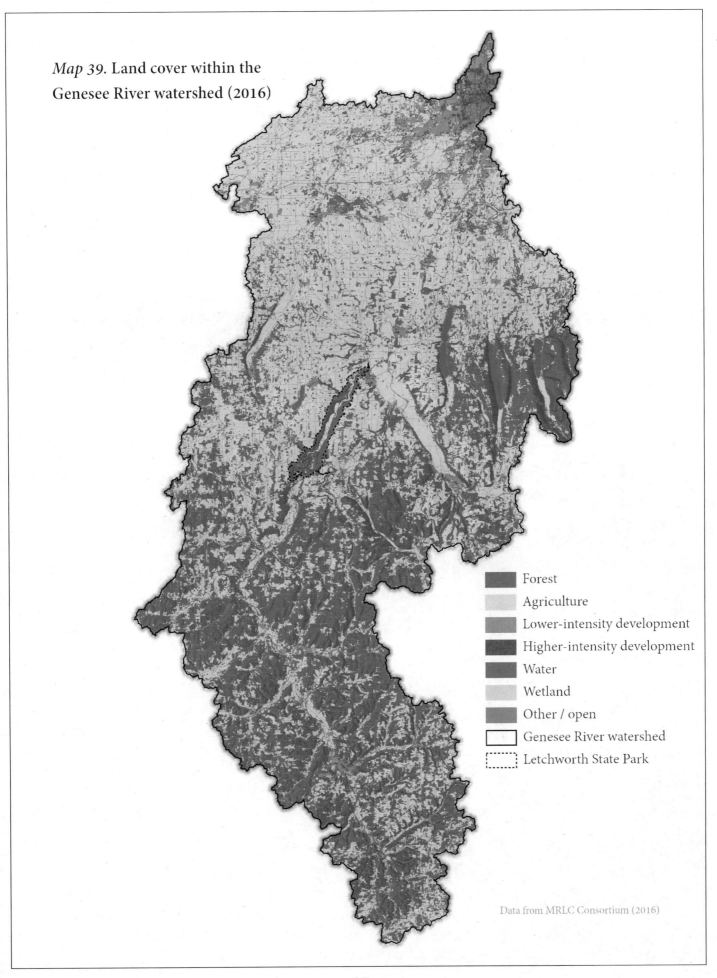

Map 39. Land cover within the Genesee River watershed (2016)

Forest
Agriculture
Lower-intensity development
Higher-intensity development
Water
Wetland
Other / open
Genesee River watershed
Letchworth State Park

Data from MRLC Consortium (2016)

85

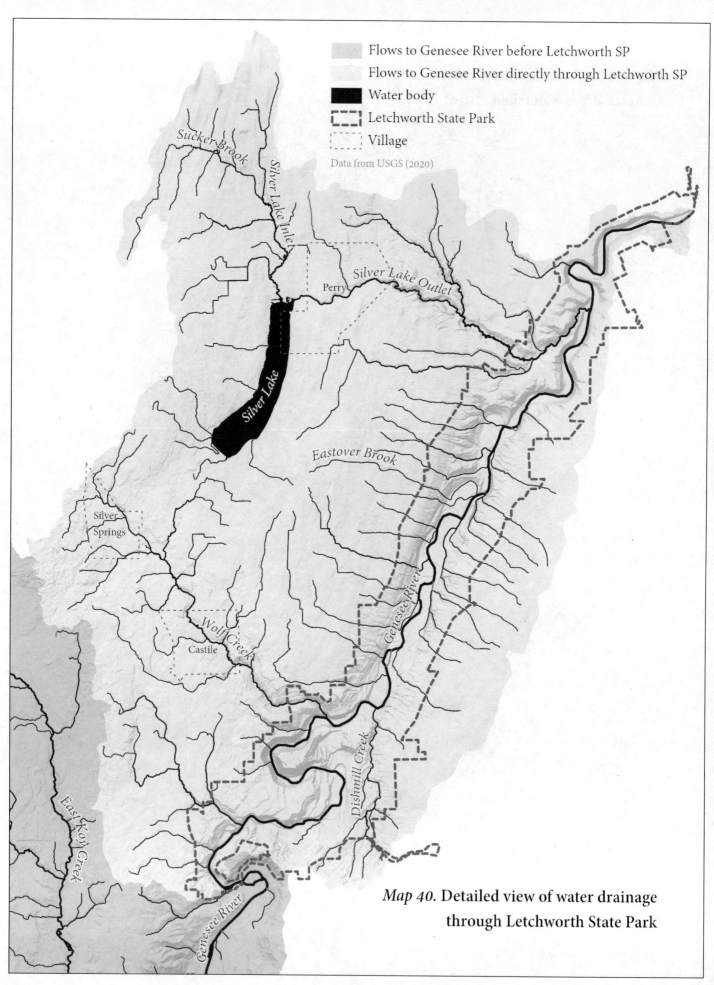

Legend:

Flows to Genesee River before Letchworth SP
Flows to Genesee River directly through Letchworth SP
Water body
Letchworth State Park
Village

Data from USGS (2020)

Sucker Brook

Silver Lake Inlet

Silver Lake Outlet

Perry

Silver Lake

Eastover Brook

Silver Springs

Genesee River

Wolf Creek

Castile

Dishmill Creek

East Koy Creek

Genesee River

Map 40. Detailed view of water drainage through Letchworth State Park

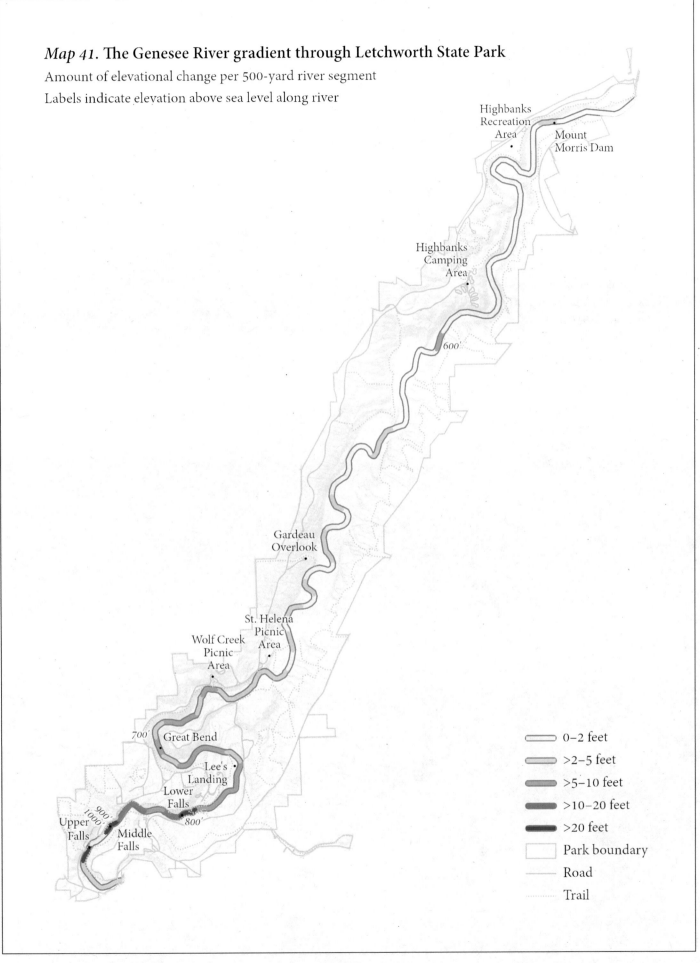

Map 41. The Genesee River gradient through Letchworth State Park

Amount of elevational change per 500-yard river segment

Labels indicate elevation above sea level along river

Highbanks Recreation Area

Mount Morris Dam

Highbanks Camping Area

600'

Gardeau Overlook

St. Helena Picnic Area

Wolf Creek Picnic Area

700' Great Bend

Lee's Landing

Lower Falls

900' 1000'

Upper Falls

800'

Middle Falls

0–2 feet

>2–5 feet

>5–10 feet

>10–20 feet

>20 feet

Park boundary

Road

Trail

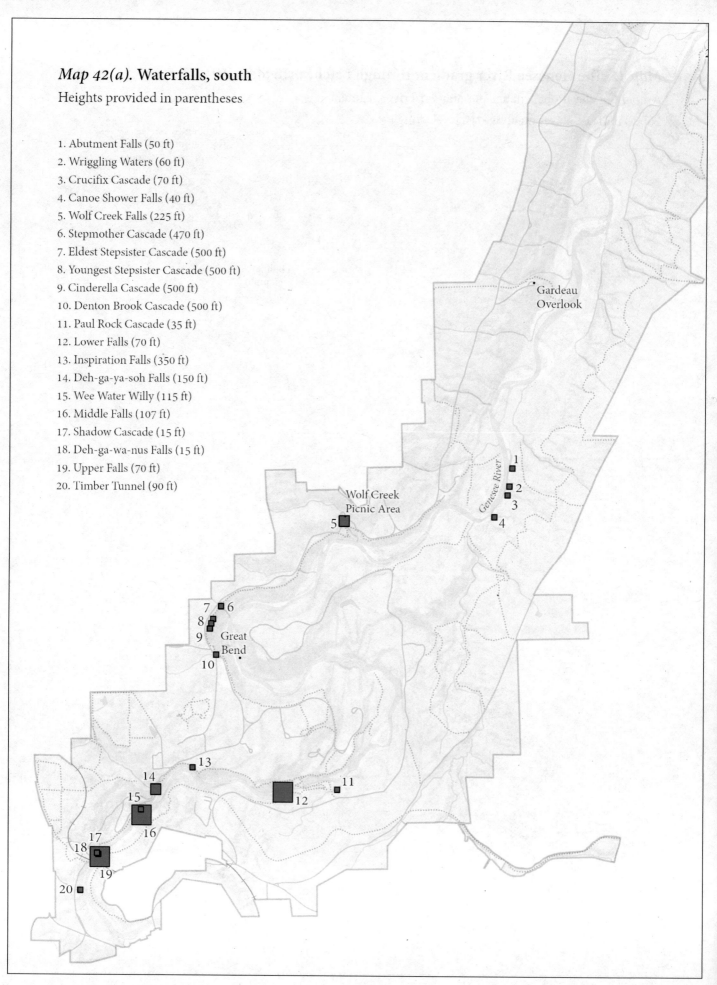

Map 42(a). Waterfalls, south

Heights provided in parentheses

1. Abutment Falls (50 ft)
2. Wriggling Waters (60 ft)
3. Crucifix Cascade (70 ft)
4. Canoe Shower Falls (40 ft)
5. Wolf Creek Falls (225 ft)
6. Stepmother Cascade (470 ft)
7. Eldest Stepsister Cascade (500 ft)
8. Youngest Stepsister Cascade (500 ft)
9. Cinderella Cascade (500 ft)
10. Denton Brook Cascade (500 ft)
11. Paul Rock Cascade (35 ft)
12. Lower Falls (70 ft)
13. Inspiration Falls (350 ft)
14. Deh-ga-ya-soh Falls (150 ft)
15. Wee Water Willy (115 ft)
16. Middle Falls (107 ft)
17. Shadow Cascade (15 ft)
18. Deh-ga-wa-nus Falls (15 ft)
19. Upper Falls (70 ft)
20. Timber Tunnel (90 ft)

Gardeau Overlook

Genesee River

Wolf Creek Picnic Area

Great Bend

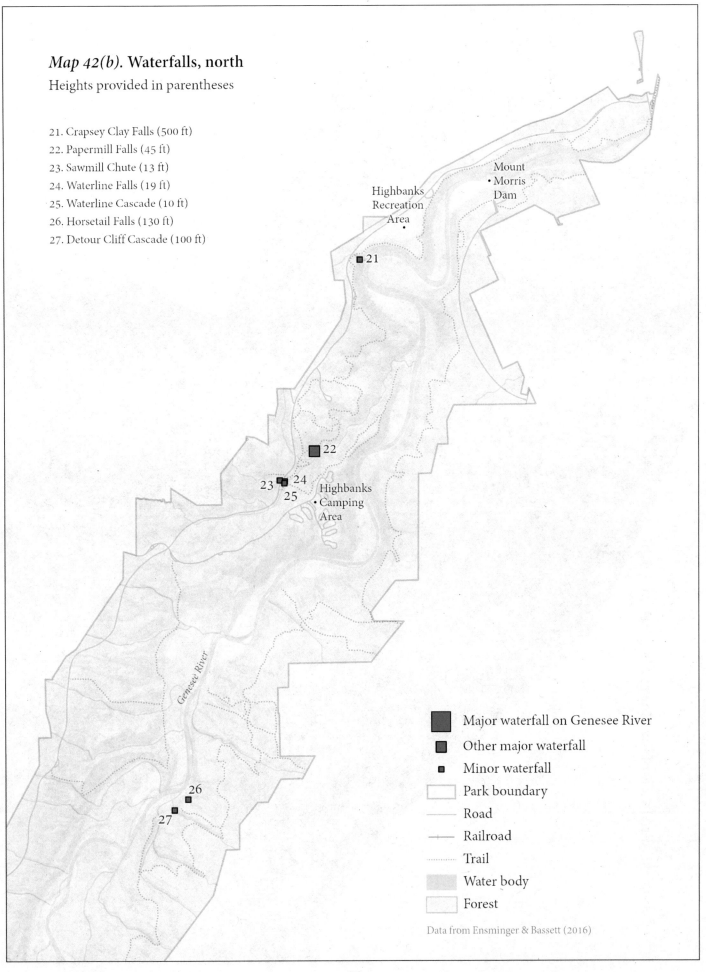

Map 42(b). Waterfalls, north

Heights provided in parentheses

21. Crapsey Clay Falls (500 ft)
22. Papermill Falls (45 ft)
23. Sawmill Chute (13 ft)
24. Waterline Falls (19 ft)
25. Waterline Cascade (10 ft)
26. Horsetail Falls (130 ft)
27. Detour Cliff Cascade (100 ft)

Mount
• Morris
Dam

Highbanks
Recreation
Area
•

■ 21

22

23 ■ 24
25

Highbanks
• Camping
Area

Genesee River

26
27

■ Major waterfall on Genesee River

■ Other major waterfall

■ Minor waterfall

Park boundary

Road

Railroad

Trail

Water body

Forest

Data from Ensminger & Bassett (2016)

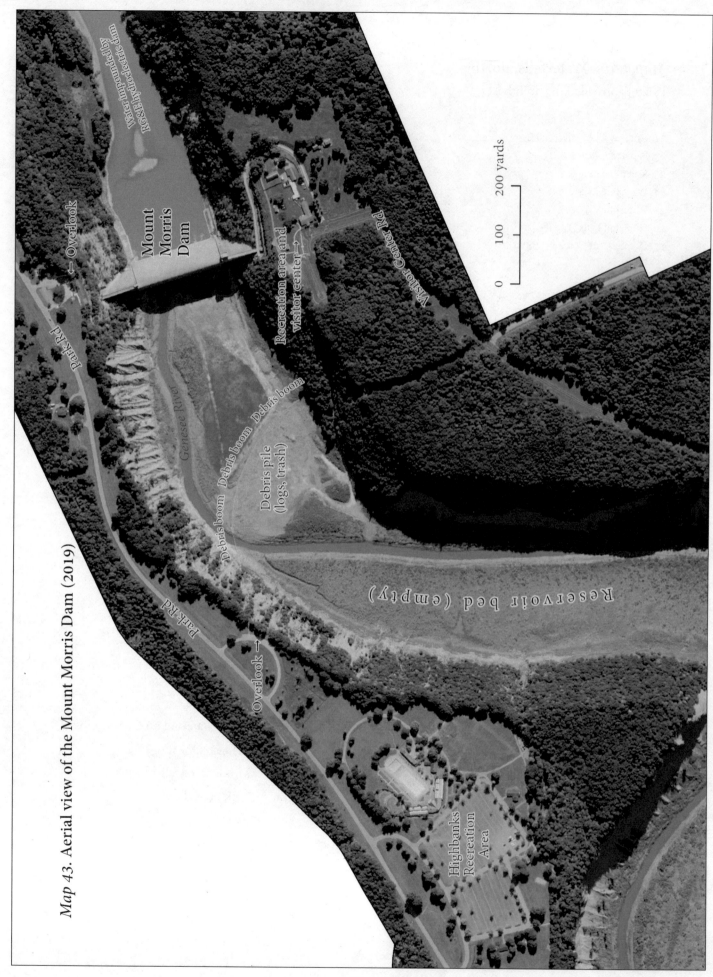

Map 43. Aerial view of the Mount Morris Dam (2019)

Water impounded by
RG&E hydroelectric dam

← Overlook

Park Rd

Mount
Morris
Dam

Recreation area and
visitor center →

Visitor Center Rd

Genesee River

Debris boom   Debris boom   Debris boom

Debris pile
(logs, trash)

Park Rd

Overlook →

Reservoir bed (empty)

Highbanks
Recreation
Area

0   100   200 yards

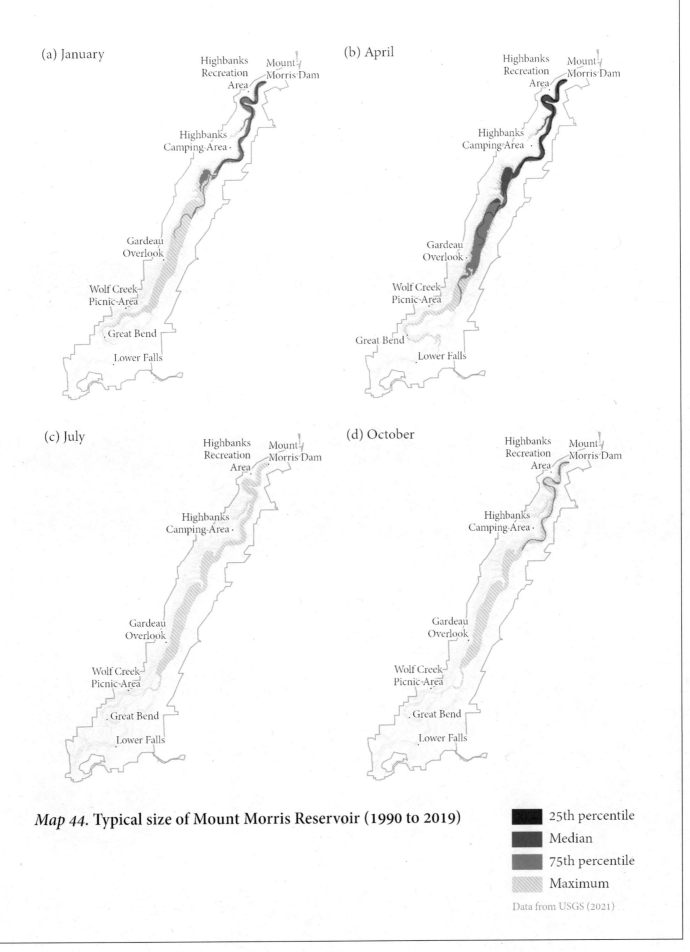

(a) January

Highbanks Recreation Area

Mount Morris Dam

Highbanks Camping Area

Gardeau Overlook

Wolf Creek Picnic Area

Great Bend

Lower Falls

(b) April

Highbanks Recreation Area

Mount Morris Dam

Highbanks Camping Area

Gardeau Overlook

Wolf Creek Picnic Area

Great Bend

Lower Falls

(c) July

Highbanks Recreation Area

Mount Morris Dam

Highbanks Camping Area

Gardeau Overlook

Wolf Creek Picnic Area

Great Bend

Lower Falls

(d) October

Highbanks Recreation Area

Mount Morris Dam

Highbanks Camping Area

Gardeau Overlook

Wolf Creek Picnic Area

Great Bend

Lower Falls

Map 44. **Typical size of Mount Morris Reservoir (1990 to 2019)**

- 25th percentile
- Median
- 75th percentile
- Maximum

Data from USGS (2021)

Chapter 3

Human History

The human history of Letchworth State Park is long, complicated, and sometimes controversial—and spans back long before its creation. Its history includes Native American settlement, abandoned "ghost villages" of European-American settlers, early land protection efforts, Civilian Conservation Corps projects, German prisoners of war, contentious dam proposals, a heroic role during a natural catastrophe, and moments of national attention.

Before proceeding chronologically, the atlas first provides maps that summarize aspects of the park's history since the arrival of Mary Jemison in 1779. Map 45 shows the locations of historical events and key moments in park history, which correspond to numbered events in the timeline on the next pages. Map 46 shows the locations of roads and the estimated locations of buildings in 1850, 1900, 1950, and 2020 to capture shifting patterns of settlement and development over this time. Map 47 portrays population and population density, as well as changing town boundaries, from 1820 to 2019 in towns that contain (or contained) the present-day park area. Map 48 shows both the number and types of historic (i.e., pre-1953) resources such as buildings and stone structures in different areas of the park before 2005 when the National Park Service added the park to its National Register of Historic Places (most historic resources symbolized in the map are still present today). Finally, Map 49 shows the number of historic resources in different areas of the park that were constructed during five eras in park history: before William P. Letchworth, the William P. Letchworth era, the early park era, the Civilian Conservation Corps era, and the modern era.

Photo 17. The Glen Iris Inn, the former home of William P. Letchworth.

Complete Timeline
(numbers in parentheses correspond to locations in Map 45)

1779: Mary Jemison and family relocate to Gardeau Flats (1).

1785: Flood on Genesee River.

1792: Ebenezer "Indian" Allen settles (2).

1797: Gardeau and Squawkie Hill Reservations created under the Treaty of Big Tree.

1803: Flood on Genesee River.

1805: Flood on Genesee River.

1807: Elisha Johnson surveys the Cottringer Tract in south half of park area.

1808 (circa): Early mill erected (3).

1813: Flood on Genesee River.

1816 (circa): Early white settlers Reuben and Perry Jones purportedly settle (4).

1817: Mary Jemison leases or sells large portions of Gardeau Reservation.

1817: Great landslide (5).

1821: Early white settler Alvah Palmer settles (6).

1823 (circa): Gibsonville settled (2).

1823: Mary Jemison sells all but two square miles of land at Gardeau Reservation.

1823 (circa): Early mill erected at Middle Falls (7).

1824: Early sawmill constructed (8).

1826: Seneca sell Squawkie Hill Reservation.

1826 (circa): St. Helena settled (9).

1827 (circa): Early sawmill erected (10).

1828: Seneca leave Squawkie Hill Reservation.

1830 (circa): Cabin is built that will become Letchworth home and later Glen Iris Inn; subsequent renovations or additions occur in 1830s, 1880, and 1913 (6).

1831: Mary Jemison sells lands, moves to Buffalo Creek Reservation, where she dies in 1833.

1835 (circa): Early sawmill constructed (11).

1835 (circa): Early sawmill constructed (12).

1835: Flood on Genesee River.

1835 (circa): First school built within current park boundary (13).

1840 (circa): Hornby Lodge constructed (14).

1845 (circa): Canal construction triggers landslide; aftermath still visible today (15).

1849: Hornby Lodge torn down (14).

1852: Portage wooden bridge opens; Erie's Buffalo & NYC Railroad opens (16).

1855 (circa): Cascade House built (17).

1856 (circa): Genesee Valley Canal portion within present-day park area completed.

1857: William P. Letchworth views Portage Glen for first time from the Portage wooden bridge (16).

1857: Flood on Genesee River.

1858: William P. Letchworth purchases first lands comprising the Glen Iris property.

1862: Entire Genesee Valley Canal completed.

1862: Civil War troops (1st New York Dragoons Regiment) train at Parade Grounds (18).

1865: Flood on Genesee River.

1872: Council House rededicated (19).

1874: Mary Jemison reburied at Council Grounds (19).

1875: Portage wooden bridge burns down and the Portage iron bridge is built (16).

1875: Flood on Genesee River.

1870s: Annual Soldiers' Picnic, hosting thousands of Civil War veterans, begins at the Portage bridge (16).

1876: Tornado near southern border of park in Portageville (20).

1878: Genesee Valley Canal abandoned.

1882: Genesee Valley Canal Railroad opens.

1889: Flood on Genesee River.

1890: Flood on Genesee River.

1894: Flood on Genesee River.

1896: Flood on Genesee River.

1898: William P. Letchworth purchases final lands comprising the Glen Iris property.

1900 (circa): Gibsonville abandoned (2).

1902: Two floods on Genesee River.

1903: Dragoons Monument dedicated at western end of the Portage iron bridge (16).

1904: Flood on Genesee River.

1906: Letchworth donates Glen Iris Estate to State, forming Letchworth State Park.

1910: William P. Letchworth dies at the age of 87; Glen Iris Estate makes formal transition to park.

1913: William P. Letchworth Museum completed (21).

1913: Flood on Genesee River.

1914: Glen Iris Inn, formerly Letchworth's home, opens to guests (6).

1915: American Scenic and Historic Preservation Society begins first plantings for arboretum

1916: Two floods on Genesee River.

1919: Dragoons Monument relocated to present location near Inspiration Point (22).

1923: Camping ground opens at Lower Falls area (23).

1927: Stone arch bridge over Deh-ga-ya-soh Creek built (24).

1927: Flood on Genesee River.

1929: Flood on Genesee River.

1930: Wolf Creek Bridge constructed (25).

1933: CCC Big Bend Camp #23 established (26).

1933: CCC Gibsonville Camp #40 established (2).

1934: CCC St. Helena Camp #76 established (27).

1934: Cabin Area E completed by CCC (28).

1934: Parade Grounds Picnic Area completed by CCC (18).

1934: Kisil Point Picnic Area completed (29).

1935: CCC Lower Falls Camp #49 established (30).

1935: Cabin Area C completed by CCC (31).

1935: Cabin Area D completed by CCC (32).

1935: St. Helena Picnic Area completed by CCC (33).

1935: CCC Big Bend Camp #23 closed (26).

1935: Flood on Genesee River.

1935 (circa): Gardeau Overlook built by CCC (34).

1936: Cabin Area B completed by CCC (35).

1936: CCC St. Helena Camp #76 closed (27).

1936 (circa): Lower Falls Road completed by CCC.

1936: Flood on Genesee River.

1937: CCC Gibsonville Camp #40 closed (2).

1938: Lower Falls Footbridge and approaches completed by CCC (36).

1938 (circa): Park Road from Wolf Creek to Gibsonville completed by CCC.

1939: Lower Falls Picnic Area completed by CCC (37).

1940 (circa): Eddy's Picnic Area completed by CCC (38).

1940: Flood on Genesee River.

1941: CCC Lower Falls Camp #49 closed (30).

1942: Wolf Creek Picnic Area completed (25).

1942: Tea Table Picnic Area completed (39).

1942: Flood on Genesee River.

1944: CCC Lower Falls Camp #49 converted to German prisoner-of-war camp (30).

1946: German prisoner-of-war camp demolished (30).

1948: Mount Morris Dam construction begins (40).

1950: St. Helena Bridge torn down (41).

1950: Original swimming pool completed (23).

1950: Flood on Genesee River.

1952: Mount Morris Dam completed (40).

1952: St. Helena abandoned and cemetery relocated due to imminent flooding from reservoir (9).

1956: Flood on Genesee River.

1963: Highbanks Recreation Area opens (42).

1963: Rochester Branch of the Pennsylvania Railroad (formerly the Genesee Valley Canal Railroad) abandoned.

1967 (circa): Highbanks Camping Area opens (43).

1969: Cascade House burns down (17).

1970: Cabin Area A completed (44).

1972: Rain from Hurricane Agnes raises reservoir to height of dam, causing major flooding of park.

1975: Letchworth Arts and Craft Show holds first annual show (42).

1983: Mary Jemison Day holds first annual event; this day is later renamed Native American Heritage Day, then Native American & Pioneer Heritage Days (45).

1989: Genesee River Protection Act limits operation of Mount Morris Dam to flood control purposes only.

1990: Annual Stone Tool Craftsman Show holds first show (42).

Late 1990s: One of the largest rockslides in park history occurs (46).

2001: Letchworth Balloon Festival holds first annual festival (47).

2003: State adds most recent parcel of land to the park.

2005: Park is added to National Register of Historic Places.

2015: "Ice volcano" attracts national attention (48).

2015: Park named "Best State Park" in USA Today Readers' Choice contest.

2016: Humphrey Nature Center opens (49).

2017: Steel Genesee Arch Bridge built (16).

2018: Portage iron bridge torn down (16).

2020: Original Lower Falls Pool is filled in and recreation area is constructed in its place (23).

2020: Park temporarily imposes access restrictions due to COVID-19 pandemic.

2020: Park receives highest attendance recorded.

2021: Autism Nature Trail opens (49).

Historical Events and News, North End
(see Map 45a)

1792: Ebenezer "Indian" Allen settles (2).

1823 (circa): Gibsonville settled (2).

1900 (circa): Gibsonville abandoned (2).

1933: CCC Gibsonville Camp #40 established (2).

1934: Kisil Point Picnic Area completed (29).

1935: Cabin Area C completed by CCC (31).

1937: CCC Gibsonville Camp #40 closed (2).

1948: Mount Morris Dam construction begins (40).

1952: Mount Morris Dam completed (40).

1963: Highbanks Recreation Area opens (42).

1967 (circa): Highbanks Camping Area opens (43).

1975: Letchworth Arts and Craft Show holds first annual show (42).

1990: Annual Stone Tool Craftsman Show holds first show (42).

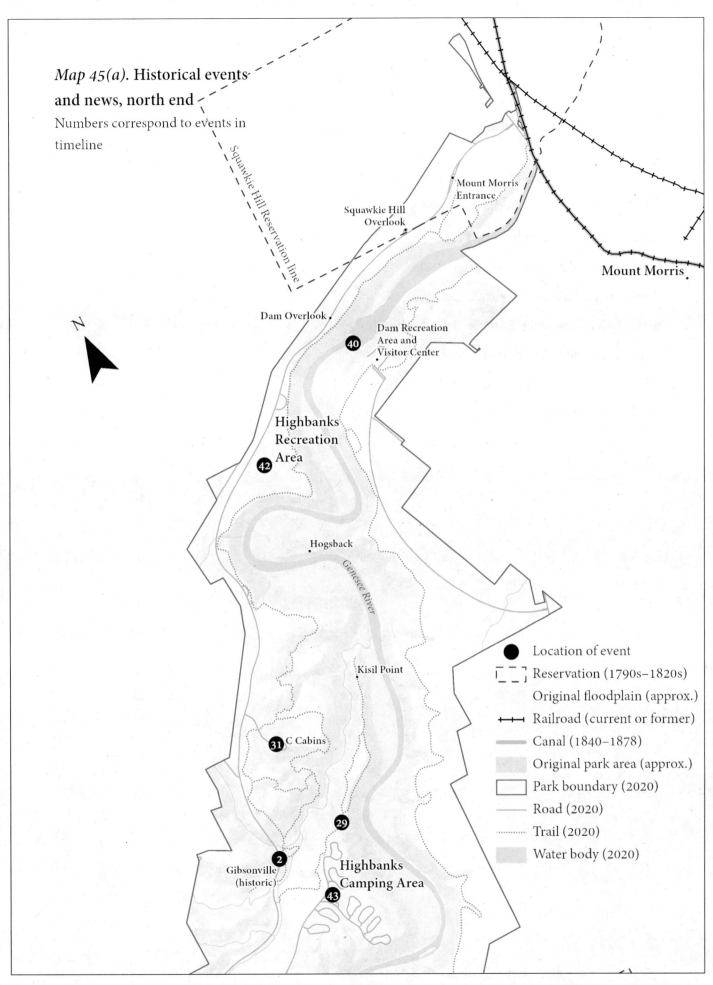

Map 45(a). Historical events and news, north end
Numbers correspond to events in timeline

Squawkie Hill Reservation line

Mount Morris Entrance

Squawkie Hill Overlook

Mount Morris

Dam Overlook

40

Dam Recreation Area and Visitor Center

Highbanks Recreation Area

42

Hogsback

Genesee River

Kisil Point

31 C Cabins

29

2

Gibsonville (historic)

Highbanks Camping Area

43

● Location of event
Reservation (1790s–1820s)
Original floodplain (approx.)
╂╂ Railroad (current or former)
── Canal (1840–1878)
Original park area (approx.)
── Park boundary (2020)
── Road (2020)
⋯ Trail (2020)
Water body (2020)

Historical Events and News, North-central

(see Map 45b)

1779: Mary Jemison and family relocates to Gardeau Flats (1).

1792: Ebenezer "Indian" Allen settles (2).

1823 (circa): Gibsonville settled (2).

1827 (circa): Early sawmill erected (10).

1900 (circa): Gibsonville abandoned (2).

1933: CCC Gibsonville Camp #40 established (2).

1934: Kisil Point Picnic Area completed (29).

1937: CCC Gibsonville Camp #40 closed (2).

1967 (circa): Highbanks Camping Area opens (43).

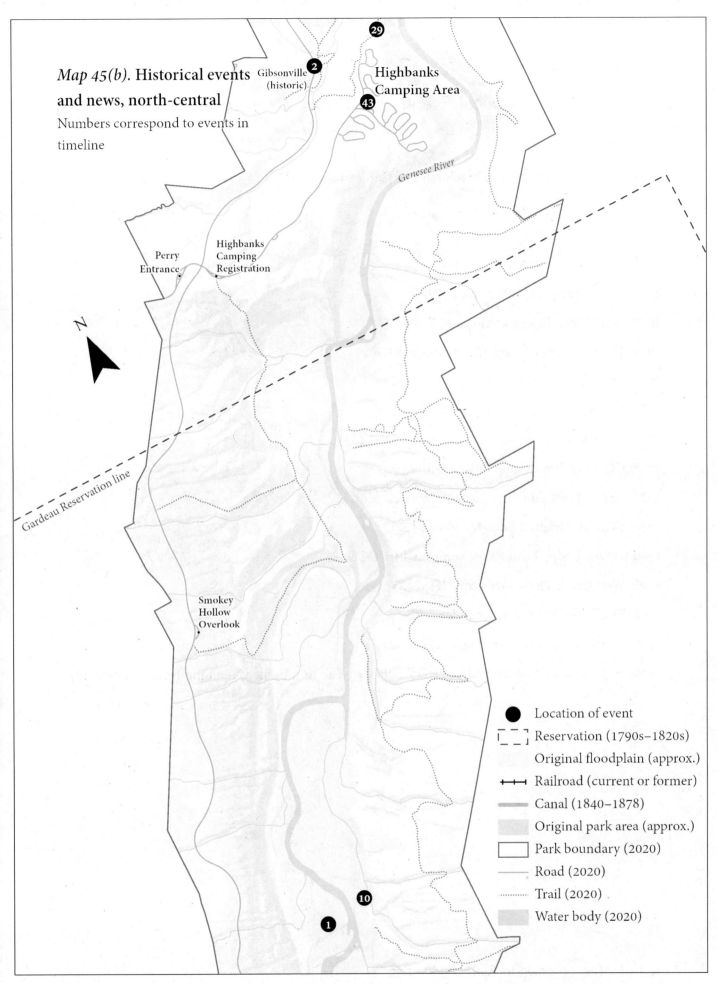

Map 45(b). **Historical events and news, north-central**

Numbers correspond to events in timeline

29

2

Gibsonville (historic)

Highbanks Camping Area

43

Genesee River

N

Perry Entrance

Highbanks Camping Registration

Gardeau Reservation line

Smokey Hollow Overlook

10

1

● Location of event

Reservation (1790s–1820s)

Original floodplain (approx.)

Railroad (current or former)

Canal (1840–1878)

Original park area (approx.)

Park boundary (2020)

Road (2020)

Trail (2020)

Water body (2020)

Historical Events and News, South-central
(see Map 45c)

1779: Mary Jemison and family relocates to Gardeau Flats (1).

1808 (circa): Early mill erected (3).

1817: Great landslide (5).

1826 (circa): St. Helena settled (9).

1827 (circa): Early sawmill erected (10).

1930: Wolf Creek Bridge constructed (25).

1933: CCC Big Bend Camp #23 established (26).

1934: CCC St. Helena Camp #76 established (27)

1934: Cabin Area E completed by CCC (28).

1935: St. Helena Picnic Area completed by CCC (33).

1935: CCC Big Bend Camp #23 closed (26).

1935 (circa): Gardeau Overlook built by CCC (34).

1936: CCC St. Helena Camp #76 closed (27).

1940 (circa): Eddy's Picnic Area completed by CCC (38).

1942: Wolf Creek Picnic Area completed (25).

1942: Tea Table Picnic Area completed (39).

1950: St. Helena Bridge torn down (41).

1952: St. Helena abandoned and cemetery relocated due to imminent flooding from reservoir (9).

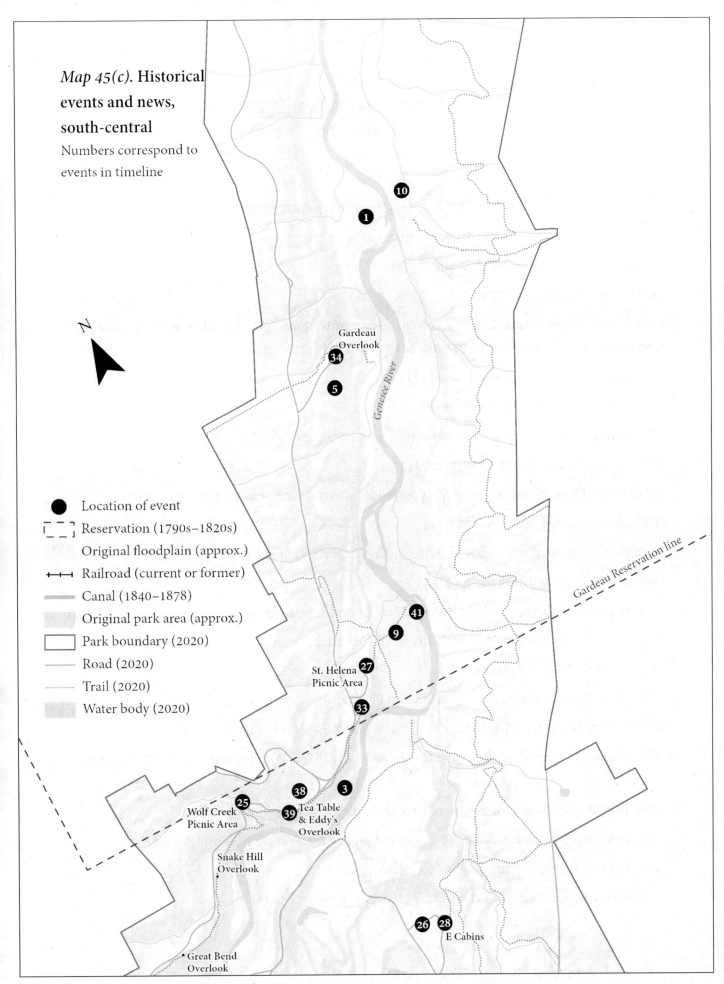

Map 45(c). Historical
events and news,
south-central

Numbers correspond to
events in timeline

● Location of event

▢ Reservation (1790s–1820s)

Original floodplain (approx.)

├─┤ Railroad (current or former)

━━ Canal (1840–1878)

Original park area (approx.)

▢ Park boundary (2020)

Road (2020)

Trail (2020)

Water body (2020)

N

Gardeau
Overlook

Genesee River

Gardeau Reservation line

St. Helena
Picnic Area

Wolf Creek
Picnic Area

Tea Table
& Eddy's
Overlook

Snake Hill
Overlook

E Cabins

Great Bend
Overlook

10
1
34
5
41
9
27
33
38
3
25
39
26
28

Historical Events and News, South End
(see Map 45d)

1808 (circa): Early mill erected (3).

1816 (circa): Early white settlers Reuben and Perry Jones purportedly settle (4).

1821: Early white settler, Alvah Palmer, settles (6).

1823 (circa): Early mill erected at Middle Falls (7).

1824: Early sawmill constructed (8).

1830 (circa): Cabin is built that will become Letchworth home and later Glen Iris Inn; subsequent renovations or additions occur in 1830s, 1880, and 1913 (6).

1835 (circa): Early sawmill constructed (11).

1835 (circa): Early sawmill constructed (12).

1835 (circa): First school built within current park boundary (13).

1840 (circa): Hornby Lodge constructed (14).

1845 (circa): Canal construction triggers landslide; aftermath remains visible today (15).

1849: Hornby Lodge torn down (14).

1852: Portage wooden bridge opens; Erie's Buffalo & NYC Railroad opens (16).

1855 (circa): Cascade House built (17).

1857: William P. Letchworth views Portage Glen for first time from the Portage wooden bridge (16).

1862: Civil War troops (1st New York Dragoons Regiment) train at Parade Grounds (18).

1872: Council House rededicated (19).

1874: Mary Jemison reburied at Council Grounds (19).

1875: Portage wooden bridge burns down and the Portage iron bridge is built (16).

1870s: Annual Soldiers' Picnic, hosting thousands of Civil War veterans, begins at the Portage bridge (16).

1876: Tornado near southern border of park in Portageville (20).

1903: Dragoons Monument dedicated at western end of the Portage iron bridge (16).

1913: William P. Letchworth Museum completed (21).

1914: Glen Iris Inn, formerly Letchworth's home, opens to guests (6).

1919: Dragoons Monument relocated to present location near Inspiration Point (22).

1923: Camping ground opens at Lower Falls area (23).

1927: Stone arch bridge over Deh-ga-ya-soh Creek built (24).

1930: Wolf Creek Bridge constructed (25).

1933: CCC Big Bend Camp #23 established (26).

1934: CCC St. Helena Camp #76 established (27).

1934: Cabin Area E completed by CCC (28).

1934: Parade Grounds Picnic Area completed by CCC (18).

1935: CCC Lower Falls Camp #49 established (30).

1935: Cabin Area D completed by CCC (32).

1935: St. Helena Picnic Area completed by CCC (33).

1935: CCC Big Bend Camp #23 closed (26).

1936: Cabin Area B completed by CCC (35).

1936: CCC St. Helena Camp #76 closed (27).

1938: Lower Falls Footbridge and approaches completed by CCC (36).

1939: Lower Falls Picnic Area completed by CCC (37).

1940 (circa): Eddy's Picnic Area completed by CCC (38).

1941: CCC Lower Falls Camp #49 closed (30).

1942: Wolf Creek Picnic Area completed (25).

1942: Tea Table Picnic Area completed (39).

1944: CCC Lower Falls Camp #49 converted to German prisoner-of-war camp (30).

1946: German prisoner-of-war camp demolished (30).

1950: Original swimming pool completed (23).

1969: Cascade House burns down (17).

1970: Cabin Area A completed (44).

1983: Mary Jemison Day holds first annual event; this day is later renamed Native American Heritage Day, then Native American & Pioneer Heritage Days (45).

Late 1990s: One of the largest rockslides in park history occurs (46).

2001: Letchworth Balloon Festival holds first annual festival (47).

2015: "Ice volcano" attracts national attention (48).

2016: Humphrey Nature Center opens (49).

2017: Steel Genesee Arch Bridge built (16).

2018: Portage iron bridge torn down (16).

2020: Original Lower Falls Pool is filled in and recreation area is constructed in its place (23).

2021: Autism Nature Trail opens (49).

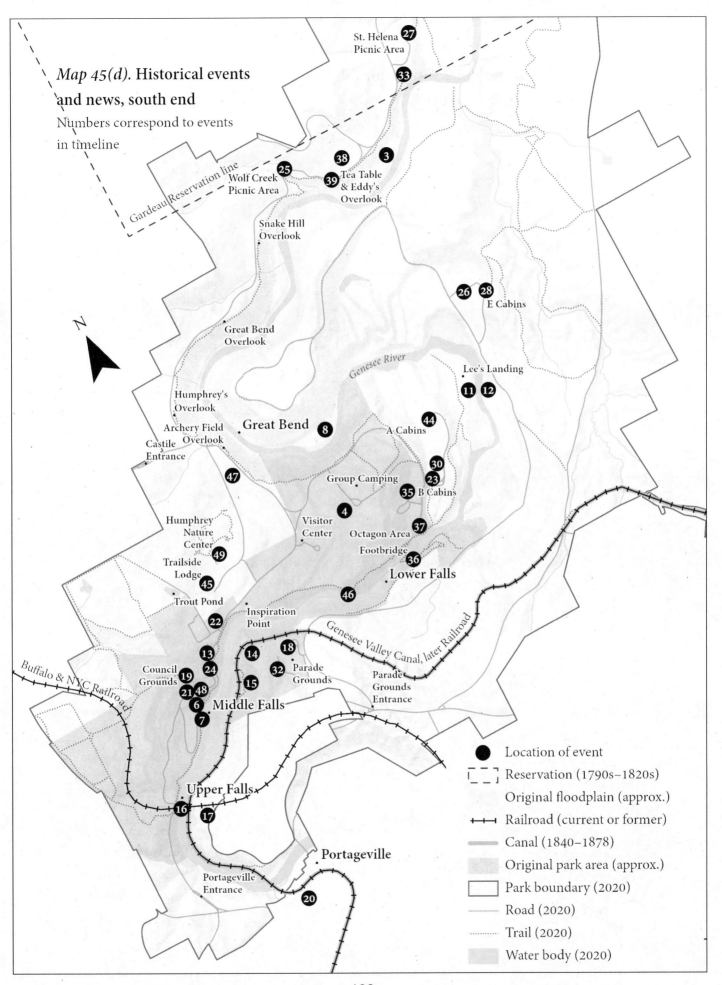

Map 45(d). Historical events and news, south end

Numbers correspond to events in timeline

St. Helena Picnic Area

Gardeau Reservation line

Wolf Creek Picnic Area

Tea Table & Eddy's Overlook

Snake Hill Overlook

E Cabins

Great Bend Overlook

Genesee River

Lee's Landing

Humphrey's Overlook

Archery Field Overlook

Great Bend

A Cabins

Castile Entrance

Group Camping

B Cabins

Visitor Center

Octagon Area

Footbridge

Lower Falls

Humphrey Nature Center

Trailside Lodge

Trout Pond

Inspiration Point

Genesee Valley Canal, later Railroad

Council Grounds

Parade Grounds

Parade Grounds Entrance

Buffalo & NYC Railroad

Middle Falls

Upper Falls

Portageville

Portageville Entrance

● Location of event

▯ Reservation (1790s–1820s)

Original floodplain (approx.)

+ Railroad (current or former)

— Canal (1840–1878)

Original park area (approx.)

▭ Park boundary (2020)

Road (2020)

Trail (2020)

Water body (2020)

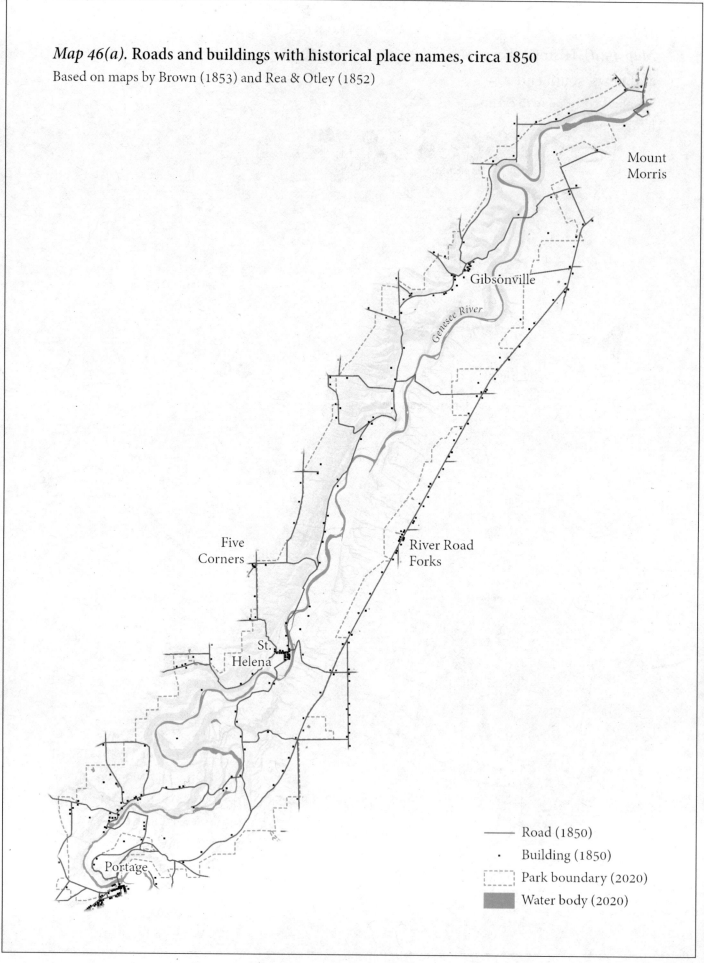

Map 46(a). **Roads and buildings with historical place names, circa 1850**

Based on maps by Brown (1853) and Rea & Otley (1852)

Mount Morris

Gibsonville

Genesee River

Five Corners

River Road Forks

St. Helena

Portage

—— Road (1850)

· Building (1850)

⸗⸗⸗ Park boundary (2020)

▬ Water body (2020)

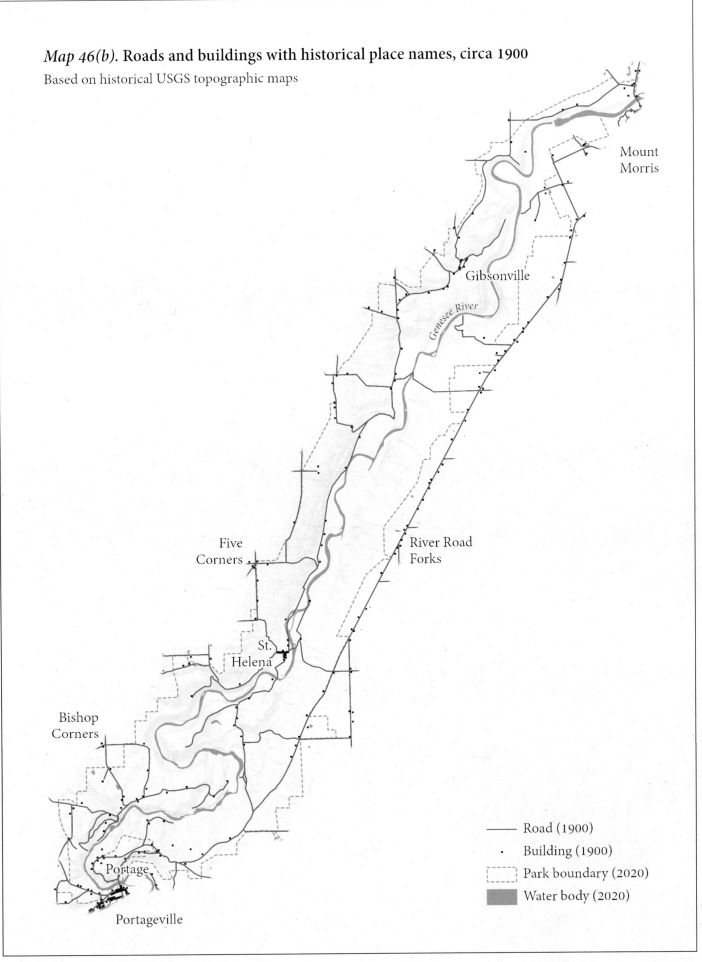

Map 46(b). **Roads and buildings with historical place names, circa 1900**
Based on historical USGS topographic maps

Mount
Morris

Gibsonville

Genesee River

Five
Corners

River Road
Forks

St.
Helena

Bishop
Corners

Portage

Portageville

— Road (1900)
· Building (1900)
⬚ Park boundary (2020)
▬ Water body (2020)

111

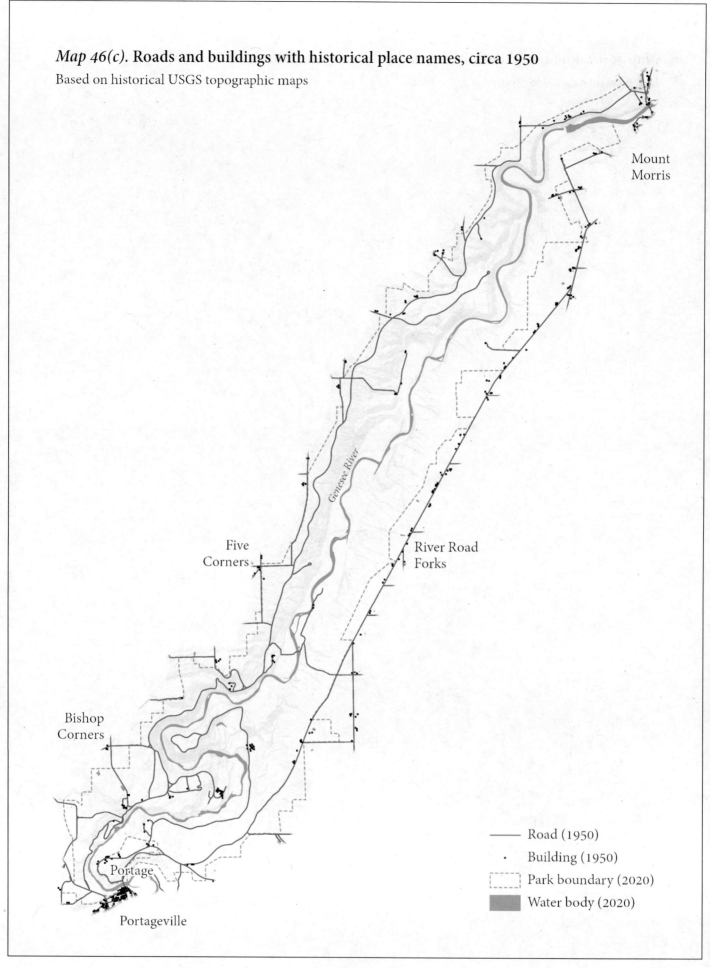

Map 46(c). **Roads and buildings with historical place names, circa 1950**
Based on historical USGS topographic maps

Genesee River

Mount
Morris

Five
Corners

River Road
Forks

Bishop
Corners

Portage

Portageville

——— Road (1950)

· Building (1950)

⌐ ⌐ Park boundary (2020)

▬ Water body (2020)

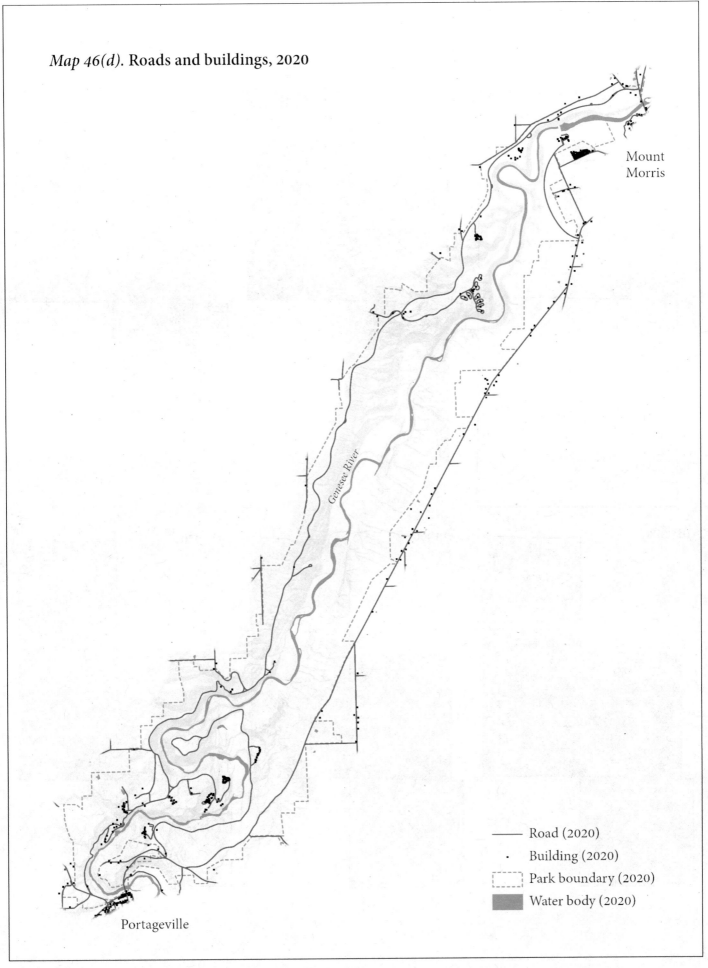

Map 46(d). **Roads and buildings, 2020**

Mount
Morris

Genesee River

Portageville

——— Road (2020)

• Building (2020)

Park boundary (2020)

Water body (2020)

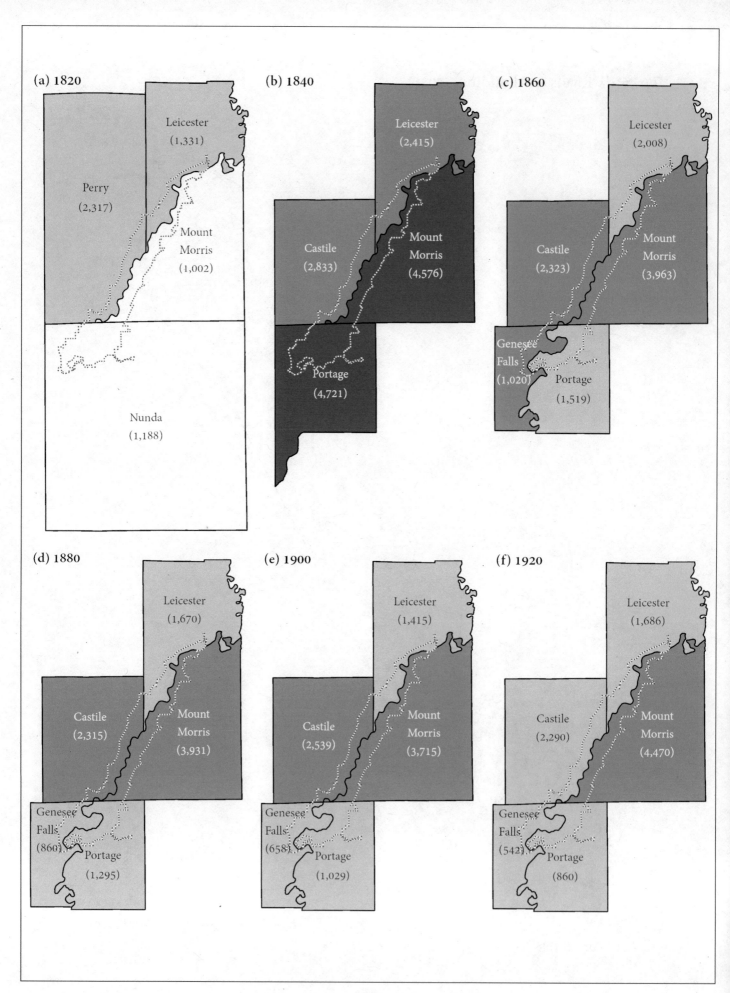

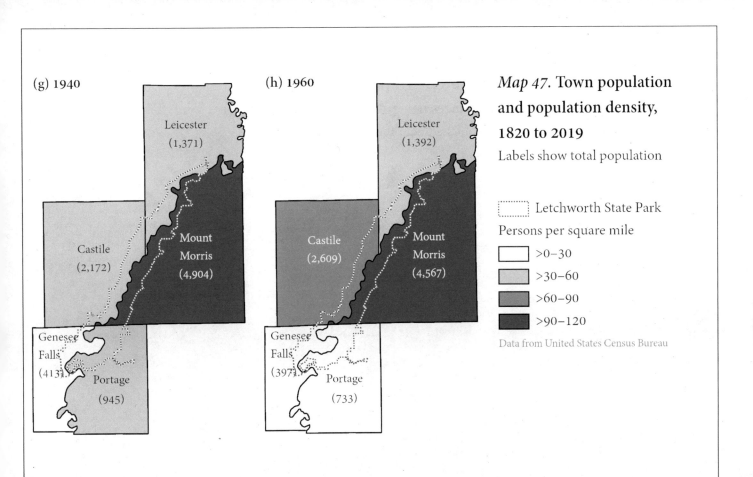

(g) 1940

Leicester
(1,371)

Castile
(2,172)

Mount
Morris
(4,904)

Genesee
Falls
(413)

Portage
(945)

(h) 1960

Leicester
(1,392)

Castile
(2,609)

Mount
Morris
(4,567)

Genesee
Falls
(397)

Portage
(733)

Map 47. Town population
and population density,
1820 to 2019

Labels show total population

┈┈┈ Letchworth State Park

Persons per square mile

□ >0–30

■ >30–60

■ >60–90

■ >90–120

Data from United States Census Bureau

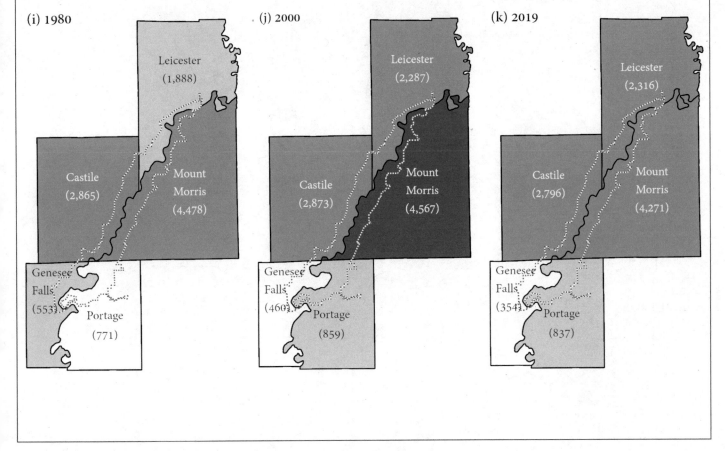

(i) 1980

Leicester
(1,888)

Castile
(2,865)

Mount
Morris
(4,478)

Genesee
Falls
(553)

Portage
(771)

(j) 2000

Leicester
(2,287)

Castile
(2,873)

Mount
Morris
(4,567)

Genesee
Falls
(460)

Portage
(859)

(k) 2019

Leicester
(2,316)

Castile
(2,796)

Mount
Morris
(4,271)

Genesee
Falls
(354)

Portage
(837)

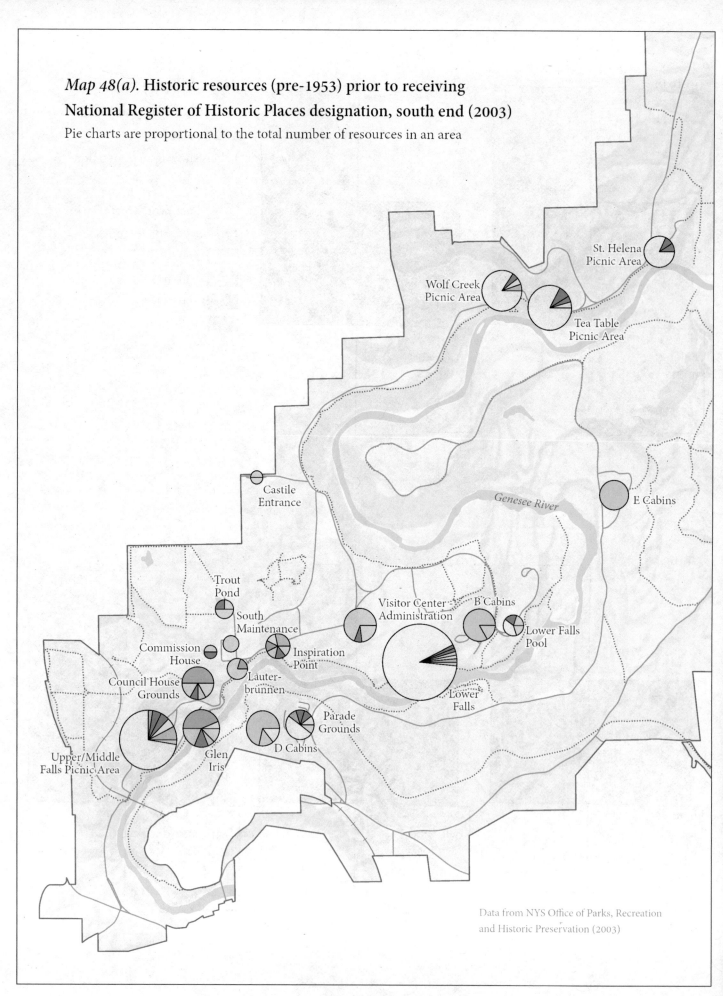

Map 48(a). **Historic resources (pre-1953) prior to receiving National Register of Historic Places designation, south end (2003)**

Pie charts are proportional to the total number of resources in an area

St. Helena Picnic Area

Wolf Creek Picnic Area

Tea Table Picnic Area

Castile Entrance

Genesee River

E Cabins

Trout Pond

South Maintenance

Visitor Center Administration

B Cabins

Lower Falls Pool

Commission House

Inspiration Point

Council House Grounds

Lauter- brunnen

Lower Falls

Upper/Middle Falls Picnic Area

Glen Iris

D Cabins

Parade Grounds

Data from NYS Office of Parks, Recreation and Historic Preservation (2003)

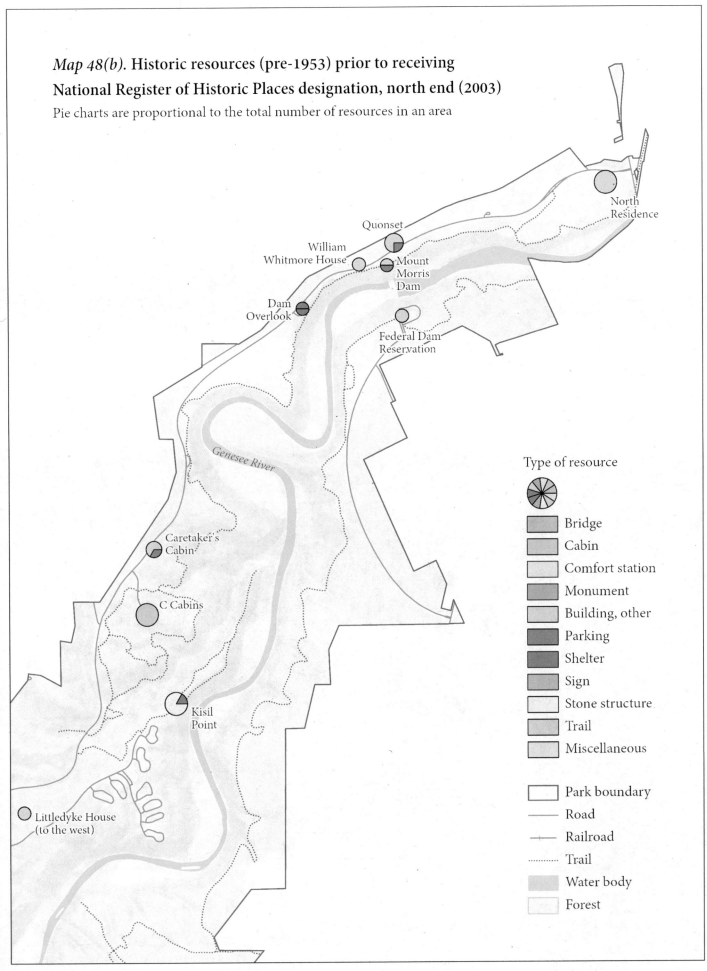

Map 48(b). **Historic resources (pre-1953) prior to receiving National Register of Historic Places designation, north end (2003)**

Pie charts are proportional to the total number of resources in an area

North Residence

Quonset

William Whitmore House

Mount Morris Dam

Dam Overlook

Federal Dam Reservation

Genesee River

Caretaker's Cabin

C Cabins

Kisil Point

Littledyke House (to the west)

Type of resource

Bridge
Cabin
Comfort station
Monument
Building, other
Parking
Shelter
Sign
Stone structure
Trail
Miscellaneous

Park boundary
Road
Railroad
Trail
Water body
Forest

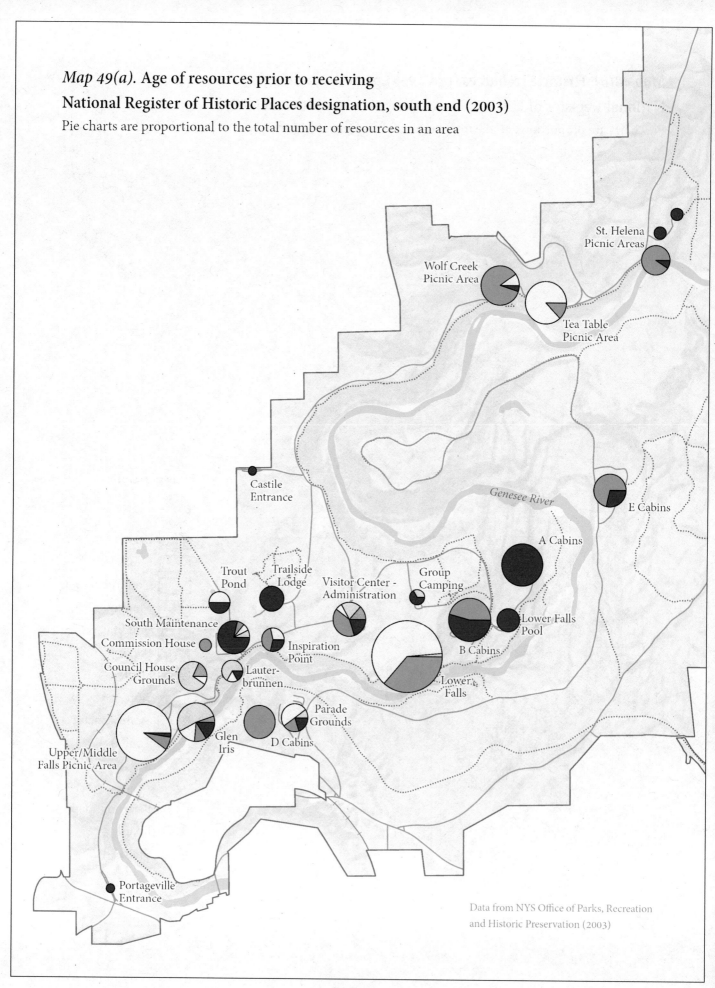

Map 49(a). Age of resources prior to receiving
National Register of Historic Places designation, south end (2003)
Pie charts are proportional to the total number of resources in an area

St. Helena
Picnic Areas

Wolf Creek
Picnic Area

Tea Table
Picnic Area

Genesee River

E Cabins

Castile
Entrance

A Cabins

Trout
Pond

Trailside
Lodge

Visitor Center -
Administration

Group
Camping

Lower Falls
Pool

South Maintenance

Commission House

Inspiration
Point

B Cabins

Council House
Grounds

Lauter-
brunnen

Lower
Falls

Parade
Grounds

Glen
Iris

D Cabins

Upper/Middle
Falls Picnic Area

Portageville
Entrance

Data from NYS Office of Parks, Recreation
and Historic Preservation (2003)

118

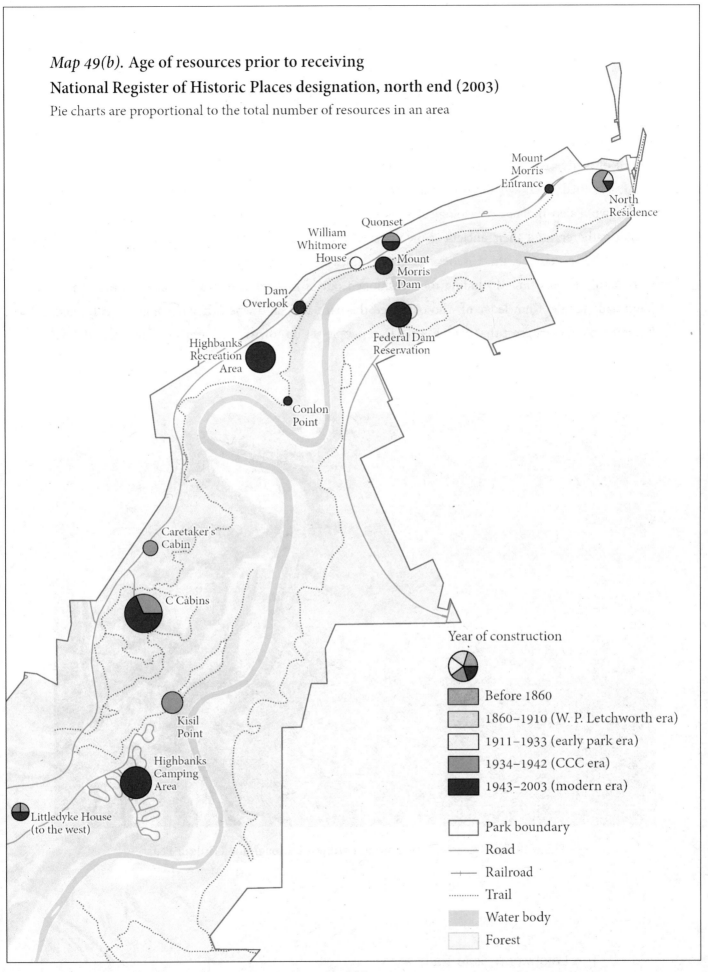

Map 49(b). Age of resources prior to receiving
National Register of Historic Places designation, north end (2003)

Pie charts are proportional to the total number of resources in an area

Mount
Morris
Entrance

North
Residence

Quonset

William
Whitmore
House

Mount
Morris
Dam

Dam
Overlook

Federal Dam
Reservation

Highbanks
Recreation
Area

Conlon
Point

Caretaker's
Cabin

C Cabins

Kisil
Point

Highbanks
Camping
Area

Littledyke House
(to the west)

Year of construction

Before 1860

1860–1910 (W. P. Letchworth era)

1911–1933 (early park era)

1934–1942 (CCC era)

1943–2003 (modern era)

Park boundary

Road

Railroad

Trail

Water body

Forest

Native American Settlement to circa 1830

Human history in the park area stretches back thousands of years and includes a long yet incomplete record of Native American settlement. Overall, the park is an archaeologically sensitive area, but it is not a hotbed of known sites in comparison to the high-density areas just to the northeast. While no known Paleo-Indian archaeological sites exist in Letchworth State Park itself, evidence places hunter-gatherers and their ancient game species in western New York as early as roughly 11,000 years ago. For example, the Hiscock site thirty miles north of the park has yielded numerous artifacts dating to this time, including tools fashioned out of mastodon bones and even a fragment of handmade textile. Knowledge of who occupied the park area, and when they occupied it, is limited, but available data suggest that Native American people set up towns and camps nearby around 3000

Photo 18. The Genesee River flowing northward through the Gardeau Flats.

BCE or earlier. Offering a rough sketch of where Native American activity occurred over the last few millennia is Map 50, showing archaeological sites—from major town sites to unidentified stonework fragments—in and around the park area. The map also shows the locations of notable archaeological sites within the park. Map 50 shows only approximate locations of sites to help ensure that they remain unvisited and undisturbed.

The most notable archaeological site investigated within the park boundary predating the Iroquois occurred at Squawkie Hill at the park's northern end. Archaeologists led by New York State Archaeologist William Ritchie in the 1930s studied earthen burial mounds here dating to as early as 140 CE. Containing graves and numerous artifacts, the mounds themselves were discovered by a property owner around the year 1900, and each of the three (or possibly four) circular mounds was thirty feet in diameter and four feet high when discovered. Archaeological evidence from sites

Photo 19. The Nancy Jemison cabin, Mary Jemison grave, and Seneca Council House at Council Grounds.

around the park suggest that residents living in the region around this time, including those who built mounds at Squawkie Hill, were a sparse population found at the periphery of regional population centers. They were part of the Point Peninsula cultural tradition with groups around Lake Ontario to the north, yet adopted aspects of the wide-spanning Ohio Hopewell "horizon"—a term to describe common characteristics of cultural groups also connected by trade—to the southwest. Available data also suggest that of any area in the park, Squawkie Hill was both occupied the longest and most consistently—but still discontinuously—over a span of nearly 1,800 years, whether in the form of towns or camps. A few other towns and camps existed at various points throughout prehistory both on the valley floor and in the upland areas within the park, and additional burial mounds are located within and near the park, but the cultural affiliation and date of occupation for most sites are uncertain. Other cultural groups inhabited western and central New York aside from those associated with Squawkie Hill sites, such as the earlier Meadowood Phase culture and the later Owasco culture, though few if any sites associated with those cultures have been definitively identified and described within Letchworth State Park.

From around 1500 to 1700, the towns of the Seneca (Onöndowa'ga:') formed the closest dense area of Native American settlement to the park, located around where Livingston, Monroe, and Ontario Counties meet today—about 15 miles (24 km) northeast of the park's northern end. Living in longhouses, the Seneca were primarily farming communities that also collected wild plant resources, and who hunted deer and other game for food and resources. In their fields they grew staples such as corn (*Zea mays*), beans (*Phaseolus vulgaris*), and squash (*Cucurbita pepo*), and tended to nut-bearing and fruit-bearing trees. As mentioned in chapter 2, Native Americans would burn upland forests to create beneficial open environments. They moved and rebuilt their towns every few decades as they used up firewood and exhausted farmland soils. Farther west and closer to the modern-day City of Buffalo was a region of diverse but related Iroquoian cultures and nations, notably the Erie, Neutral, Wenro, and Kahkwa. During these centuries, the park area was either a less-utilized buffer zone between nations, or an area the Seneca occasionally visited to hunt and acquire resources. The Seneca called the valley where the current park is located "Seh-ga-hun-da," or the "Vale of Three Falls." The Genesee River Valley was likely a major travel corridor via both land and water—a portage route around the falls to the east of the river is purported to have existed between canoe "carrying places" at Portageville and St. Helena.

Due to factors that included conflict with white settlers, their colonization of other Native American territories, and trade opportunities, Seneca settlement shifted geographically in the 1700s, dispersing across western New York and beyond. Becoming a center of Native American settlement by the end of the eighteenth century was an area just northeast of the park area centered upon modern-day Geneseo that included a part of the park's northern end. Living here were the Seneca along with various Native Americans including other Iroquois Five Nations (Haudenosaunee) groups, forming mixed-ethnicity communities. The eighteenth century was not a period of decline for the Seneca. Archaeological and historical evidence suggest that they carefully and shrewdly made decisions—such as where to live, and what elements of European-American housing construction and food procurement to adopt—to better their position in response to political and economic forces in the region. They also retained some elements of their material culture while also adopting certain European elements.

Map 51 shows Native American town populations in 1790 just before white settlement. The map also shows their approximate overland travel routes, one of which was located where River Road on the park's east side is today. Nearly 750 persons lived in a five-town area that included Squawkie Hill within the park. Near its southern end was the town of Deowesto (Nunda) with 48 persons counted. Note that these population totals are mostly from 1790, just eleven years after American forces destroyed Seneca towns—due to their support of the British during the Revolutionary War— around present-day Geneseo. Population numbers were likely much higher prior to 1779: for example, Chenussio (Little Beard's Town) alone had more than 100 houses when destroyed.

Native Americans moved onto reservations established by the Treaty of Big Tree of 1797, a complex treaty involving various parties including the Seneca, the States of New York and Massachusetts, Thomas Morris (son and agent of Robert Morris, financier of the American Revolution), and the Holland Land Company, all of which was overseen by the United States government. In addition to establishing reservations, the treaty also extinguished Native American title to lands west of the Genesee River for a sum of money paid to the Seneca among other ends. Like many other treaties involving Native Americans, this treaty is highly controversial to modern scholars and Native American communities in that it involved bribery and deception of the Seneca at the treaty signing.

Maps 51 and 52 show the locations of reservations established by the aforementioned treaty, two of which—Squawkie Hill Reservation and Gardeau Reservation—overlapped with the present-day park area. The Squawkie Hill Reservation was located at the park's northern end and totaled about 1,300 acres (526 ha), whereas the much larger Gardeau Reservation sprawled across the center of the park and totaled nearly 18,000 acres (7,284 ha). Over one third of the current park area was once reservation land: about 36 percent of the park was part of the Gardeau Reservation, and another 1 percent of the park was part of the Squawkie Hill Reservation. Map 52 additionally shows western New York circa 1800 as a mix of both white settlements and Native American reservations.

The park area falls in a swath of land once known as the Morris Reserve, a twelve-mile-wide tract with a complicated ownership and development history that also involves Native Americans (Map 52). First controlled by the Seneca, the State of Massachusetts obtained its preemption rights (sole right to purchase land from Native Americans, in this context) along with much of western New York in 1786 under the Treaty of Hartford. Massachusetts then sold those rights in 1788 to Oliver Phelps and Nathaniel Gorham, two leaders of a syndicate of land speculators. When Phelps and Gorham could not make its payments, the preemption rights for this tract and additional lands in western New York reverted to Massachusetts in 1791. Robert Morris purchased the preemption rights from Massachusetts in 1791 for lands west of the Genesee River in New York, and later obtained full title to the Morris Reserve from the Seneca in 1797 via the Treaty of Big Tree (lands farther west went to the Holland Land Company; compare Maps 52 and 53). Morris then fell into debt, and the Morris Reserve was auctioned off to speculators piecemeal. The result: comprising the area that would become Letchworth State Park was a patchwork of small land tracts once owned by Morris but subdivided by different developers, with names such as the Cottringer Tract, Honorary Creditors Tract, and Mount Morris Tract. Original land surveys of these tracts provided some of the forest descriptions in Map 19.

The time from 1790 to 1830 was a transitional period between Native American and white settlement in the park area and surrounding region. Small Native American communities persisted on the Squawkie Hill and Gardeau Reservations, whereas the Seneca sold off other reservations nearby such as Little Beard's Town. Some early white settlers lived among the Seneca: the surveyor of the Cottringer Tract, Elisha Johnson, observed a community of six white families and five Native American families farming along the Genesee River on the Gardeau Reservation in 1807. Native Americans moved elsewhere including to other reservations west, and the Seneca sold off portions of the reservations in the park area in the 1820s. About eighty people were living at Squawkie Hill in 1816. Also living on the Gardeau Reservation since 1779 were Mary Jemison and her children, who acquired the reservation lands under the Treaty of Big Tree. The life of Mary Jemison (Deh-ga-wa-nus, or "Two Falling Voices")—the "White Woman of the Genesee" who was captured and adopted by the Seneca as a child, and who later chose to live as a Seneca—is covered in the following section and later in Map 57. The Seneca sold the last of the reservations as part of the first Buffalo Creek Treaty of 1826, another treaty some view as illegitimate since it was never ratified by the U.S. Senate nor proclaimed by the President. The last Seneca left Squawkie Hill in 1828, and Jemison left Gardeau in 1831. With those sales and departures, a land the Seneca long possessed—including the land that would become Letchworth State Park—was now fully under white ownership.

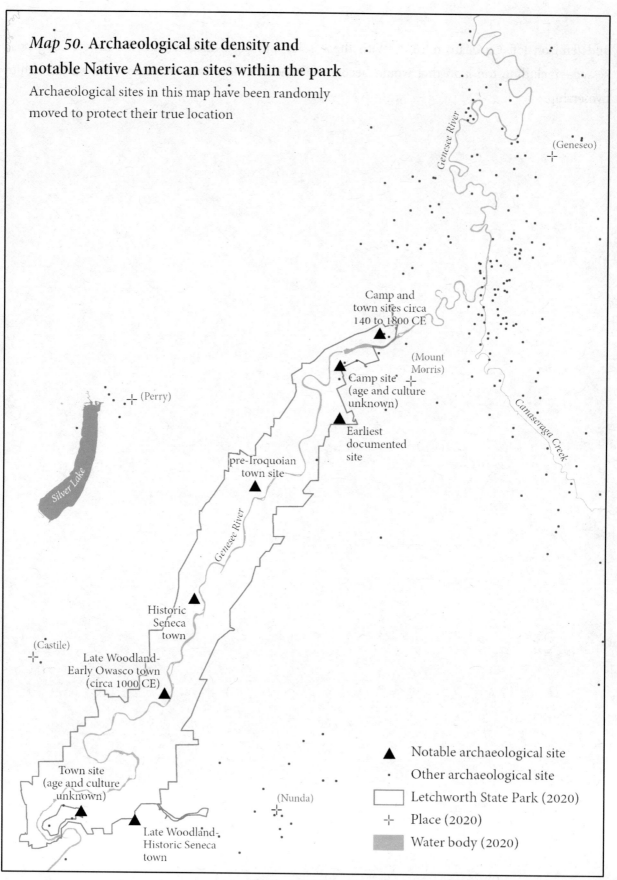

Map 50. Archaeological site density and notable Native American sites within the park

Archaeological sites in this map have been randomly moved to protect their true location

Genesee River

(Geneseo)

Camp and town sites circa 140 to 1800 CE

(Mount Morris)

Camp site (age and culture unknown)

Canaseraga Creek

Earliest documented site

(Perry)

pre-Iroquoian town site

Silver Lake

Genesee River

Historic Seneca town

(Castile)

Late Woodland-Early Owasco town (circa 1000 CE)

Town site (age and culture unknown)

(Nunda)

Late Woodland-Historic Seneca town

▲ Notable archaeological site

· Other archaeological site

☐ Letchworth State Park (2020)

+ Place (2020)

▨ Water body (2020)

Data from NYS Office of Parks, Recreation and Historic Preservation (2003, 2020)

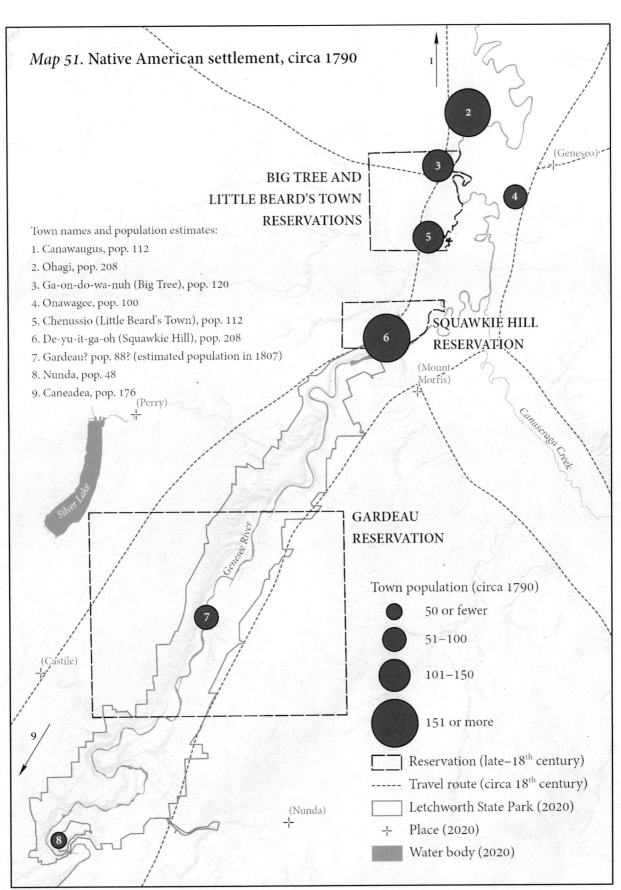

Map 51. Native American settlement, circa 1790

BIG TREE AND
LITTLE BEARD'S TOWN
RESERVATIONS

Town names and population estimates:

1. Canawaugus, pop. 112
2. Ohagi, pop. 208
3. Ga-on-do-wa-nuh (Big Tree), pop. 120
4. Onawagee, pop. 100
5. Chenussio (Little Beard's Town), pop. 112
6. De-yu-it-ga-oh (Squawkie Hill), pop. 208
7. Gardeau? pop. 88? (estimated population in 1807)
8. Nunda, pop. 48
9. Caneadea, pop. 176

SQUAWKIE HILL
RESERVATION

GARDEAU
RESERVATION

Town population (circa 1790)

- 50 or fewer
- 51–100
- 101–150
- 151 or more

▢ Reservation (late–18th century)

---- Travel route (circa 18th century)

▢ Letchworth State Park (2020)

+ Place (2020)

▬ Water body (2020)

(Geneseo)

(Mount Morris)

Canaseraga Creek

(Perry)

Silver Lake

Genesee River

(Castile)

(Nunda)

Population data from Kirkland (1791) and Johnson (1807); travel route data from Morgan (1851)

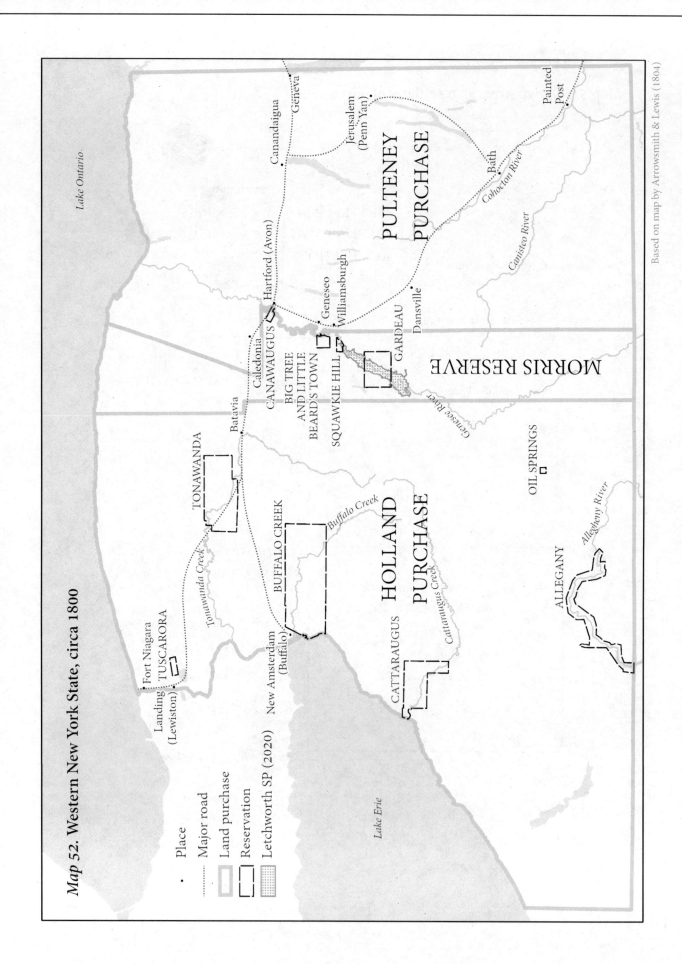

Map 52. Western New York State, circa 1800

Place

Major road

Land purchase

Reservation

Letchworth SP (2020)

Lake Ontario.

Fort Niagara

Landing (Lewiston)

TUSCARORA

New Amsterdam (Buffalo)

TONAWANDA

Tonawanda Creek

Batavia

Caledonia

BUFFALO CREEK

Buffalo Creek

Canandaigua

Geneva

Jerusalem (Penn Yan)

Painted Post

PULTENEY PURCHASE

Bath

Cohocton River

Canisteo River

Hartford (Avon)

CANAWAUGUS

BIG TREE AND LITTLE BEARD'S TOWN

SQUAWKIE HILL

Geneseo

Williamsburgh

GARDEAU

Dansville

MORRIS RESERVE

Genesee River

OIL SPRINGS

HOLLAND PURCHASE

Cattaraugus Creek

CATTARAUGUS

ALLEGANY

Allegheny River

Lake Erie

Based on map by Arrowsmith & Lewis (1804)

128

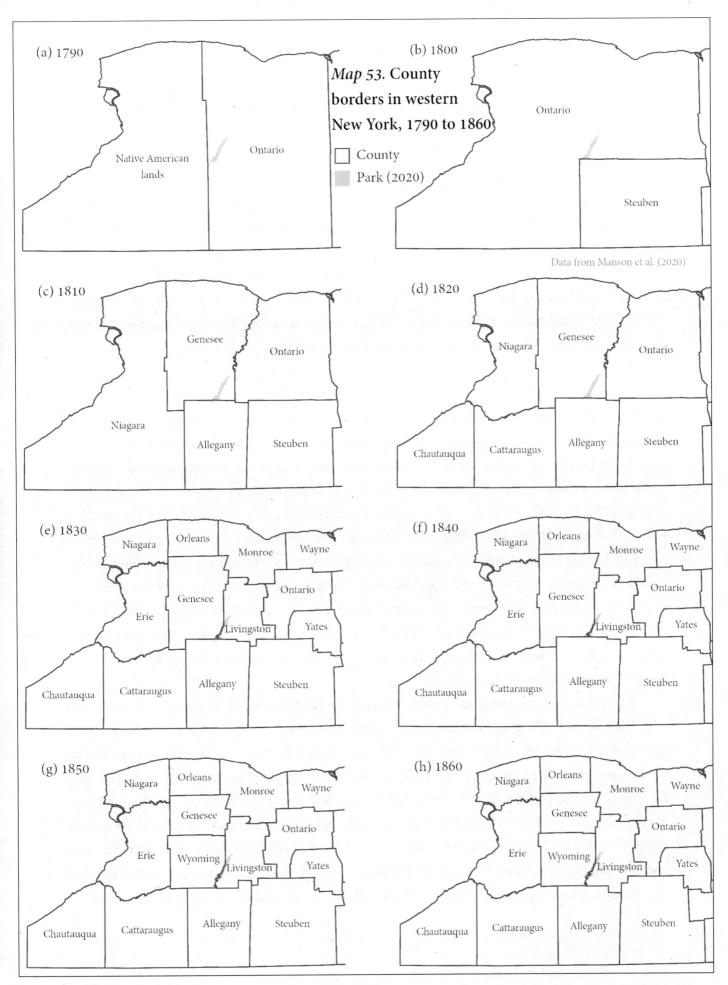

Map 53. County borders in western New York, 1790 to 1860

□ County
▨ Park (2020)

Data from Manson et al. (2020)

(a) 1790
Native American lands
Ontario

(b) 1800
Ontario
Steuben

(c) 1810
Genesee
Ontario
Niagara
Allegany
Steuben

(d) 1820
Niagara
Genesee
Ontario
Chautauqua
Cattaraugus
Allegany
Steuben

(e) 1830
Niagara
Orleans
Monroe
Wayne
Genesee
Erie
Ontario
Livingston
Yates
Chautauqua
Cattaraugus
Allegany
Steuben

(f) 1840
Niagara
Orleans
Monroe
Wayne
Genesee
Erie
Ontario
Livingston
Yates
Chautauqua
Cattaraugus
Allegany
Steuben

(g) 1850
Niagara
Orleans
Monroe
Wayne
Genesee
Erie
Wyoming
Ontario
Livingston
Yates
Chautauqua
Cattaraugus
Allegany
Steuben

(h) 1860
Niagara
Orleans
Monroe
Wayne
Genesee
Erie
Wyoming
Ontario
Livingston
Yates
Chautauqua
Cattaraugus
Allegany
Steuben

Settlement before Park Creation (circa 1790 to 1910)

The history of European-American settlement in the park area begins in the 1790s. Overall, though settlers heavily used the land for timber and farmland throughout the next two centuries, white settlements within the current park boundary were not extensive, and population in towns comprising the present park area peaked around 1840 before declining until the start of the twentieth century. To summarize some trends in the immediate region, Map 47 shows changes to population, population density, and town borders every twenty years from 1820 onward, and Map 53 shows changes to county borders every ten years from 1790 to 1860. Over the first half of the nineteenth century, the area that would become the park was in the jurisdiction of various towns and counties that were frequently splitting and merging, before modern borders solidified around 1860.

White settlement was sporadic from 1790 to 1830. Map 45 and the associated timeline provides some illustrative key dates as to when white settlement began. Ebenezer "Indian" Allen settled in 1792 on Silver Lake Outlet west of the current Highbanks Camping Area, and Reuben and Perry Jones settled around 1816 near the present location of the visitor center near the southern end (though some think they arrived in the 1820s). Alvah Palmer settled in 1821 and built the original cabin that would later become William P. Letchworth's home, and later known as the Glen Iris Inn. Colonel George Williams, land agent for the Cottringer Tract, created an estate in and near the southern end of the park by 1833. The earliest mills for timber and other industries were established in the first few decades of the nineteenth century to exploit the waterpower and navigability (during high water) of the Genesee River. In 1820, population densities of towns making up the future park area were only 39, 31, 20, and 8 persons per square mile in Leicester, Perry, Mount Morris, and Nunda, respectively—and the total population of these towns combined was less than 6,000 people (Map 47a). By modern definitions, the population density of these towns would almost classify them as sparsely populated frontier communities.

By 1850, foci of white settlement within the park area were the hamlet of Gibsonville, the hamlet of St. Helena, and milling operations around Middle Falls (Maps 46a and 54). Just outside the park were the larger clusters of settlement in Mount Morris and Portage, and smaller clusters at Five Corners and River Road Forks. By 1840, population density increased to 115, 91, 74, and 71 persons per square mile in Portage, Mount Morris, Castile, and Leicester, respectively (Map 47b)—and population increased to over 14,000. Map 54 shows roads and notable buildings in the mid–nineteenth century: within the modern park boundary were about 160 main buildings including twelve mills and five schools, as estimated from historical maps. Around 1850, St. Helena had numerous mills and stores, a school, and a few dozen dwellings; Gibsonville likewise had mills and stores, a school,

Photo 20. The gorge bottom at sunset upstream from the former site of St. Helena in autumn.

and over a dozen dwellings. North–south roads existed along the valley bottom. Many early farmers sold timber and potash (a byproduct of burned vegetation used in various industries) from clearing their land, shipping it via the Genesee River or later by canal. They grew corn and wheat before realizing the limitations of the soil, and instead transitioned toward raising livestock and diversifying the crops they grew. Although rough terrain and lack of bridges have limited travel between west and east sides historically, in the mid–nineteenth century there were numerous crossings over the Genesee River within the modern-day park boundary, some at bridges and others at low-water fords—compare that with the single footbridge crossing within the park today. One bridge crossed just above Middle Falls.

Map 55 shows the birthplaces of residents living in 1855—the earliest New York State census to record these data—in the five-town area that would eventually contain the park: Leicester, Castile, Mount Morris, Genesee Falls, and Portage. Mid-nineteenth-century residents within and around the park area were mainly born in New York State (71%), but a notable number were not. Almost half (44%) in the five-town area were born in Livingston or Wyoming Counties, and over a quarter (27%) were born in other counties in New York, led by Cayuga County (over 4%). Roughly an equal number were born in other states in the United States (15%) and other countries (14%). Connecticut and Vermont (3% per state) provided the most settlers out of all states other than New York, and Ireland (9%) provided the most immigrants from a foreign country, some of whom were likely workers on the Genesee Valley Canal. Four residents were born at sea. By 1900, as immigration numbers slowed over the nineteenth century, just a few percent of citizens in each of the five towns were born outside the United States.

Two major engineering projects linked to the park's history were the Genesee Valley Canal and the railroad, focused at the northern and southern ends of the park. The Genesee Valley Canal was a 124-mile (200 km) long and 42-foot (13 m) wide canal with an accompanying towpath that connected the Erie Canal at the City of Rochester with the Allegany River at the City of Olean. Taking decades to construct and fully completed in 1862 (only to be defunct by 1878), the most difficult portion to build was the 5.5 miles (9 km) through what became the southern end of the park (see Maps 54d and 56). Construction here involved a failed attempt at a tunnel on the east side opposite from Inspiration Point (the entrance to which is viewable from Trail #7), blasting away rock along the gorge wall when the tunnel construction failed, and the creation of several canal locks that allowed boats to change elevation. The byproduct of blasting is still visible on the opposite side of the gorge from Inspiration Point as a talus slope of rock debris now overgrown with vegetation. Much of the canal was dug by hand including the "Deep Cut," a two-mile-long and fifty-foot-deep section preserved within the narrow strip of park jutting out to the east at the park's south end. Elisha Johnson, surveyor of the

Photo 21. Papermill Falls on Silver Lake Outlet in winter, the former site of a mill in Gibsonville.

Cottringer Tract (see chapter 2) and former mayor of Rochester, was now a businessman and engineer building the canal's ill-fated tunnel section, who also built his rustic-yet-gaudy Hornby Lodge in the 1840s atop this section—the Lodge collapsed from land disturbance caused by tunnel blasting. The canal cost over $6 million at the time, more than three times the original estimate. While the Genesee Valley Canal lost money annually, it stimulated economic development along its length, facilitated travel, and contributed to the success of the Erie Canal that connected to it.

The arrival of the railroad made the Genesee Valley Canal obsolete. Completed in 1852 was an important portion of the Buffalo and New York City Railroad, connecting the communities of Attica and Hornellsville and more efficiently connecting Buffalo to New York City. The railroad crossed the gorge just upstream from Upper Falls and just north of the modern bridge via the Portage wooden bridge (also known as the Portage High Bridge), which for many years was the largest wooden bridge in the world at over 230 feet (70 m) tall and 800 feet (244 m) long. After only twenty-three years of use, it burned down in 1875 and was replaced with the Portage iron bridge (also known as the Portage trestle bridge). Other railroads crossed the extreme northern and southern ends of the park area, including one built directly atop the former towpath of the Genesee Valley Canal in 1882. Map 56 shows the route of the Genesee Valley canal until 1878, along with railroads and railroad stations circa 1900. Trail #7 within the park today follows the towpath beside the exact route of the Genesee Valley Canal and the railroad later constructed atop it. The railroads and hotel industry facilitated early tourism to the park area, developing in the nineteenth century—for example, visitors came from New York and beyond (see Map 74 later) to stay at the Cascade House, built around 1855 and located in Portage at the intersection of two railroad lines. Trains stopped on the Portage wooden bridge to let passengers admire the view.

Living in the nineteenth century within the park area were two of its most famous historical figures: Mary Jemison from 1779 to 1831, and William P. Letchworth from 1858 to 1910. Map 57 presents important locations in the lives of both. Born at sea on a ship from Ireland around 1743, Jemison was captured as a teen by the Shawnee along with French soldiers (during the French and Indian War) at her home near Gettysburg, Pennsylvania, and was later adopted by the Seneca. She then spent years in towns along the Ohio River, moved to the Genesee River Valley, and was eventually displaced to what would become the Gardeau Reservation within the current park area. In the early nineteenth century, those Gardeau lands made her one of the largest landowners in the region. Along the way she had a tumultuous personal life: she was married, widowed, and remarried; had children and lost children; saw her town (Chenussio, or Little Beard's Town) destroyed by American forces in the American Revolution; and sold her land (some of the last Seneca-owned) to white settlers in the Genesee Valley. In addition to mapping important locations, Map 57 provides a timeline of notable events in the life of Mary Jemison. The lives of Jemison and Letchworth did not intersect until after her death in 1833: when development threatened her grave on the then–Buffalo Creek Reservation, Letchworth agreed at her grandsons' request to have her reburied at the Council Grounds on his Glen Iris Estate in 1874. Visitors can view her grave today. Given how essential he was to the modern existence of the park, the next section of this chapter is devoted entirely to Letchworth.

During the second half of the nineteenth century, the collective population of the surrounding towns steadily declined: from around 13,000 in 1850 to 9,000 in 1900. Sawmills had exploited the forests of the area and were closing in the middle of the century, but agriculture persisted. By around

1900, about 140 buildings stood within the park area as estimated from historical maps—still five schools, as in the middle of the nineteenth century, but fewer signs of industry (Map 58). The number of river crossings shrank. Both the villages of Gibsonville and St. Helena within the park area had seen their peak in the middle of the century. Many pieces of evidence suggest their decline: decreasing populations, fewer houses, post office closures, damaged mills not rebuilt, damaged bridges not replaced. Being located on the valley bottom, compounding problems for St. Helena were regular floods on the Genesee River from rains and ice jams that inundated roads and buildings.

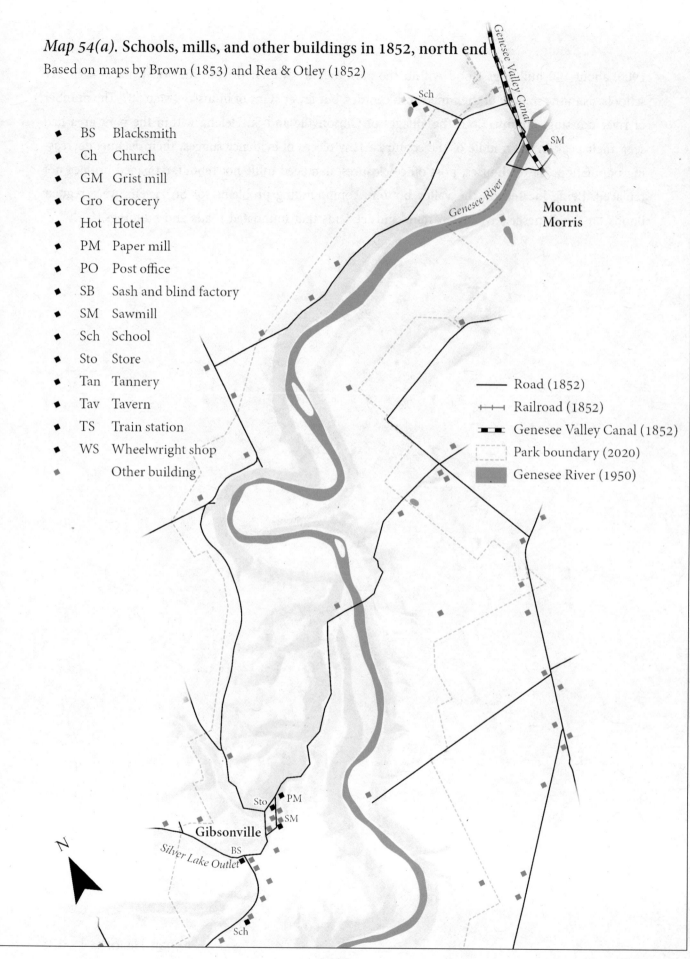

Map 54(a). **Schools, mills, and other buildings in 1852, north end**
Based on maps by Brown (1853) and Rea & Otley (1852)

- BS   Blacksmith
- Ch   Church
- GM   Grist mill
- Gro   Grocery
- Hot   Hotel
- PM   Paper mill
- PO   Post office
- SB   Sash and blind factory
- SM   Sawmill
- Sch   School
- Sto   Store
- Tan   Tannery
- Tav   Tavern
- TS   Train station
- WS   Wheelwright shop
-     Other building

Genesee Valley Canal

Genesee River

Mount Morris

Sch

SM

—— Road (1852)

⊢+⊣ Railroad (1852)

■■■ Genesee Valley Canal (1852)

Park boundary (2020)

Genesee River (1950)

Sto   PM

SM

Gibsonville

BS

Silver Lake Outlet

Sch

N

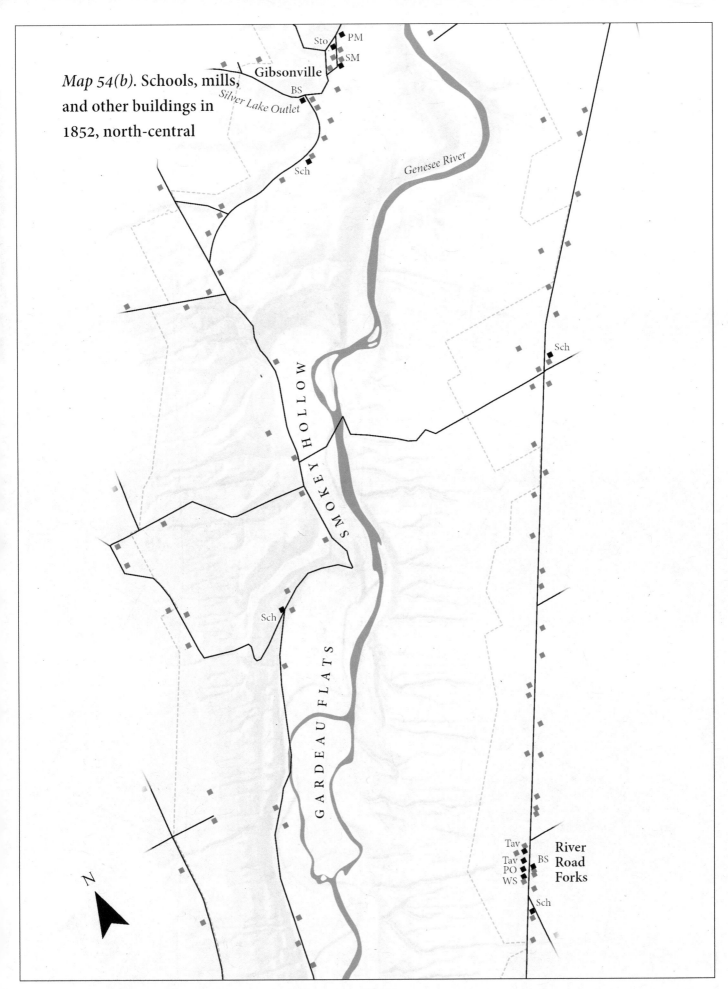

Map 54(b). Schools, mills, and other buildings in 1852, north-central

Gibsonville

Sto
PM
SM
BS

Silver Lake Outlet

Sch

Genesee River

Sch

S M O K E Y   H O L L O W

Sch

G A R D E A U   F L A T S

N

Tav
Tav
PO
WS

BS

River Road Forks

Sch

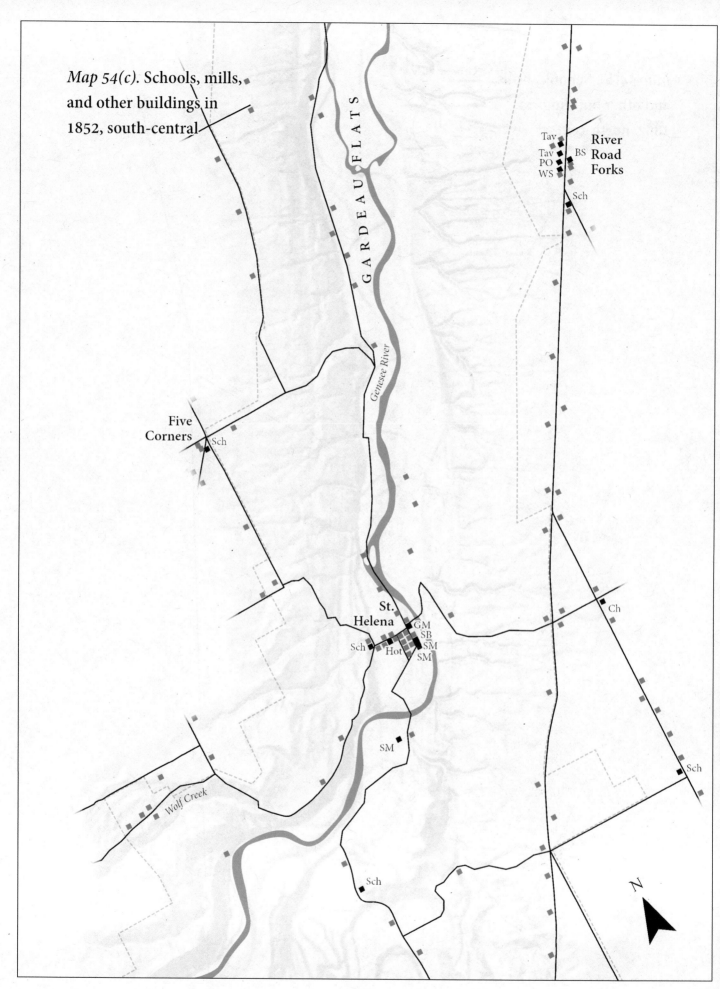

Map 54(c). Schools, mills, and other buildings in 1852, south-central

GARDEAU FLATS

Genesee River

Tav
Tav
PO
WS
BS

River Road Forks

Sch

Five Corners Sch

Ch

St. Helena
GM
SB
SM
Sch Hot SM

SM

Wolf Creek

Sch

Sch

N

138

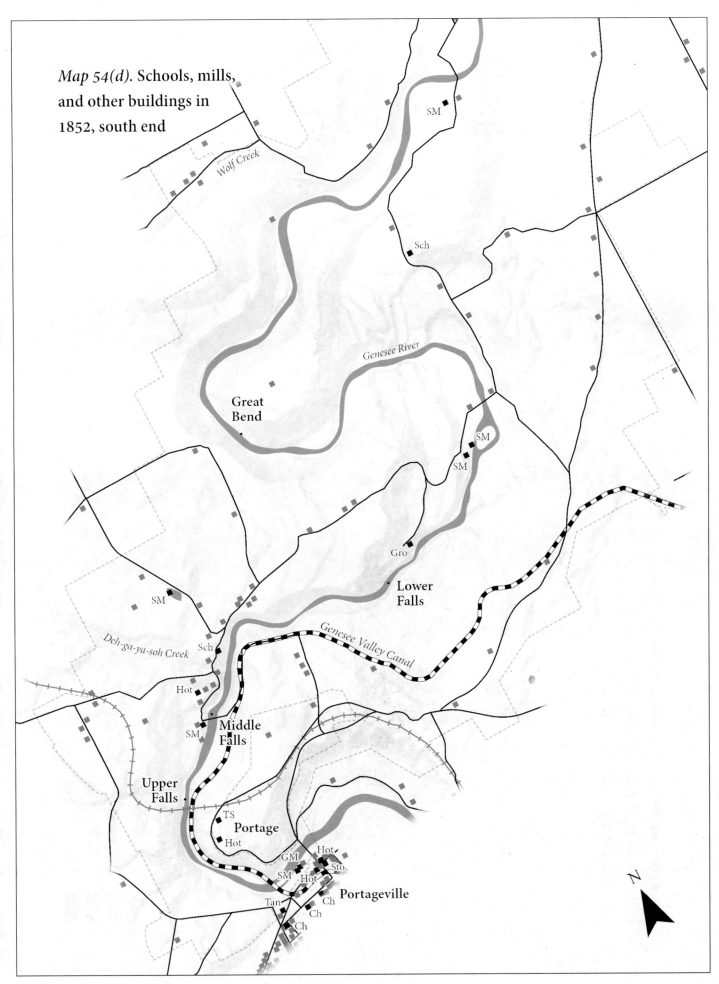

Map 54(d). Schools, mills, and other buildings in 1852, south end

Wolf Creek

SM

Sch

Genesee River

Great Bend

SM

SM

Gro

Lower Falls

Genesee Valley Canal

SM

Deh-ga-ya-soh Creek

Sch

Hot

SM

Middle Falls

Upper Falls

TS

Portage

Hot

GM

Hot

SM

Sto

Hot

Tan

Ch

Portageville

Ch

Ch

N

139

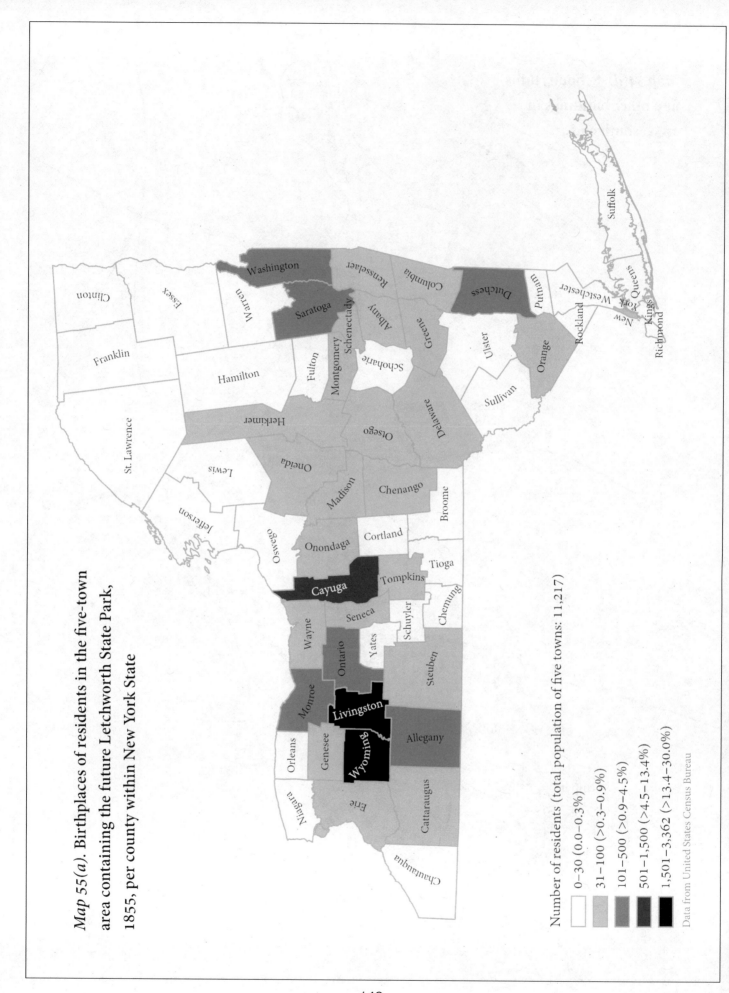

Map 55(a). Birthplaces of residents in the five-town area containing the future Letchworth State Park, 1855, per county within New York State

Number of residents (total population of five towns: 11,217)

- 0–30 (0.0–0.3%)
- 31–100 (>0.3–0.9%)
- 101–500 (>0.9–4.5%)
- 501–1,500 (>4.5–13.4%)
- 1,501–3,362 (>13.4–30.0%)

Data from United States Census Bureau

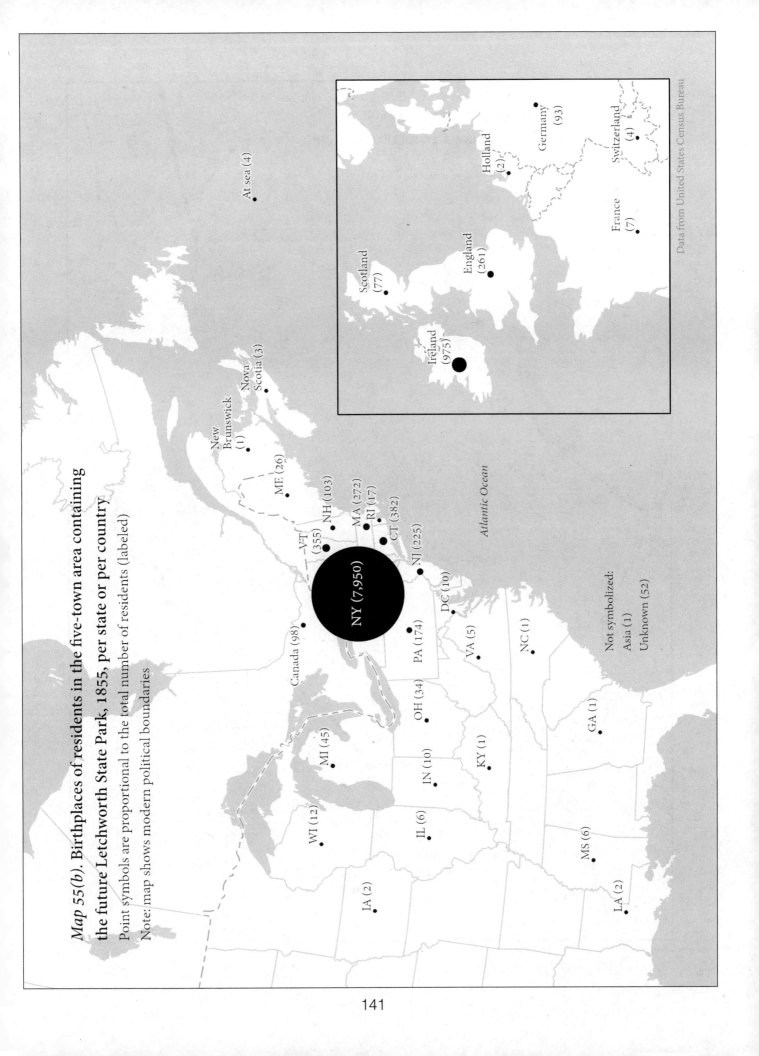

Map 55(b). Birthplaces of residents in the five-town area containing the future Letchworth State Park, 1855, per state or per country

Point symbols are proportional to the total number of residents (labeled)

Note: map shows modern political boundaries

At sea (4)

Scotland (77)

Ireland (975)

England (261)

Holland (2)

Germany (93)

Switzerland (4)

France (7)

Data from United States Census Bureau

Nova Scotia (3)

New Brunswick (1)

ME (26)

NH (103)

MA (272)

RI (17)

CT (382)

VT (355)

NY (7,950)

NJ (225)

Canada (98)

PA (174)

DC (10)

VA (5)

NC (1)

OH (34)

MI (45)

IN (10)

KY (1)

GA (1)

WI (12)

IL (6)

MS (6)

IA (2)

LA (2)

Atlantic Ocean

Not symbolized:
Asia (1)
Unknown (52)

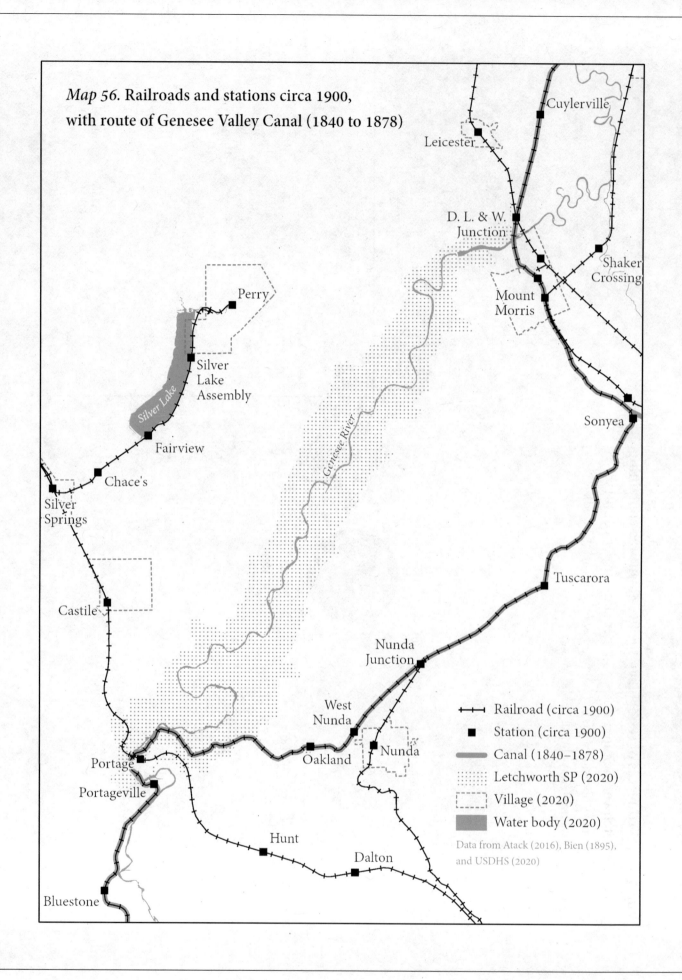

Map 56. Railroads and stations circa 1900, with route of Genesee Valley Canal (1840 to 1878)

Cuylerville

Leicester

D. L. & W. Junction

Shaker Crossing

Mount Morris

Perry

Silver Lake Assembly

Silver Lake

Fairview

Genesee River

Sonyea

Chace's

Silver Springs

Castile

Tuscarora

Nunda Junction

West Nunda

Nunda

Oakland

Portage

Portageville

Hunt

Dalton

Bluestone

	Railroad (circa 1900)
■	Station (circa 1900)
	Canal (1840–1878)
	Letchworth SP (2020)
	Village (2020)
	Water body (2020)

Data from Atack (2016), Bien (1895), and USDHS (2020)

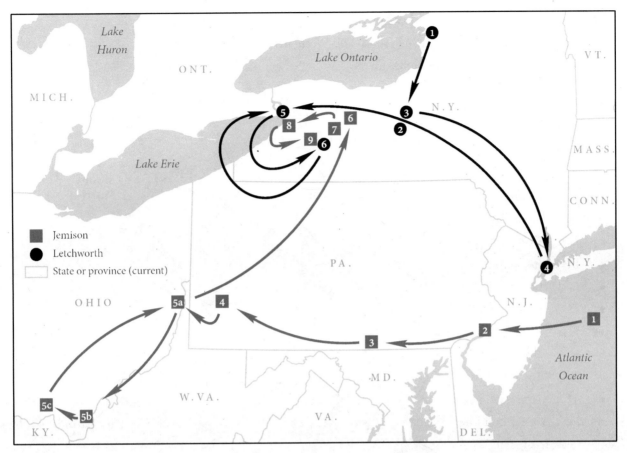

Map 57. **Important places in the lives of Mary Jemison and William P. Letchworth**

Numbers in parentheses below correspond to numbers in map

Jemison timeline

1743: Born at sea on ship from Belfast, Ireland (1)

1743: Family arrives in Philadelphia, PA (2)

1744: Family moves to Marsh Creek, PA (3)

1758: Captured by the Shawnee (3)

1758: Taken to Fort Duquesne, present-day Pittsburgh, PA (4)

1758: Taken by two Seneca women to "Mingo Town", present-day Mingo Junction, OH, and adopted (5a)

1760: Moves with Seneca family to Wiishto, near present-day Gallipolis, OH (5b)

1760-1762: Moves seasonally among Native American villages; marries and has children (5a, 5b, and 5c)

1762: Moves to Chenussio, present-day Geneseo, NY, with husband and child; separates from husband during trip (6)

1779: Sullivan campaign destroys Chenussio (6)

1779: Moves to Gardeau Flats, present-day Letchworth State Park, with children from second marriage (7)

1831: Sells last of her lands; moves to Buffalo Creek Reservation, Buffalo, NY, with family (8)

1833: Dies; buried at Buffalo Creek Reservation (8)

1874: Body exhumed and reburied on Glen Iris Estate (9)

Letchworth timeline

1823: Born in Brownville, NY (1)

circa 1830: Family moves to Sherwood, NY (2)

circa 1838: Becomes clerk at Hayden & Holmes, a hardware and saddlery business, in Auburn, NY (3)

1845: Moves to New York City, NY, to work for P. and T. Hayden Company (4)

1848: Moves to Buffalo, NY; becomes partner in Pratt & Letchworth, a malleable iron business (5)

1857: First views Portage Glen from railroad bridge (6)

1858: Acquires first lands to form Glen Iris Estate (6)

1906: Donates Glen Iris Estate to New York State (6)

1910: Dies on Glen Iris Estate (6); buried in Buffalo, NY (5)

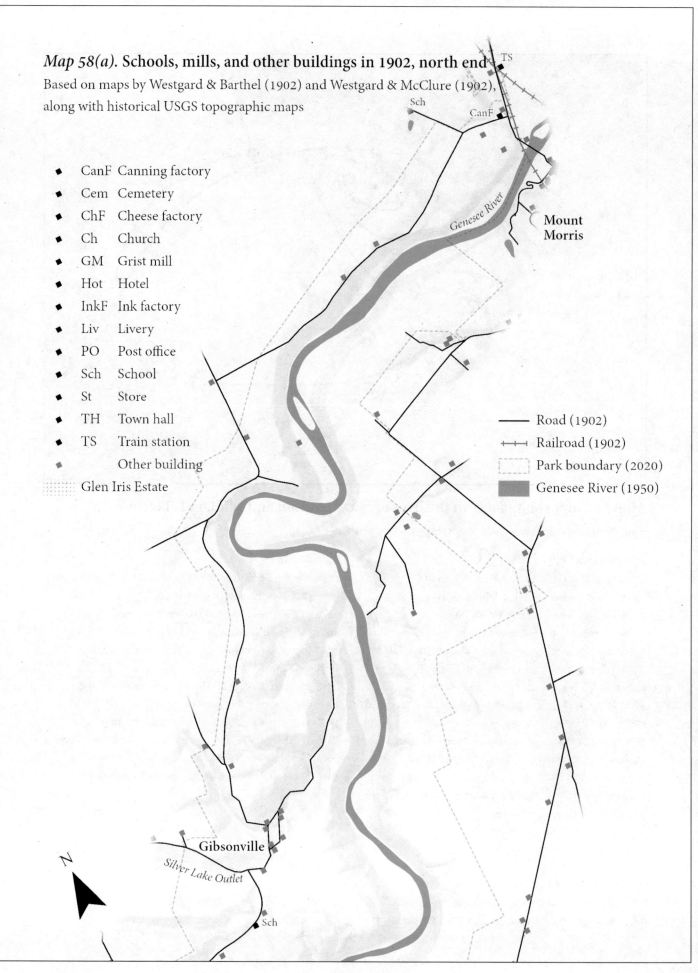

Map 58(a). **Schools, mills, and other buildings in 1902, north end**
Based on maps by Westgard & Barthel (1902) and Westgard & McClure (1902),
along with historical USGS topographic maps

◆	CanF	Canning factory
◆	Cem	Cemetery
◆	ChF	Cheese factory
◆	Ch	Church
◆	GM	Grist mill
◆	Hot	Hotel
◆	InkF	Ink factory
◆	Liv	Livery
◆	PO	Post office
◆	Sch	School
◆	St	Store
◆	TH	Town hall
◆	TS	Train station
◆		Other building
░░	Glen Iris Estate	

TS

Sch

CanF

Genesee River

**Mount
Morris**

Road (1902)

Railroad (1902)

Park boundary (2020)

Genesee River (1950)

N

Gibsonville

Silver Lake Outlet

Sch

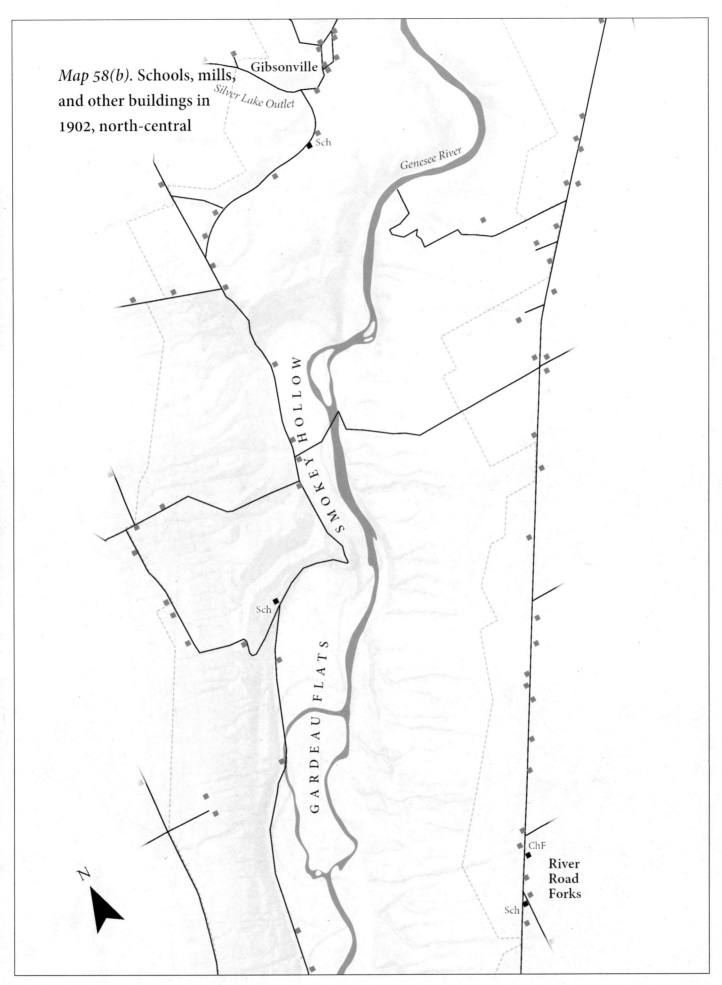

Map 58(b). Schools, mills, and other buildings in 1902, north-central

Gibsonville

Silver Lake Outlet

Sch

Genesee River

S M O K E Y   H O L L O W

G A R D E A U   F L A T S

Sch

ChF

River Road Forks

Sch

N

145

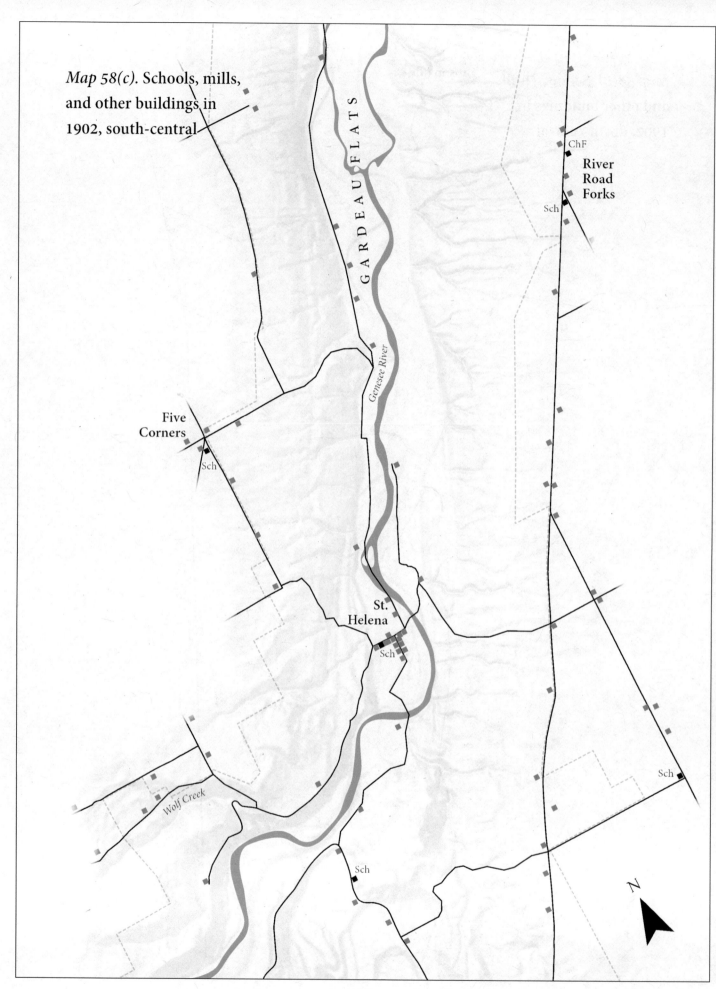

Map 58(c). Schools, mills, and other buildings in 1902, south-central

GARDEAU FLATS

Genesee River

River Road Forks

ChF

Sch

Five Corners

Sch

St. Helena

Sch

Wolf Creek

Sch

Sch

N

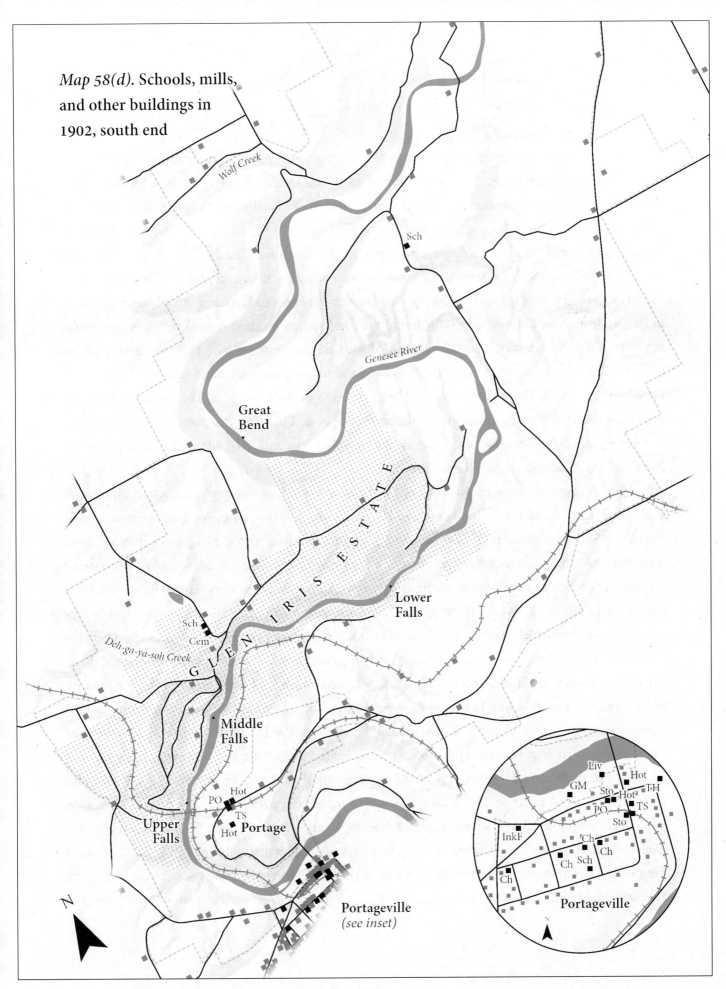

Map 58(d). Schools, mills, and other buildings in 1902, south end

Wolf Creek

Sch

Genesee River

Great Bend

G L E N   I R I S   E S T A T E

Lower Falls

Sch
Cem

Deh-ga-ya-soh Creek

Middle Falls

Hot
PO
TS
Hot **Portage**

Upper Falls

N

Portageville
(see inset)

Liv
GM   Hot
Sto Hot   TH
PO   TS
Sto
InkF
Ch
Ch   Sch   Ch
Ch

Portageville

N

147

The William P. Letchworth Era (circa 1860 to 1910)

The park owes its existence almost solely to William Pryor Letchworth, whose estate formed the first 1,000 acres (405 ha) of the park in 1906. Born in 1823 to a Quaker family in Brownville, New York (near Watertown), and growing up near Auburn, New York, Letchworth was a businessman and philanthropist who made his fortune with Pratt & Letchworth in the City of Buffalo, manufacturing hardware for horses, saddles, carriages, and trains. Map 57 manifests his life journey and important events. In 1857, he sought to purchase a country estate when, at the suggestion of a friend, he took the train to the Portage wooden bridge to view the waterfalls on the Genesee River while returning to Buffalo from New York City. Here he found the ideal spot: a location replete with natural beauty, but also abused by industry. In 1875, he recalled his first glance at the land that would become his Glen Iris Estate: "There were unsightly objects in the form of ruinous buildings, wrecks of abandoned enterprises and bare points that had been stripped of their foliage . . . in every direction the eye encountered something that shocked the aesthetic sense. But I saw that nature was endeavoring to recover herself." Before his fateful trip to Portage, he had considered situating his estate on the shores of Lake Ontario or the Niagara River.

Map 59 shows the progresssion of Letchworth's land purchases to create his estate, along with some modern-day landmarks for reference. He purchased the first parcel of land around Middle Falls in 1858, but it took until 1898 for him to acquire the final parcel of land—a span of about forty years. At times his land holdings were not contiguous, but he eventually pieced together one continuous property on both sides of the gorge above Upper Falls to below Lower Falls, and lands from Lower Falls to the river at Great Bend. Letchworth commissioned various improvements to the property, many of which still exist: additions to his home residence (now known as the Glen Iris Inn), stonework, water features, landscaping, and tree plantings. Noted landscape architect William Webster, a student of Frederick Law Olmsted, designed much of Letchworth's estate. Letchworth owned and ran farms—Lauterbrunnen, Prospect Home, and Chestnut Lawn—on his property near where the park's visitor center is located today. He allowed visitors on his estate and even made improvements (such as benches and shelters) to facilitate viewing the gorge scenery, believing that allowing people to connect with nature could help cure some of the ills of society. Map 58 shows his 1,000-acre (405 ha) estate in 1902 situated alongside other settlement within the present park area.

Letchworth also played a role in preserving the legacy of the Iroquois in the Genesee Valley, likely motivated by his early reading of Mary Jemison's biography first published in 1824. He formed the Council Grounds area on a bluff above his Glen Iris home, where he relocated the Seneca Council House shipped from Caneadea via the Genesee Valley Canal in 1872, and the cabin of Nancy Jemison

Photo 22. Close-up view from Inspiration Point in autumn.

(daughter of Mary) from the Gardeau Flats in 1881. He also allowed the reburial of Mary Jemison's remains at Council Grounds in 1874 at the request of her grandchildren made at the Council House dedication two years earlier, and placed a bronze statue of Mary atop her grave in 1910.

Retiring in 1873, he split his time thereafter between the Glen Iris Estate and traveling extensively stateside and abroad to advocate for societal causes such as developing epileptic centers, improving the foster care system, and prison reform. In 1906, Letchworth, at eighty-three years old, donated his estate to the State of New York, and designated the American Scenic and Historic Preservation Society as its manager and protector. Organized in 1895, the Society was one of the earliest land conservation groups and lobbies in the State of New York. Map 60 portrays the park in 1907, still with features of Letchworth's estate and with Letchworth still residing there, since the state would not fully convert the estate into a park until his passing. Letchworth had considered making his estate a refuge for poor or orphaned children associated with his Wyoming Benevolent Institute, and some speculate that he had long considered donating his property to the State—but the donation was largely an effort to protect the estate from destructive dam projects along the Genesee River proposed around the turn of the twentieth century. The Portageville Dam was one such project: a 130-foot-tall (40 m) dam proposed just upstream from the Glen Iris Estate, which threatened to alter the flow of the Genesee River over the falls and to bring major construction to the area (covered in the next section). In rejecting the proposed dam on various legal grounds, the State Water Supply Commission ruled that the issue was "complicated by the existence of Letchworth Park."

Letchworth resided at his Glen Iris home until his passing in 1910. He was buried in Buffalo's Forest Lawn Cemetery, where a simple engraved stone quarried from the riverbed above Middle Falls marks his final resting place. Long before his death, at the rededication ceremony of the Council Grounds in 1872, the Seneca adopted Letchworth into the Wolf Clan tribe and bestowed upon him the name Hai-wa-ye-is-tah, meaning "the Man Who Always Does Right."

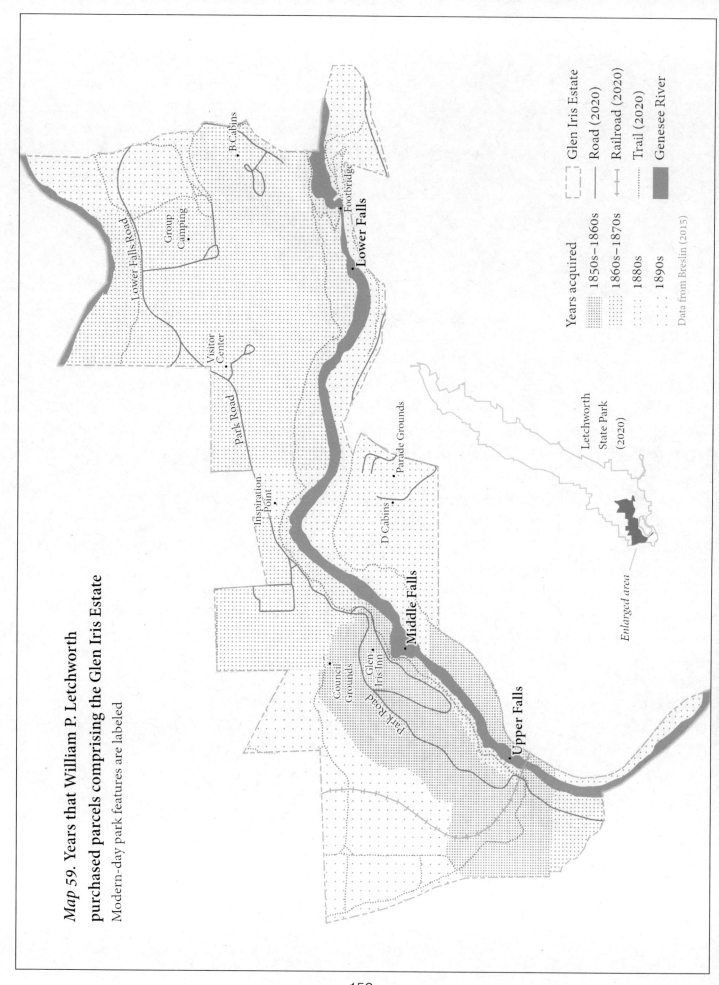

Map 59. Years that William P. Letchworth purchased parcels comprising the Glen Iris Estate

Modern-day park features are labeled

Upper Falls

Middle Falls

Lower Falls

Footbridge

B Cabins

Group Camping

Lower Falls Road

Visitor Center

Park Road

Inspiration Point

Parade Grounds

D Cabins

Council Grounds

Glen Iris Inn

Park Road

Letchworth State Park (2020)

Enlarged area

Years acquired

1850s–1860s

1860s–1870s

1880s

1890s

Glen Iris Estate

Road (2020)

Railroad (2020)

Trail (2020)

Genesee River

Data from Breslin (2015)

152

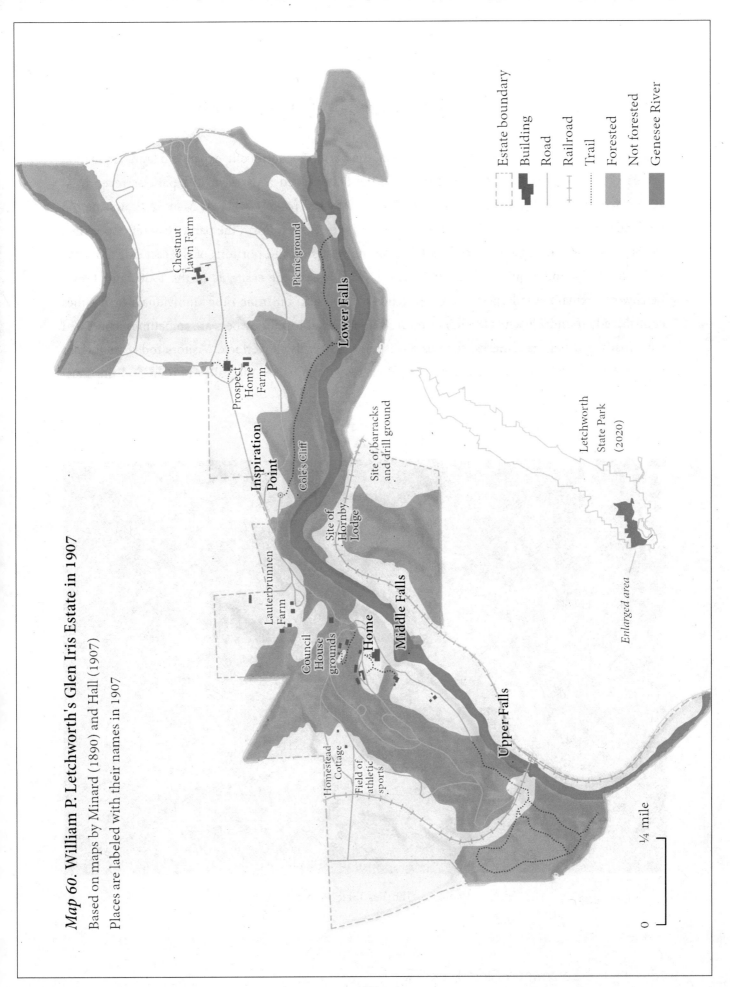

Map 60. William P. Letchworth's Glen Iris Estate in 1907
Based on maps by Minard (1890) and Hall (1907)
Places are labeled with their names in 1907

Chestnut Lawn Farm

Picnic ground

Lower Falls

Prospect Home Farm

Inspiration Point

Cole's Cliff

Site of barracks and drill ground

Site of Hornby Lodge

Lauterbrunnen Farm

Council House grounds

Home

Middle Falls

Upper Falls

Homestead Cottage

Field of athletic sports

Enlarged area

Letchworth State Park (2020)

Estate boundary
Building
Road
Railroad
Trail
Forested
Not forested
Genesee River

0   ¼ mile

153

After Park Creation (circa 1910 until present)

Since Letchworth's 1,000-acre (405 ha) donation, the park has continually expanded: land acquisition occurred mostly from the 1920s to 1960s, but the State added a parcel to the park as recently as 2003. Map 61 shows the years in which the State purchased parcels, whereas Map 62 shows the top ten landowners who sold or donated the most land to the State to form the park. Generally speaking, the State acquired over 6,000 acres (2,428 ha) on the west side and portions of the east side from the 1920s to 1940s, and acquired over 3,000 acres (1,214 ha), on the east side in the 1950s and 1960s. Letchworth remains the largest grantor of lands to the park, but nine other individuals or families contributed around 200 acres (81 ha) or more. The names of former owners are sometimes associated with roads and park landmarks, such as Kisil Point and Eddy's Overlook. Visitors today might not realize that the federal government owns 3,500 acres (1,416 ha) of the valley bottom and northern

Photo 23. The Tea Table Picnic Area.

end for dam operation and flood management (land purchased from earlier landowners and power companies), though it leases most of those lands to the State of New York.

The 1910s and 1920s were the era of the American Scenic and Historic Preservation Society, an organization that advocated for the protection of natural scenery and historic landmarks. During this time, the organization managed the park, acquired additional parcels on behalf of the State, and brought about many changes and improvements. Society projects included planting an arboretum to continue Letchworth's reforestation efforts in 1912, building the William P. Letchworth Museum in 1913 to display Letchworth's artifact collection, and modernizing Letchworth's home into the Glen Iris Inn that opened to guests in 1914. They built comfort stations and widened existing park roads to increase visitor access, and later added new roads and entrances to further accommodate increasing demand brought by the automobile. Perhaps symbolic as much as practical, they removed Letchworth's rustic yet narrow wooden gate marking the original entrance to his Glen Iris Estate along Park Road sometime in the 1920s. The Society also built visitor facilities near Lower Falls where the first park campground was located. Two of their most notable projects were bridges still used today over Wolf Creek and Deh-ga-ya-soh Creek toward the park's southern end. The Society made some alterations to the estate that today seem surprising and drastic: at the Council Grounds they removed structures deemed unnecessary (such as a cottage and an entrance lodge) and cut down trees to achieve a more open park-like appearance, and also removed farm outbuildings from the Glen Iris Inn. Some projects were proposed but never begun, such as a 112-room hotel near Inspiration Point. In 1930, the Society transferred control of the park to the State's new Genesee State Park Commission.

The 1930s and 1940s were the era of the Civilian Conservation Corps (CCC) who, perhaps along with Letchworth himself, contributed most to the architectural character of the park. A program to employ and train young men during the Great Depression, CCC members stayed in four camps within the park that each held 200 men (Map 63). Camps contained barracks that housed the men, along with dining halls, infirmaries, lavatories, storage sheds, garages, shops, and administrative buildings. The CCC constructed numerous park features such as picnic areas, roads, park entrances, overlooks, cabins, shelters, culverts, and bridges including the iconic Lower Falls Footbridge, perhaps its signature work. They completed major tree planting efforts throughout the park. They also built or improved much of Park Road, which would become the most important north–south access road through the park's west side. While their impact upon the park was lasting, their actual time within the park was brief, spanning only from the mid-1930s to the early 1940s.

After the CCC left, camp buildings found other uses: for example, the Gibsonville camp housed female workers of a local canning factory, and the Lower Falls camp housed German prisoners of war

Photo 24. The stone arch bridge above Deh-ga-ya-soh Falls, viewed from the east side of the park.

from 1944 to 1946. In addition to showing the locations of CCC camps, Map 63 shows the locations of their notable projects, which were mainly clustered toward the park's southern end. Noted Rochester architect Charles Cromwell designed the CCC-constructed structures in the rustic Adirondack style, which were so renowned that the National Park Service included photos of the structures in a publication that provided guidance to designers nationwide on best architectural choices for parks. Map 64 shows the locations of notable historic structures, including those built both under the CCC and in earlier eras. Finally, Map 65 compares the park in 1945 (just after the CCC era concluded) and in 2020 by mapping differences in the park area along with roads and notable park areas (both tourist and administrative) then and now.

Maps 67 and 68 show a mosaic of the earliest aerial photos of the park area in 1938, and Map 66 shows modern aerial photos to allow a side-by-side comparison of change over time. Though the 1938 photos show marginalia and signs of wear and tear, they capture a transition in time from a settled area to the modern park (also see Map 69 later). They show a patchwork of farmland (solid,

Photo 25. A stone staircase constructed by the Civilian Conservation Corps leading to Lower Falls.

lighter colors) and forests (grainy, darker colors) both within and outside the park boundary—a landscape more utilized and less forested than the park today. Roads, houses, fields, and forests appeared in areas now inundated beneath the Mount Morris Reservoir. Roads led to the village of St. Helena, where a few houses remained as well as a bridge crossing the Genesee River. They show the natural flow of the Genesee River before construction of the Mount Morris Dam began in 1948. CCC camps are visible. The Highbanks Recreation Area and Highbanks Camping Area do not exist yet.

One of the most controversial and recurring topics in Letchworth State Park's history was dam construction. Governments and power companies eyed the steep canyon walls of the park and vicinity as ideal sites for dams both to control floods and for hydroelectric power. From 1865 to 1950, the Genesee River flooded on average once every five to seven years, damaging farms in the middle Genesee Valley and flooding portions of the City of Rochester downstream. Various dam proposals surfaced in the late nineteenth and early twentieth centuries hoping to exploit the ideal sites within and near the present park, proposals that continued all the way into the 1970s. Companies studied sites near Mount Morris within the northern end of the park, as well as a Portageville site upstream from the park's southern end.

Although some proposals failed, the U.S. Congress approved one project as part of the Flood Control Act of 1944: the Mount Morris Dam. Constructed from 1948 to 1952, the massive concrete dam is over 1,000 feet (305 m) long at its top, stands 230 feet (70 m) above the riverbed near the northern end of the park, and is one of the largest dams east of the Mississippi River. Unlike many other major dams in the United States, it is a "dry dam"—a dam not constructed to provide hydroelectric power but to control floods. The dam was controversial due to its price tag ($25 million at the time), impacts on natural ecosystems, and flooding of former Native American and white settlement sites. Construction of the dam, and the impending flooding from the reservoir, required the removal of remains in the St. Helena Cemetery and their reburial in Grace Cemetery within the Village of Castile. Although contentious, according to one estimate the dam has prevented over $3 billion in flooding damages downstream. To help protect archaeological sites and riverine ecosystems, the U.S. Congress passed the Genesee River Protection Act of 1989, which ensured that the U.S. Army Corps of Engineers could only operate the dam to stop floods rather than to maintain a reservoir for scenic or recreational purposes. Map 69 shows the present park area circa 1945 (see Map 61 for the actual park boundary at this time), just before the dam started to impound waters and fill the reservoir in 1952. The map also shows the path of the Genesee River before the construction of the Mount Morris Dam and creation of the reservoir.

By 1950, the State had acquired most of the west side and both ends of the park and was closing in on the middle portion of the east side. Farmland abandonment and natural reforestation had

Photo 26. The Lower Falls footbridge constructed by the Civilian Conservation Corps.

begun. Residents continued to move out of the park area, selling lands to the State. Population figures had stagnated in the surrounding towns as a whole (Map 47), and would only modestly increase for the five-town area from 1900 into the present. Map 69 shows land use, buildings, and roads in 1945: around 120 buildings existed within the present park area, according to historical maps, but most of those were associated with the park itself. Virtually all roads along the valley bottom had disappeared, except for a few that still led into the former village of St. Helena (compare the years 1850, 1900, and 1950 in Map 46). The major north–south roads along the valley bottom disappeared, made obsolete by Park Road and soon to be inundated from the Mount Morris Reservoir anyway. Aside from the Lower Falls Footbridge, one of the only remaining river crossings was the bridge at St. Helena, which was torn down later in 1950. Any remnants of St. Helena are likely now buried beneath many feet of river sediment deposited from Genesee River floods, although remnants of the bridge are visible from Trail #13.

One of the most surreal events to occur within the park was Hurricane Agnes in mid-June of 1972—at that time the costliest hurricane in United States history. Agnes formed on the Yucatán Peninsula of Mexico as a tropical depression, strengthened to a Category 1 hurricane over the Gulf of Mexico, and struck the panhandle of Florida. It weakened to a tropical depression as it moved northeasterly through the southeastern United States, but it then combined with another low-pressure system, causing it to strengthen to a tropical storm and to produce extreme rainfall. As it moved back over the Atlantic Ocean off the coasts of North Carolina and Virginia, it turned northwest and made landfall in New York. High rainfall from the slow-moving system led to devastating flooding, loss of human life, and destruction of property in riverside communities, especially in Pennsylvania and New York. Map 70 shows rainfall amounts in the region along with the final northwesterly path of the eye of the storm.

Hurricane Agnes dropped 12 to 15 inches (30 to 38 cm) of rain over southern portions of the Genesee River watershed from June 20 to June 25. The Mount Morris Dam held back the immense volume of floodwater and protected life and property downstream, but the reservoir rose to just 4 feet (1.2 m) below the top of the dam before the Corps of Engineers needed to release some water to prevent floating large debris from overtopping and damaging the dam. The reservoir was 196 feet (60 m) deep at the dam, 322,600 acre-feet (398,000 megaliters) in volume, and over 3,000 acres (1,210 ha) in area. As shown in Map 71, waters flooded most of the valley bottom, and almost completely submerged the Hogsback at the northern end and Lower Falls at the southern end. The raging river also battered the Lower Falls Footbridge and reduced the heights of Middle and Upper Falls by half. The floodwaters within the reservoir saturated and destabilized soils in some portions of the park, triggering landslides once the water receded that are still visible today.

In the second half of the twentieth century, the park emerged into its modern form. In the 1950s, the State constructed or improved entrances at Portageville, Perry, and Mount Morris. In the 1960s, notable areas such as the Highbanks Recreation Area, Highbanks Camping Area, Cabin Area A, and new portions of the St. Helena Picnic Area were constructed. Projects such as the Highbanks Recreation Area were indicative of a shift from passive recreation focused on the preservation of nature, toward attracting more visitors and providing active recreation options within the park—a shift observed both in the types of recreation afforded and in the modern architecture constructed. In the 1980s, the State constructed the modern Castile entrance that replaced the former Castile entrance near Wolf Creek, an entrance popular today for leading visitors directly to the spectacular overlooks above the cliffs at Great Bend. Most areas within the park (i.e., those shown in Map 48) have remained as once constructed, with occasional additions or demolitions, though one of the only exceptions was perhaps the Lower Falls area where the State filled in a pool built in 1950 and replaced it with a modernized recreation facility by 2020. In the last few decades, the park's popularity has increased owing to photos of its scenery shared on social media platforms, wins in "best state park" contests (see Map 79 later), and national media attention. In 2017, the new steel Genesee Arch Bridge replaced the Portage iron bridge that was torn down the next year. Other notable recent additions to the park were the Humphrey Nature Center in 2016 and the Autism Nature Trail in 2021.

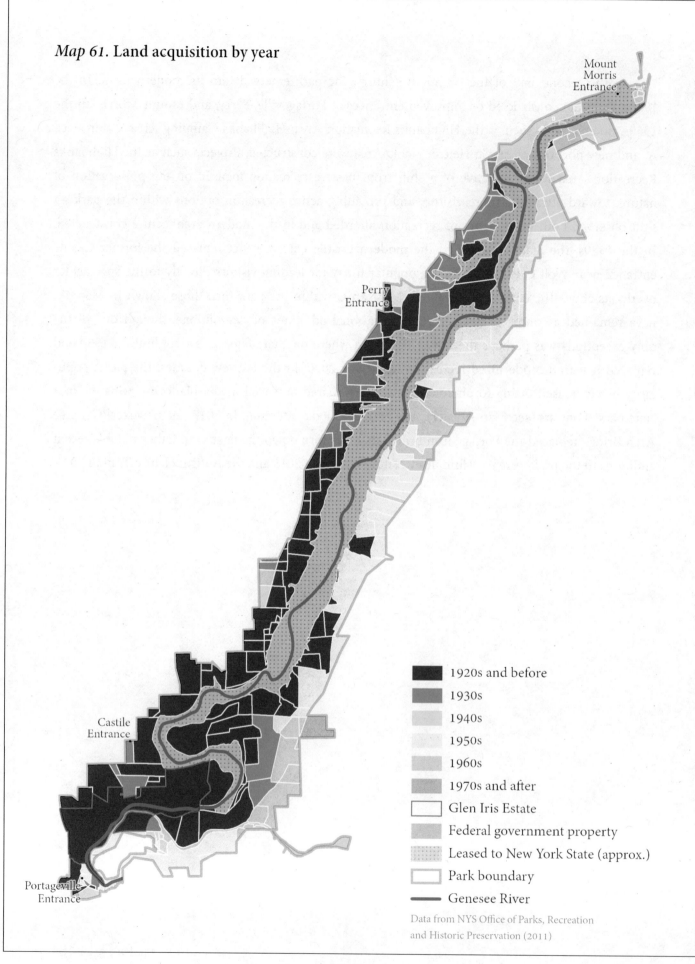

Map 61. **Land acquisition by year**

Mount
Morris
Entrance

Perry
Entrance

Castile
Entrance

Portageville
Entrance

- 1920s and before
- 1930s
- 1940s
- 1950s
- 1960s
- 1970s and after
- Glen Iris Estate
- Federal government property
- Leased to New York State (approx.)
- Park boundary
- Genesee River

Data from NYS Office of Parks, Recreation
and Historic Preservation (2011)

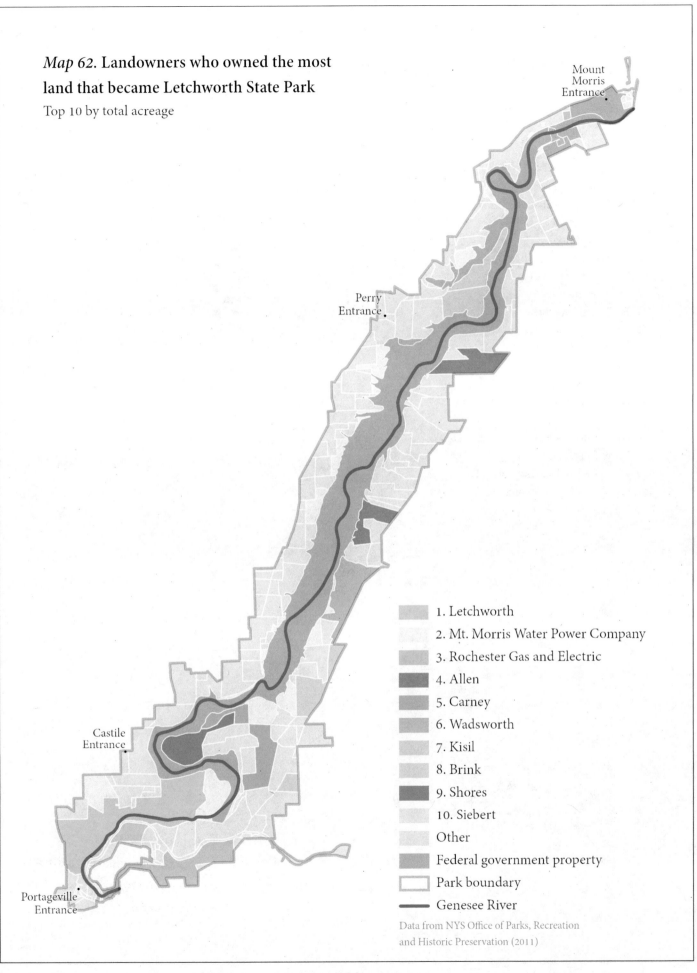

Map 62. Landowners who owned the most land that became Letchworth State Park

Top 10 by total acreage

Mount Morris Entrance

Perry Entrance

Castile Entrance

Portageville Entrance

1. Letchworth
2. Mt. Morris Water Power Company
3. Rochester Gas and Electric
4. Allen
5. Carney
6. Wadsworth
7. Kisil
8. Brink
9. Shores
10. Siebert
Other
Federal government property
Park boundary
Genesee River

Data from NYS Office of Parks, Recreation and Historic Preservation (2011)

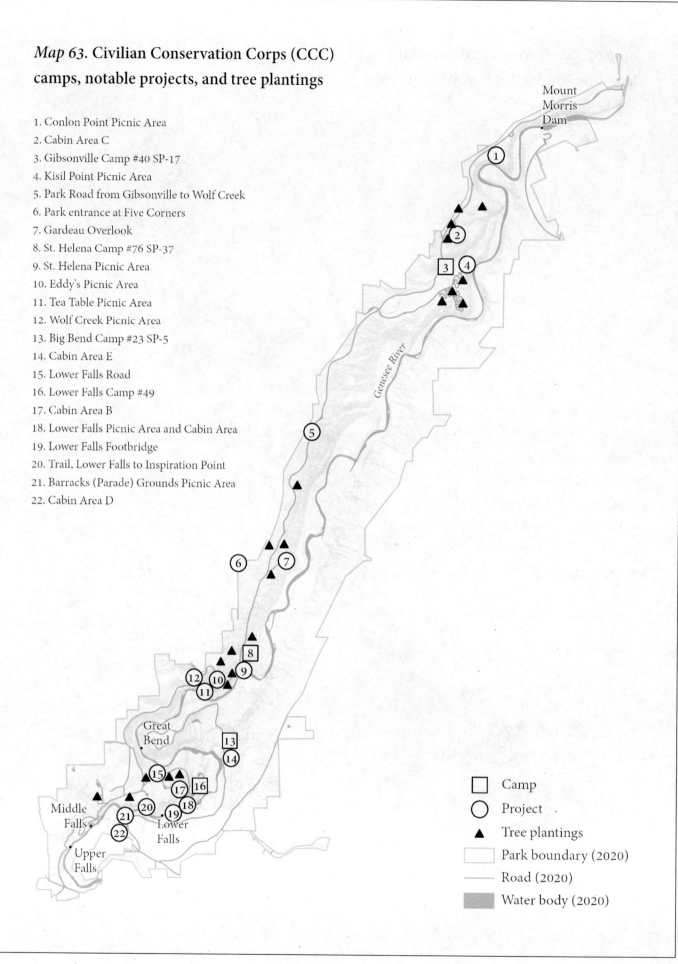

Map 63. Civilian Conservation Corps (CCC) camps, notable projects, and tree plantings

1. Conlon Point Picnic Area
2. Cabin Area C
3. Gibsonville Camp #40 SP-17
4. Kisil Point Picnic Area
5. Park Road from Gibsonville to Wolf Creek
6. Park entrance at Five Corners
7. Gardeau Overlook
8. St. Helena Camp #76 SP-37
9. St. Helena Picnic Area
10. Eddy's Picnic Area
11. Tea Table Picnic Area
12. Wolf Creek Picnic Area
13. Big Bend Camp #23 SP-5
14. Cabin Area E
15. Lower Falls Road
16. Lower Falls Camp #49
17. Cabin Area B
18. Lower Falls Picnic Area and Cabin Area
19. Lower Falls Footbridge
20. Trail, Lower Falls to Inspiration Point
21. Barracks (Parade) Grounds Picnic Area
22. Cabin Area D

Mount Morris Dam

Genesee River

Great Bend

Middle Falls

Lower Falls

Upper Falls

□ Camp
○ Project
▲ Tree plantings
▢ Park boundary (2020)
— Road (2020)
▬ Water body (2020)

Map 64. Notable extant historical structures and approximate years of completion

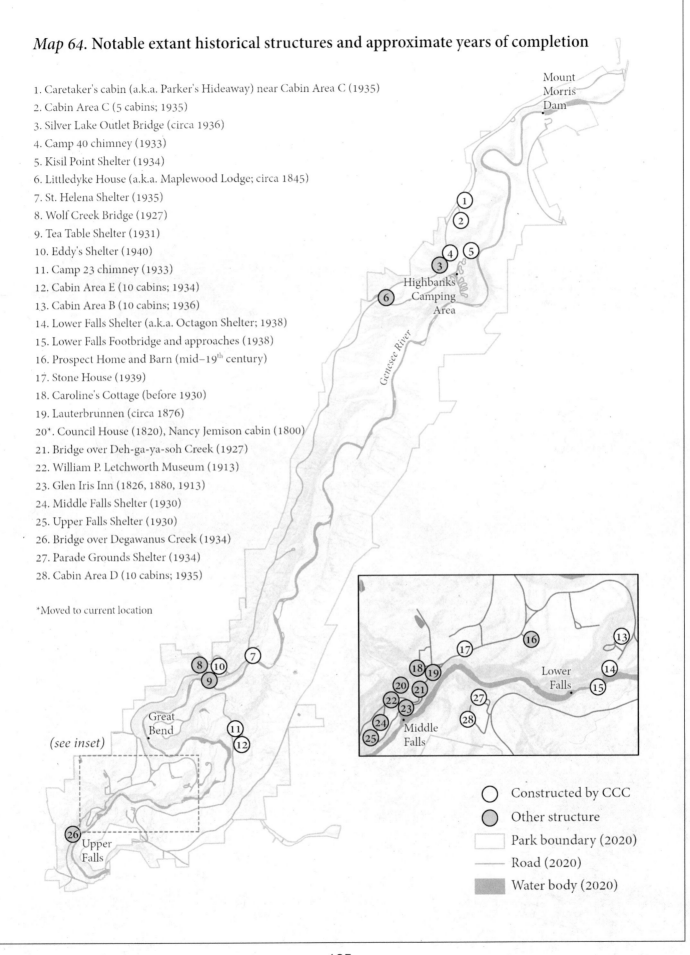

1. Caretaker's cabin (a.k.a. Parker's Hideaway) near Cabin Area C (1935)
2. Cabin Area C (5 cabins; 1935)
3. Silver Lake Outlet Bridge (circa 1936)
4. Camp 40 chimney (1933)
5. Kisil Point Shelter (1934)
6. Littledyke House (a.k.a. Maplewood Lodge; circa 1845)
7. St. Helena Shelter (1935)
8. Wolf Creek Bridge (1927)
9. Tea Table Shelter (1931)
10. Eddy's Shelter (1940)
11. Camp 23 chimney (1933)
12. Cabin Area E (10 cabins; 1934)
13. Cabin Area B (10 cabins; 1936)
14. Lower Falls Shelter (a.k.a. Octagon Shelter; 1938)
15. Lower Falls Footbridge and approaches (1938)
16. Prospect Home and Barn (mid–19th century)
17. Stone House (1939)
18. Caroline's Cottage (before 1930)
19. Lauterbrunnen (circa 1876)
20*. Council House (1820), Nancy Jemison cabin (1800)
21. Bridge over Deh-ga-ya-soh Creek (1927)
22. William P. Letchworth Museum (1913)
23. Glen Iris Inn (1826, 1880, 1913)
24. Middle Falls Shelter (1930)
25. Upper Falls Shelter (1930)
26. Bridge over Degawanus Creek (1934)
27. Parade Grounds Shelter (1934)
28. Cabin Area D (10 cabins; 1935)

*Moved to current location

Mount Morris Dam

Genesee River

Highbanks Camping Area

Great Bend

(see inset)

Upper Falls

Stone House 17
16
13
18
19
20 21
22
23
27
28
24
25 Middle Falls
Lower Falls
14
15

○ Constructed by CCC
● Other structure
▢ Park boundary (2020)
— Road (2020)
▓ Water body (2020)

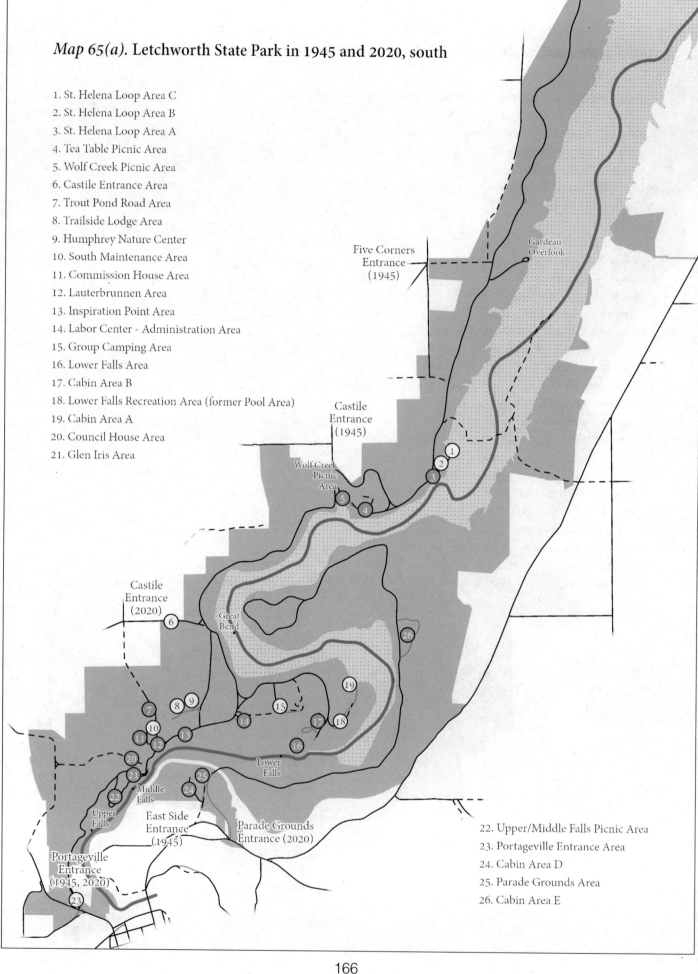

Map 65(a). Letchworth State Park in 1945 and 2020, south

1. St. Helena Loop Area C
2. St. Helena Loop Area B
3. St. Helena Loop Area A
4. Tea Table Picnic Area
5. Wolf Creek Picnic Area
6. Castile Entrance Area
7. Trout Pond Road Area
8. Trailside Lodge Area
9. Humphrey Nature Center
10. South Maintenance Area
11. Commission House Area
12. Lauterbrunnen Area
13. Inspiration Point Area
14. Labor Center - Administration Area
15. Group Camping Area
16. Lower Falls Area
17. Cabin Area B
18. Lower Falls Recreation Area (former Pool Area)
19. Cabin Area A
20. Council House Area
21. Glen Iris Area

22. Upper/Middle Falls Picnic Area
23. Portageville Entrance Area
24. Cabin Area D
25. Parade Grounds Area
26. Cabin Area E

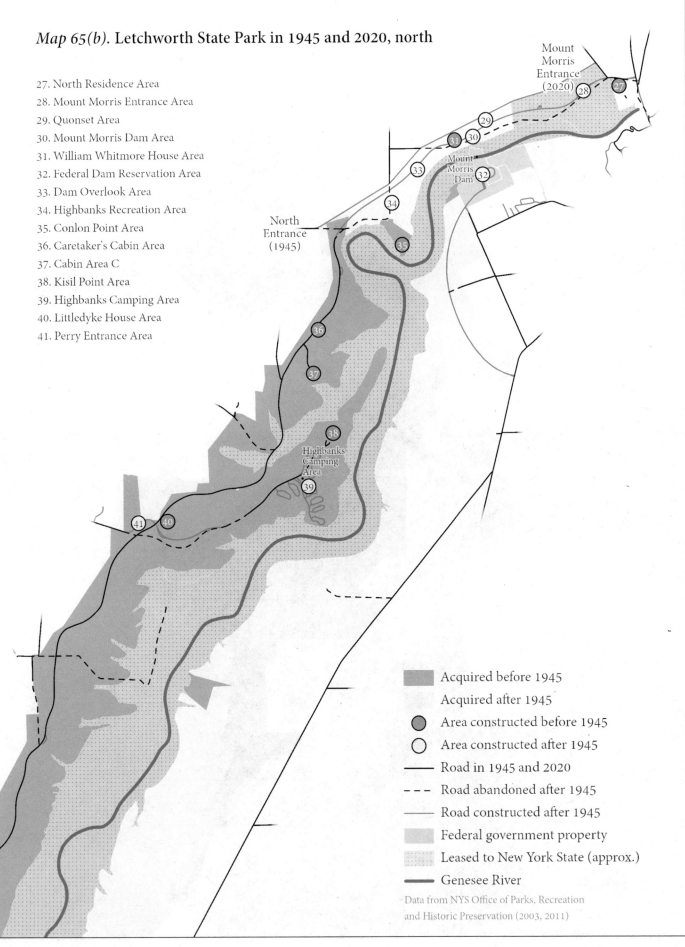

Map 65(b). Letchworth State Park in 1945 and 2020, north

27. North Residence Area
28. Mount Morris Entrance Area
29. Quonset Area
30. Mount Morris Dam Area
31. William Whitmore House Area
32. Federal Dam Reservation Area
33. Dam Overlook Area
34. Highbanks Recreation Area
35. Conlon Point Area
36. Caretaker's Cabin Area
37. Cabin Area C
38. Kisil Point Area
39. Highbanks Camping Area
40. Littledyke House Area
41. Perry Entrance Area

Mount Morris Entrance (2020)

Mount Morris Dam

North Entrance (1945)

Highbanks Camping Area

Acquired before 1945
Acquired after 1945
Area constructed before 1945
Area constructed after 1945
Road in 1945 and 2020
Road abandoned after 1945
Road constructed after 1945
Federal government property
Leased to New York State (approx.)
Genesee River

Data from NYS Office of Parks, Recreation and Historic Preservation (2003, 2011)

Map 66(a). Aerial view in 2019 with locations labeled, north end

Mount Morris
Entrance

Squawkie Hill
Overlook

Dam Overlook

Mount
Morris Dam
Dam Recreation
Area and
Visitor Center

Highbanks
Recreation
Area

Hogsback

Kisil Point

C Cabins

Gibsonville
(historic)

Highbanks
Camping Area

N

Map 67(a). Aerial view in 1938, north end

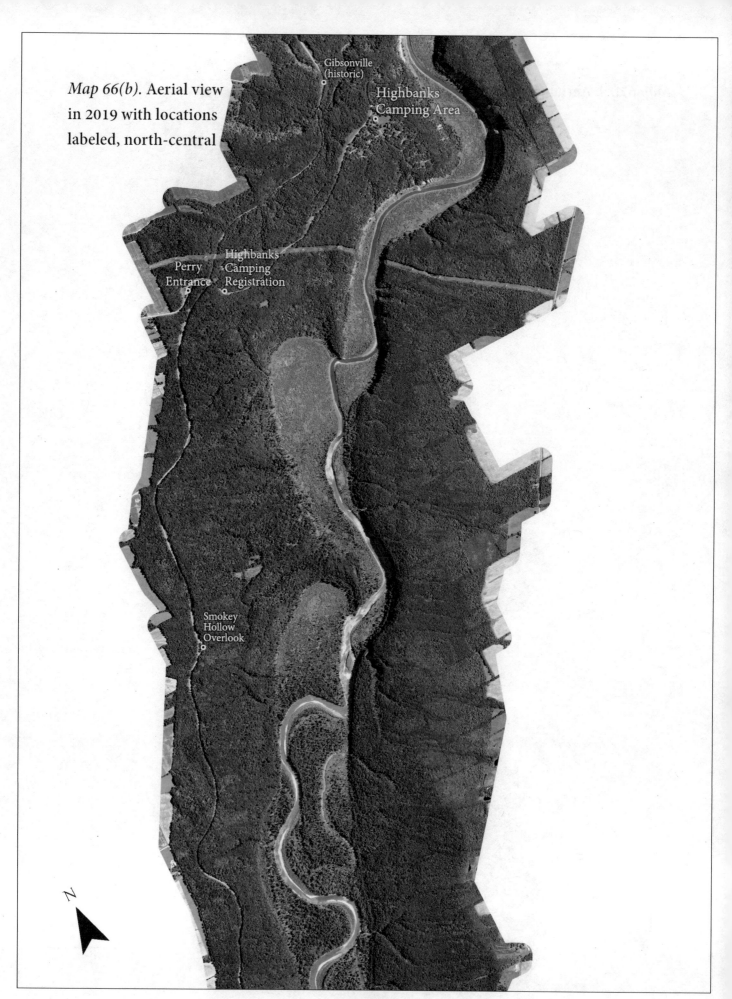

Map 66(b). Aerial view in 2019 with locations labeled, north-central

Gibsonville (historic)

Highbanks Camping Area

Perry Entrance

Highbanks Camping Registration

Smokey Hollow Overlook

N

Map 67(b). Aerial view
in 1938, north-central

N

0   ¼   ½
mile

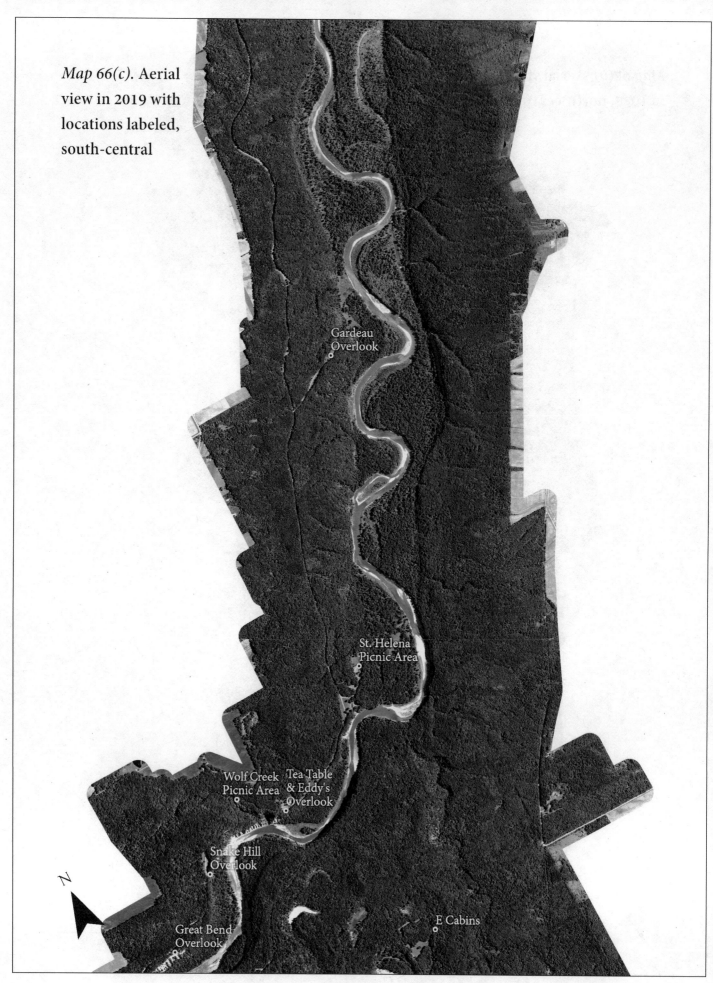

Map 66(c). Aerial view in 2019 with locations labeled, south-central

Gardeau Overlook

St. Helena Picnic Area

Wolf Creek Picnic Area

Tea Table & Eddy's Overlook

Snake Hill Overlook

Great Bend Overlook

E Cabins

N

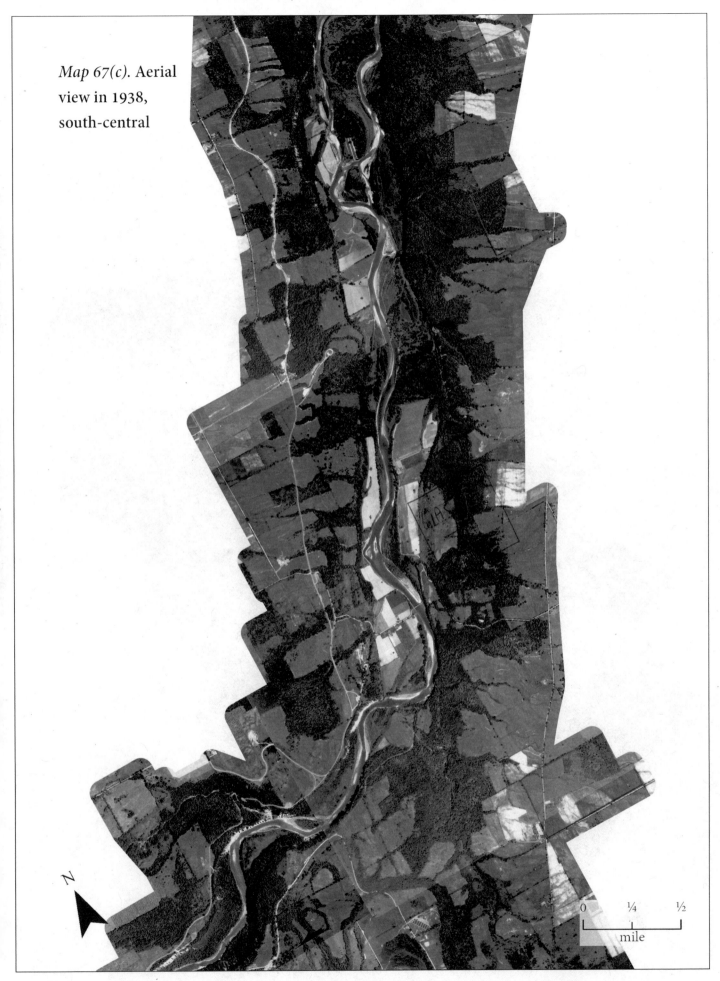

Map 67(c). Aerial view in 1938, south-central

N

0   ¼   ½
mile

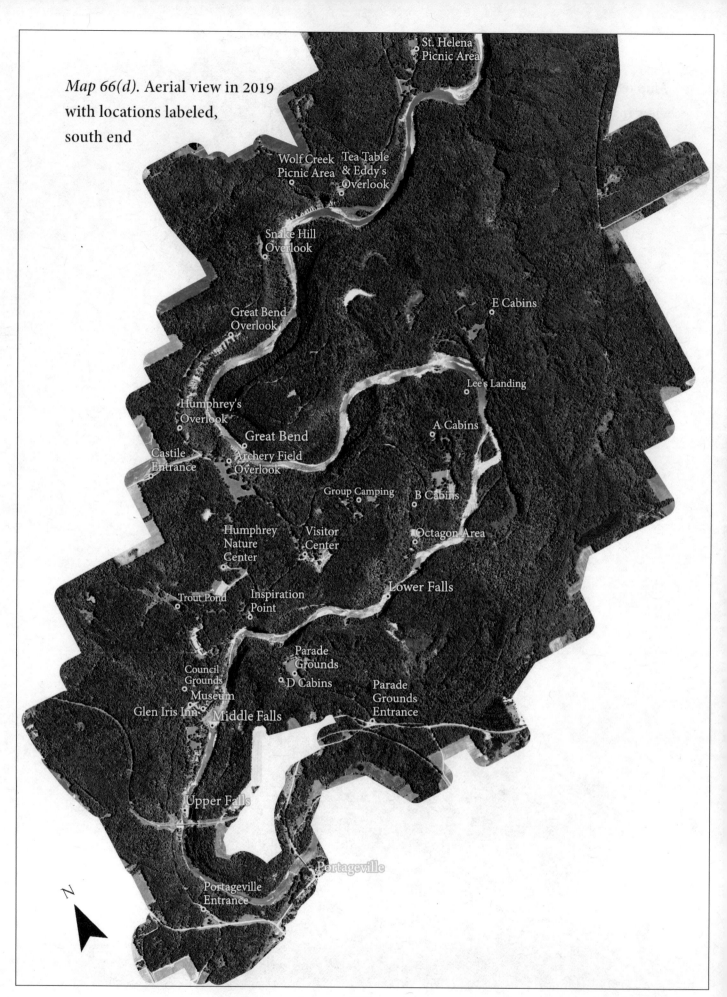

Map 66(d). Aerial view in 2019 with locations labeled, south end

St. Helena Picnic Area

Wolf Creek Picnic Area

Tea Table & Eddy's Overlook

Snake Hill Overlook

E Cabins

Great Bend Overlook

Lee's Landing

Humphrey's Overlook

A Cabins

Great Bend

Castile Entrance

Archery Field Overlook

Group Camping

B Cabins

Humphrey Nature Center

Visitor Center

Octagon Area

Lower Falls

Trout Pond

Inspiration Point

Parade Grounds

Council Grounds

D Cabins

Parade Grounds Entrance

Museum

Glen Iris Inn

Middle Falls

Upper Falls

Portageville

Portageville Entrance

N

Map 67(d). Aerial view in 1938, south end

0   ¼   ½
mile

Map 68(a). 1938 aerial view
close-up: Highbanks area

1. Future site of Mount Morris Dam
2. Future site of Highbanks Recreation Area
3. Conlon Point Picnic Area
4. Hogsback

0   100   200
yards

N

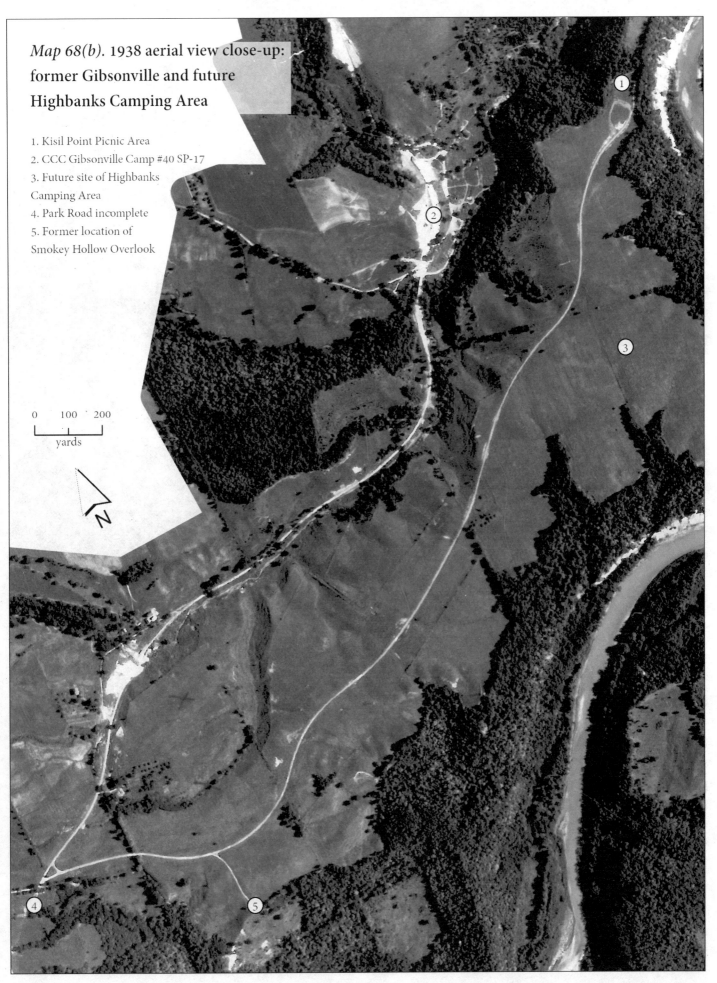

Map 68(b). 1938 aerial view close-up: former Gibsonville and future Highbanks Camping Area

1. Kisil Point Picnic Area
2. CCC Gibsonville Camp #40 SP-17
3. Future site of Highbanks Camping Area
4. Park Road incomplete
5. Former location of Smokey Hollow Overlook

0   100   200
yards

N

Map 68(c). 1938 aerial view close-up: St. Helena and Wolf Creek areas

0   100   200
yards

N

1. St. Helena Bridge
2. St. Helena
3. CCC St. Helena Camp #76 SP-37
4. St. Helena Picnic Area
5. Wolf Creek Picnic Area

Map 68(d). 1938 aerial view close-up: Lower Falls area

0   100   200
yards

N

1. CCC Big Bend Camp #23 SP-5
2. CCC Lower Falls Camp #49
3. Chestnut Lawn Farm
4. Prospect Home Farm
5. Lower Falls

179

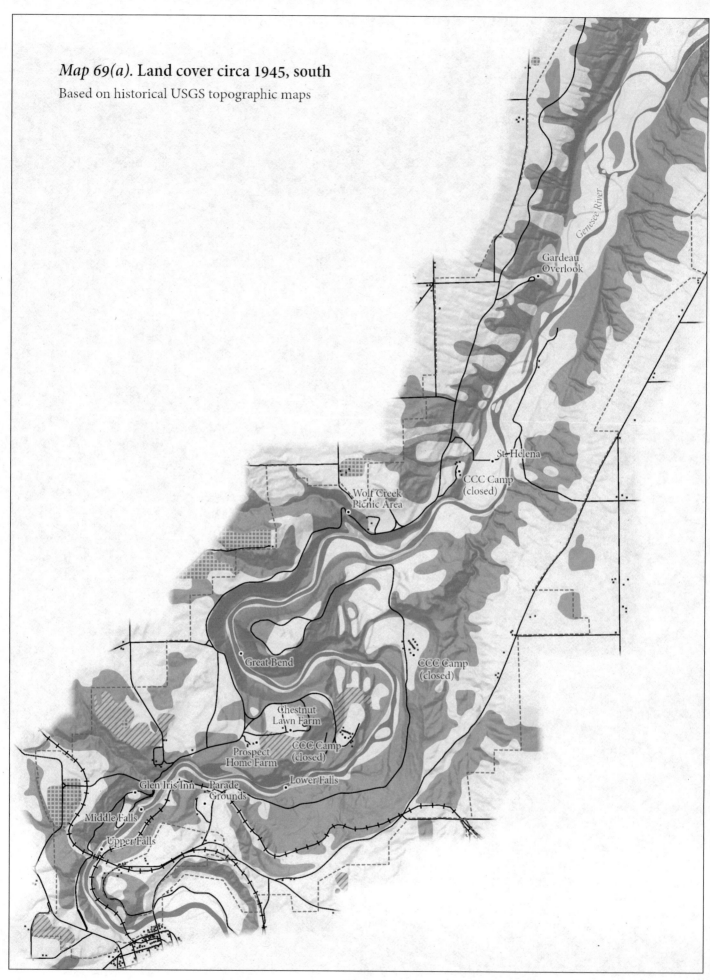

Map 69(a). Land cover circa 1945, south

Based on historical USGS topographic maps

Genesee River

Gardeau
Overlook

St. Helena

CCC Camp
(closed)

Wolf Creek
Picnic Area

Great Bend

CCC Camp
(closed)

Chestnut
Lawn Farm

CCC Camp
(closed)

Prospect
Home Farm

Lower Falls

Glen Iris Inn   Parade
                 Grounds

Middle Falls

Upper Falls

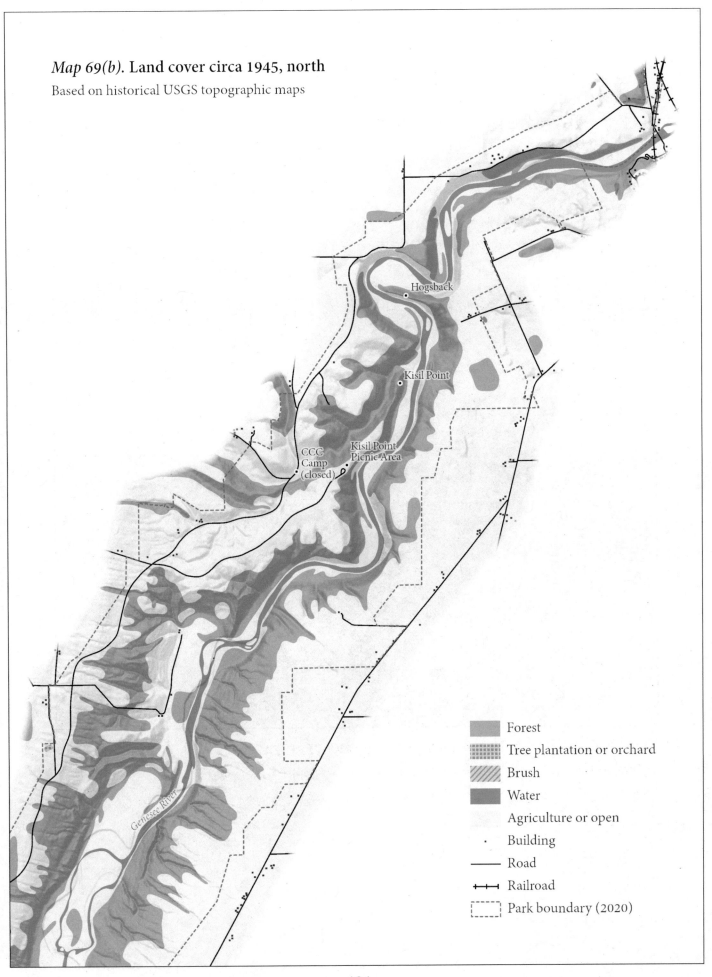

Map 69(b). Land cover circa 1945, north

Based on historical USGS topographic maps

Hogsback

Kisil Point

Kisil Point
Picnic Area

CCC
Camp
(closed)

Genesee River

Forest

Tree plantation or orchard

Brush

Water

Agriculture or open

Building

Road

Railroad

Park boundary (2020)

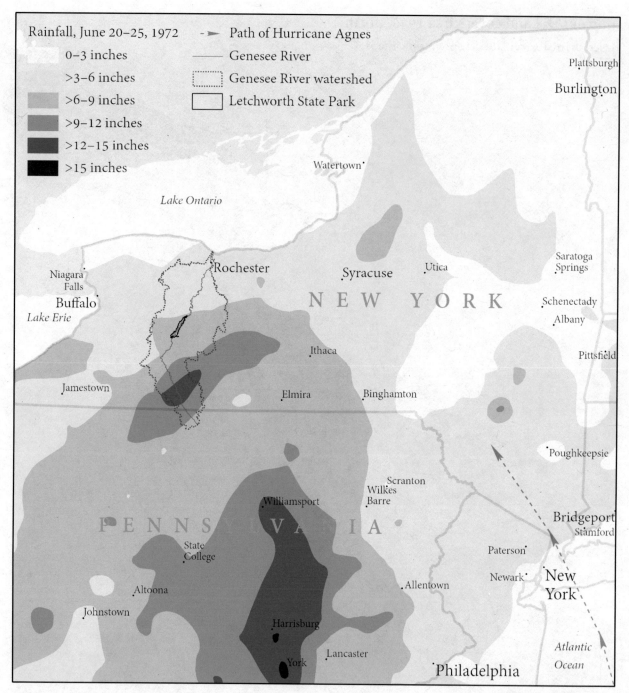

Rainfall, June 20–25, 1972

- 0–3 inches
- >3–6 inches
- >6–9 inches
- >9–12 inches
- >12–15 inches
- >15 inches

- - ➤ Path of Hurricane Agnes
- —— Genesee River
- Genesee River watershed
- Letchworth State Park

Plattsburgh
Burlington

Watertown

Lake Ontario

Niagara Falls
Buffalo
Lake Erie

Rochester

Syracuse

Utica

Saratoga Springs

Schenectady
Albany

N E W   Y O R K

Pittsfield

Jamestown

Ithaca

Elmira
Binghamton

Poughkeepsie

Scranton
Wilkes Barre

Bridgeport
Stamford

Williamsport

P E N N S Y L V A N I A

State College

Paterson

Newark

New York

Altoona

Allentown

Johnstown

Harrisburg

Lancaster

Atlantic Ocean

York

Philadelphia

Map 70. **Rainfall from Hurricane Agnes, June 20–25, 1972**
Within portions of New York State and vicinity

Data from NOAA NCEI (2020)

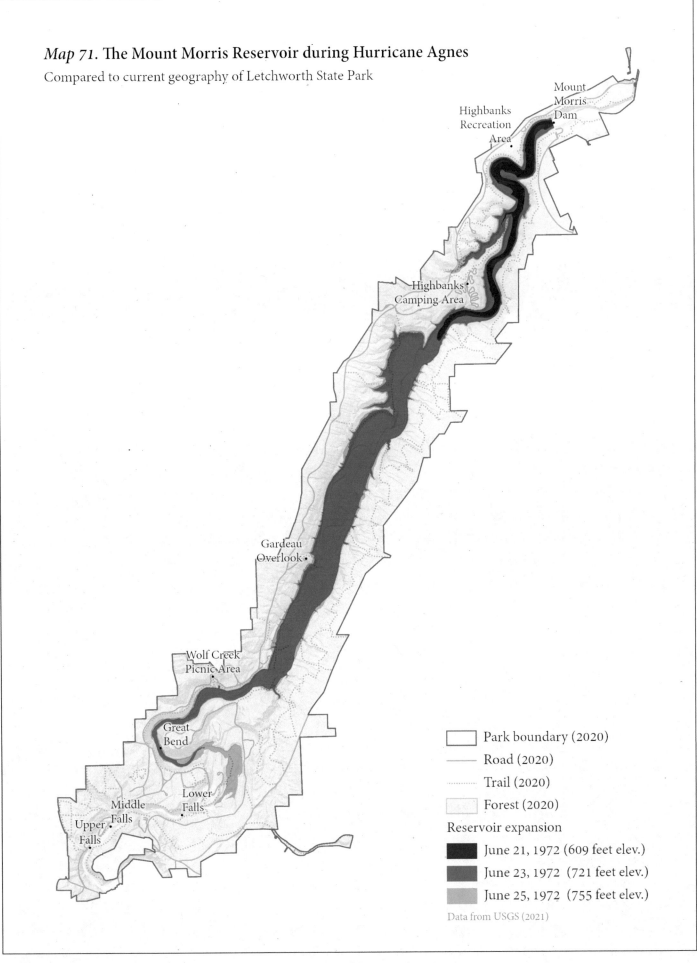

Map 71. The Mount Morris Reservoir during Hurricane Agnes

Compared to current geography of Letchworth State Park

Mount Morris Dam

Highbanks Recreation Area

Highbanks Camping Area

Gardeau Overlook

Wolf Creek Picnic Area

Great Bend

Lower Falls

Middle Falls

Upper Falls

Park boundary (2020)

Road (2020)

Trail (2020)

Forest (2020)

Reservoir expansion

June 21, 1972 (609 feet elev.)

June 23, 1972 (721 feet elev.)

June 25, 1972 (755 feet elev.)

Data from USGS (2021)

Chapter 4

Tourism

Photo 27. Visitors watching hot-air balloons above Middle Falls.

As a major tourist attraction that affords many recreational opportunities, Letchworth State Park is an economic driver in the region: according to a 2017 report, the park generates about $51 million in visitor spending in the area annually, which in turn supports nearly 600 jobs. Still, these numbers are small compared to other parks: for instance, visitors to Grand Canyon National Park in 2019 spent $890 million and supported nearly 12,000 jobs. Slightly more than half of Letchworth State Park's visitors are "day-trippers," and those who spend the night are typically from out of state and stay a few days. Age-based differences in tourism behavior are apparent: younger visitors tend to be day-trippers whereas older visitors tend to stay one or more nights. Overall, visitors also tend to be those who already know about or have already visited the park and surrounding area—perhaps testament to the park's beauty and opportunities. To explore visitation to Letchworth State Park beyond these trends, this chapter first covers geographic trends in visitation in greater depth, and then covers aspects of tourism- and recreation-based activities in the park.

Visitation

Since the mid–twentieth century, the park has received hundreds of thousands of visitors each year: in 1946 about 125,000 people visited, and by 1951 that number had increased to about 430,000.

Photo 28. Stonework and paths at Inspiration Point in autumn.

From 2003 to 2019, Letchworth State Park received on average 706,000 visitors per year (Map 72), or nearly 2,000 visitors per day. Of the twelve parks in the Genesee Region of New York, Letchworth State Park receives more than half of all visitors in a year. If Letchworth State Park were a national park, it would rank twenty-eighth out of sixty-four by visitation in 2017 (the last year without a federal government shutdown or pandemic)—it has more visitors than national parks such as Mammoth Cave and Redwood, but fewer visitors than national parks such as Canyonlands and Crater Lake (Map 73). While its visitation numbers appear impressive, its average attendance from 2003 to 2019 barely broke the top twenty New York state parks by attendance, falling behind Niagara Falls, Saratoga Springs, Allegany State Park, the New York State Fair, Green Lakes State Park, and several parks in the Hudson Valley–New York City–Long Island region (Map 72).

From 2003 to 2019, the park experienced an upward trend in attendance: about 650,000 visited in 2003 and 842,000 visited in 2019, with an average increase of 12,000 visitors per year. However, its increase in attendance over this time was not exceptional within the context of all of New York state parks, most of which also saw an increasing trend in attendance—in other words, Letchworth State Park's rank by attendance among state parks has remained virtually unchanged over the years.

Two recent years are noteworthy for park attendance: 2015 and 2020. In 2015, park attendance increased by over 200,000 people from the previous year to over 850,000 (a 32% increase) when it gained national media attention both for its "ice volcano" (a spring-fed fountain that froze outside the Glen Iris Inn) that formed during a uniquely cold winter, and for receiving first place in USA Today's "America's Favorite State Park" contest. During the COVID-19 pandemic in 2020, attendance rose by around 125,000 people to nearly one million from the previous year (a 15% increase), as park entry fees were waived for a time and as people sought socially distanced outdoor activities. All these numbers are estimates—and likely underestimates—of visitation, since they are based on counts of vehicle entrance fees paid and average number of visitors per automobile. The estimates also exclude counts of visitors to the park's east side, non-motorized visitors, and those who visit the park's west side at times when fees are not collected.

While obtaining a clear picture of the origins of Letchworth State Park visitors is challenging, available data suggest that the park's visitors are mainly from New York, along with some from the surrounding region and a small percentage from abroad. All datasets suggest a "distance decay": more visitors originate from near the park, and fewer from far away. Four maps show the origins of visitors using different datasets, one of which offers a historical perspective: visitors to the Cascade House hotel in Portage from 1886 to 1904 (Map 74), park reviewers on TripAdvisor.com (Map 75), a sample of visitors to the park museum and nature center (Map 76), and results of a survey conducted by a local economic group (Map 77). Visitors originate mainly from urban areas within

Photo 29. Upper Falls and the Genesee Arch Bridge.

the state such as Rochester, Buffalo, Syracuse, Albany, and New York City. Pennsylvania, New Jersey, and Massachusetts add sizable numbers of visitors, with Florida (possibly retirees splitting time between New York and the Sunshine State) and the Province of Ontario in Canada adding more modest numbers. Based on recent guestbook entries to the museum and nature center, if you were to ask 100 visitors where they are from, about sixty would be from New York, thirty-six would be from another state, and four would be from another country. Rates of Google searches for "Letchworth State Park" (Map 78) by U.S. state suggest that Pennsylvania, Massachusetts, Connecticut, New Jersey, and Ohio are the states most interested in the park besides New York. The top five metro areas searching for websites on the park are Rochester, Buffalo, Elmira, and Syracuse in New York, followed by Erie, Pennsylvania.

Given the park's proximity to the border, Canadians are the most common international visitor, accounting for about two-thirds of international visitation—but data used for creating Maps 75 through 77 suggest that visitors from at least thirty-five countries (such as England, Australia, and Japan) and four continents have visited the park in the last few decades. One report suggested that visitors are more geographically diverse in the autumn than the summer, when fall foliage attracts more distant visitors along with families of college students at SUNY Geneseo, just ten minutes north.

The data in Maps 74 through 77 more likely show the origins of persons who self-identify as "tourists" or "visitors" at the park. Another segment of the population—its regular users—are local recreationalists who literally or figuratively live with Letchworth State Park in their backyard. Based on a 2021 survey, members of the Facebook fan groups "Friends of Letchworth State Park," "Letchworth State Park Enthusiasts," and "Letchworth State Park Lovers" visit the park a median of five times per year, with some visiting as often as twice per week. Respondents described their top five activities in the park as sightseeing, hiking, observing wildlife, photography, and appreciating history. They reside in nearby communities like Mount Morris, Perry, and Castile, utilizing the Mount Morris and Castile entrances most frequently and eastern access points least frequently. They describe the park as a "gem," their "favorite," and the "best place on Earth," but are also concerned about overuse and about whether the current park honors Mr. Letchworth's original intentions for the donation of his estate.

Much of the park's recent popularity is due to awards and recognitions the park has received. Map 79 shows which U.S. state parks have placed on a "Best State Park" contest by *USA Today*, a "20 wild and beautiful U.S. state parks" list by *National Geographic*, and a "30 Best State Parks in America" list by *Thrillist.com* (the top hit when searching "best state parks" on Google). Only two parks placed on all three lists: Letchworth State Park, and the 5,000-acre (2,023 ha) Hunting Island State Park in coastal South Carolina. Letchworth State Park, as mentioned before, earned first place

Photo 30. The William P. Letchworth Museum.

in the *USA Today* contest. The map also shows that the park is part of a trio of recognized, water-fall-related New York state parks, alongside Niagara Falls and Watkins Glen State Parks. Letchworth State Park is also only one of about ninety state parks in the United States to be listed on the National Register of Historic Places in its entirety, and one of about 200 state parks to possess any historic resources on this list—there are over 6,600 state parks in the United States.

As seen in Map 80, the park possesses rentals for both day-trippers and overnight visitors: five cabin areas with over eighty cabins combined, a camping area with over 250 sites, a sixteen-room lodge (the Glen Iris Inn), a nine-room lodge (Pinewood), five lodge or home rentals, and ten pavilion or shelter day-use rentals. As with many park phenomena, these rentals are concentrated toward the park's northern and southern ends. Outside of the park are bed-and-breakfasts, hotels, motels, and campgrounds (Map 81), along with rentals through online lodging marketplaces like Airbnb and VRBO. Given the rural character of the region, availability of within-park lodging options, and the relatively high percentage of day-trippers, an industry for overnight accommodations is not significant in the surrounding area.

While visitation brings economic benefits to the region, and while most visits to the park are positive, tourism within the park still has negatives. Park visitation causes modest soil erosion along marked trails, and unofficial "herd paths" can trample sensitive vegetation and stifle forest regeneration. As a "Carry In Carry Out" park that does not provide waste receptacles, some visitors leave litter along trails and at popular park landmarks. And due to the steep cliffs, the allure of the river, and increasing visitor usage, accidents and tragedies do occur within the park.

Accidents have occurred for over 100 years in the park: a car crashed into the gorge near Upper Falls in 1917 causing two fatalities, and "inexperienced, careless, ignorant or overadventuresome" drivers led the American Scenic and Historic Preservation Society to exclude vehicle access from certain overlooks and to redesign roads as early as 1918. Since 2000, an accidental death due to a fall or drowning has occurred roughly once every three years, in addition to modest numbers of calls for rescues or assistance. As a comparison, the rate of accidents in the park is higher than nearby Niagara Falls State Park, but lower than Grand Canyon National Park. This atlas does not provide a map or details of accidents out of respect for the families of those involved, but these accidents cluster in the most visited portions of the park. Calls to 911 for falls and traumatic injuries generally occur near popular destinations at the southern end of the park. Park police most often self-initiate calls around Lower Falls—an area whose secluded character, illegal river access, and prohibited vantage points make it a hotspot for dangerous activity. Not only are people involved in accidents but pet dogs as well.

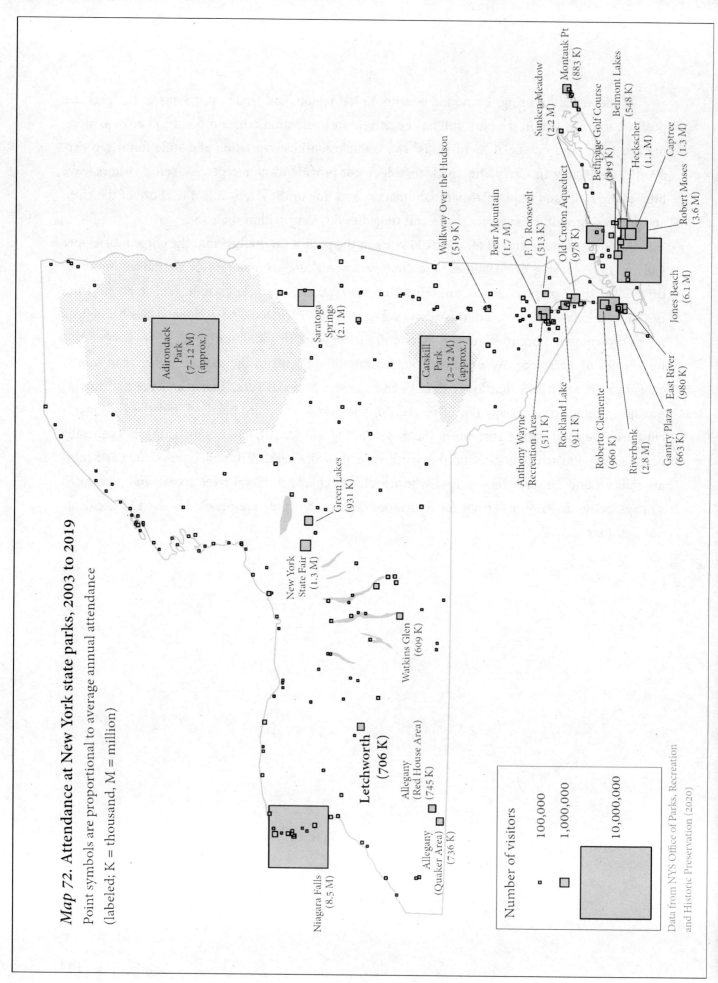

Map 72. Attendance at New York state parks, 2003 to 2019

Point symbols are proportional to average annual attendance (labeled; K = thousand, M = million)

Montauk Pt (883 K)

Sunken Meadow (2.2 M)

Belmont Lakes (548 K)

Bethpage Golf Course (819 K)

Heckscher (1.1 M)

Captree (1.3 M)

Robert Moses (3.6 M)

Walkway Over the Hudson (519 K)

Bear Mountain (1.7 M)

F. D. Roosevelt (513 K)

Old Croton Aqueduct (978 K)

Jones Beach (6.1 M)

Adirondack Park (7–12 M) (approx.)

Saratoga Springs (2.1 M)

Catskill Park (2–12 M) (approx.)

Anthony Wayne Recreation Area (511 K)

Rockland Lake (911 K)

Roberto Clemente (960 K)

Riverbank (2.8 M)

Gantry Plaza (663 K)

East River (980 K)

Green Lakes (931 K)

New York State Fair (1.3 M)

Watkins Glen (609 K)

Letchworth (706 K)

Allegany (Red House Area) (745 K)

Allegany (Quaker Area) (736 K)

Niagara Falls (8.5 M)

Number of visitors

100,000

1,000,000

10,000,000

Data from NYS Office of Parks, Recreation and Historic Preservation (2020)

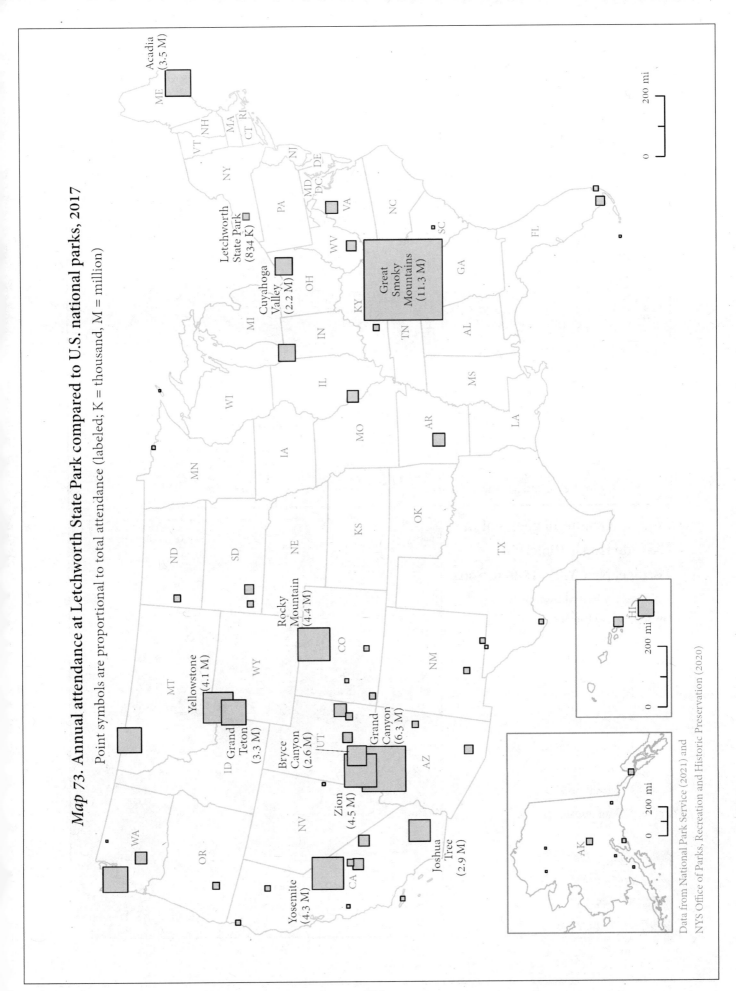

Map 73. Annual attendance at Letchworth State Park compared to U.S. national parks, 2017

Point symbols are proportional to total attendance (labeled; K = thousand, M = million)

Acadia (3.5 M)

Letchworth State Park (834 K)

Cuyahoga Valley (2.2 M)

Great Smoky Mountains (11.3 M)

Rocky Mountain (4.4 M)

Yellowstone (4.1 M)

Grand Teton (3.3 M)

Bryce Canyon (2.6 M)

Grand Canyon (6.3 M)

Zion (4.5 M)

Joshua Tree (2.9 M)

Yosemite (4.3 M)

200 mi

200 mi

200 mi

Data from National Park Service (2021) and
NYS Office of Parks, Recreation and Historic Preservation (2020)

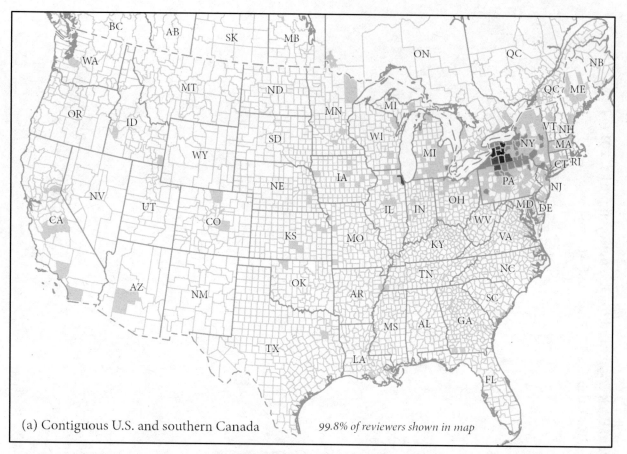

(a) Contiguous U.S. and southern Canada   *99.8% of reviewers shown in map*

Map 74. Origins of guests of the Cascade House (hotel) in Portage, New York, 1886 to 1904

Data are presented by county (modern-day borders are shown)

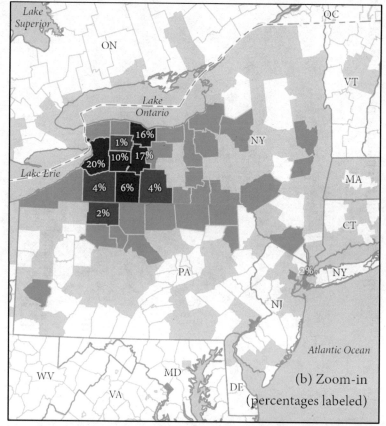

(b) Zoom-in (percentages labeled)

- Letchworth State Park
- State or province
- - - National border

Percent of all guests

- 0%
- >0.0–0.1%
- >0.1–1.0%
- >1.0–5.0%
- >5.0–20.0%

194

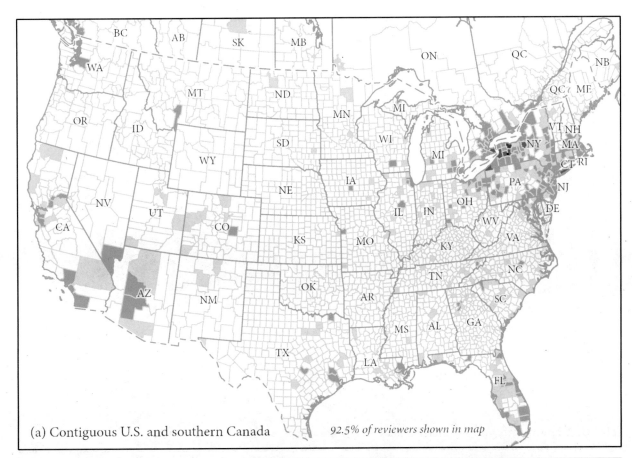

(a) Contiguous U.S. and southern Canada   *92.5% of reviewers shown in map*

Map 75. Origins of reviewers for Letchworth State Park on TripAdvisor.com, 2003 to 2019

Data are presented by county

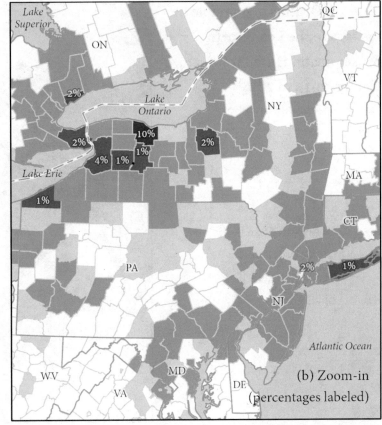

(b) Zoom-in (percentages labeled)

- •   Letchworth State Park
- ▢   State or province
- – – –   National border

Percent of all reviewers

- 0%
- >0.0–0.1%
- >0.1–1.0%
- >1.0–5.0%
- >5.0–11.0%

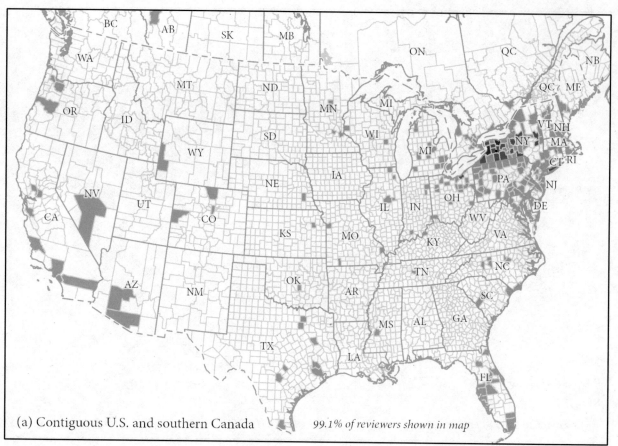

(a) Contiguous U.S. and southern Canada   *99.1% of reviewers shown in map*

Map 76. **Origins of a sample of visitors to the Letchworth Museum and Humphrey Nature Center, 2015 to 2018**

Data are presented by county

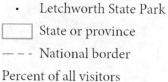

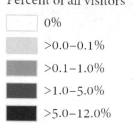

- Letchworth State Park
- State or province
- - - National border

Percent of all visitors

- 0%
- >0.0–0.1%
- >0.1–1.0%
- >1.0–5.0%
- >5.0–12.0%

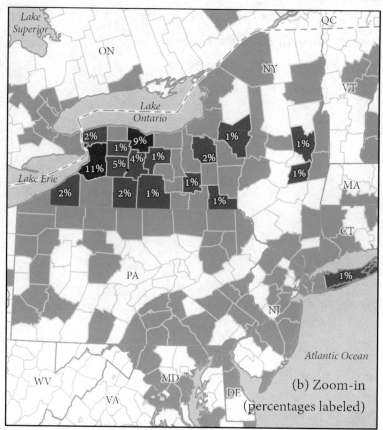

(b) Zoom-in (percentages labeled)

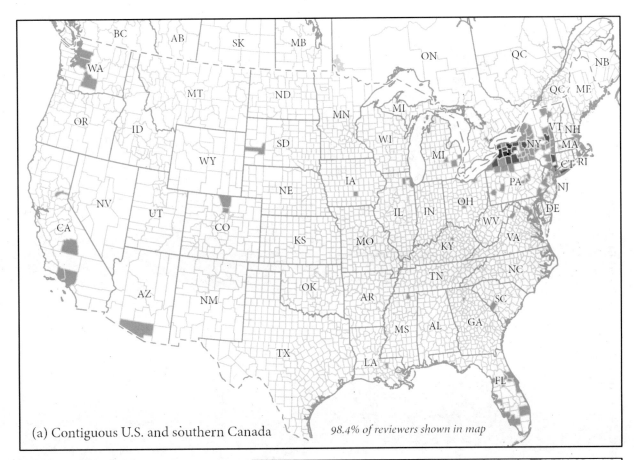

(a) Contiguous U.S. and southern Canada

98.4% of reviewers shown in map

***Map 77.* Origins of visitors based on a survey by Letchworth Gateway Villages, May to November 2017**

Data are presented by county

- Letchworth State Park
- State or province
- - - National border

Percent of all visitors

- 0%
- >0.0–0.1%
- >0.1–1.0%
- >1.0–5.0%
- >5.0–14.0%

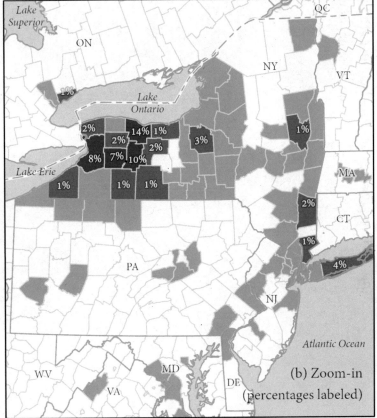

(b) Zoom-in (percentages labeled)

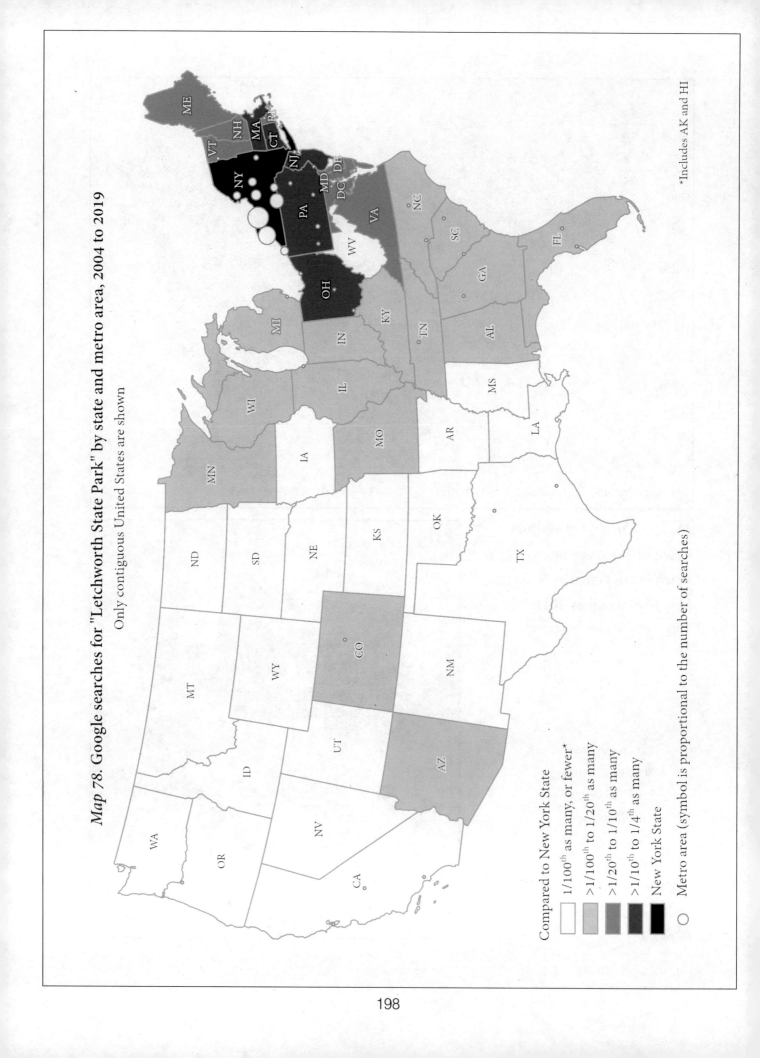

Map 78. Google searches for "Letchworth State Park" by state and metro area, 2004 to 2019

Only contiguous United States are shown

Compared to New York State

1/100th as many, or fewer*

>1/100th to 1/20th as many

>1/20th to 1/10th as many

>1/10th to 1/4th as many

New York State

○ Metro area (symbol is proportional to the number of searches)

*Includes AK and HI

198

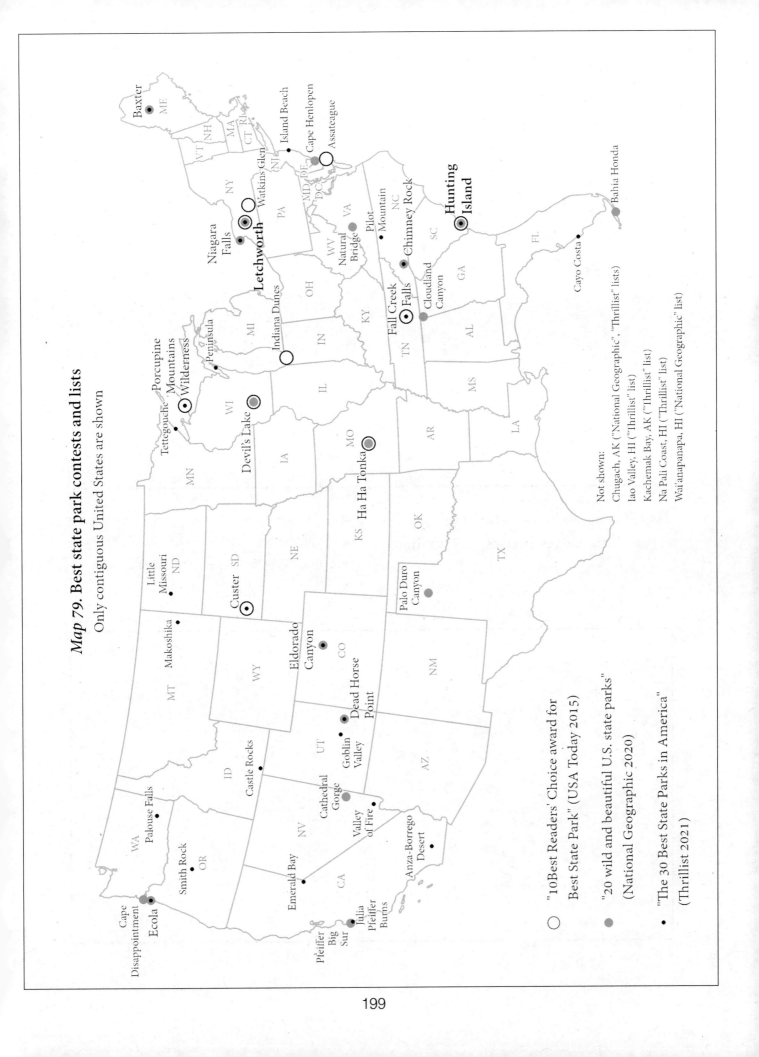

Map 79. **Best state park contests and lists**
Only contiguous United States are shown

Baxter — ME
Island Beach — NJ
Cape Henlopen
Assateague
Watkins Glen
NY
Niagara Falls
Letchworth
PA
MD DE
DC
WV
Natural Bridge
VA
Pilot Mountain
NC
Chimney Rock
SC
Hunting Island
VT NH MA
CT RI

OH
KY
Fall Creek Falls
Cloudland Canyon
TN
GA
AL
FL
Cayo Costa
Bahia Honda

MI
Peninsula
Porcupine Mountains Wilderness
Indiana Dunes
IN
IL
MS
LA

Tettegouche
MN
WI
Devil's Lake
IA
MO
Ha Ha Tonka
AR
OK
Palo Duro Canyon
TX

Little Missouri
ND
Custer SD
NE
KS

Makoshika
MT
WY
Eldorado Canyon
CO
NM

Castle Rocks
ID
Cathedral Gorge
Dead Horse Point
UT
Goblin Valley
AZ

Palouse Falls
WA
Smith Rock
OR
NV
Emerald Bay
CA
Valley of Fire
Anza-Borrego Desert

Cape Disappointment
Ecola
Pfeiffer Big Sur
Julia Pfeiffer Burns

Not shown:
Chugach, AK ("National Geographic", "Thrillist" lists)
Iao Valley, HI ("Thrillist" list)
Kachemak Bay, AK ("Thrillist" list)
Na Pali Coast, HI ("Thrillist" list)
Waiʻanapanapa, HI ("National Geographic" list)

○ "10Best Readers' Choice award for Best State Park" (USA Today 2015)

● "20 wild and beautiful U.S. state parks" (National Geographic 2020)

• "The 30 Best State Parks in America" (Thrillist 2021)

199

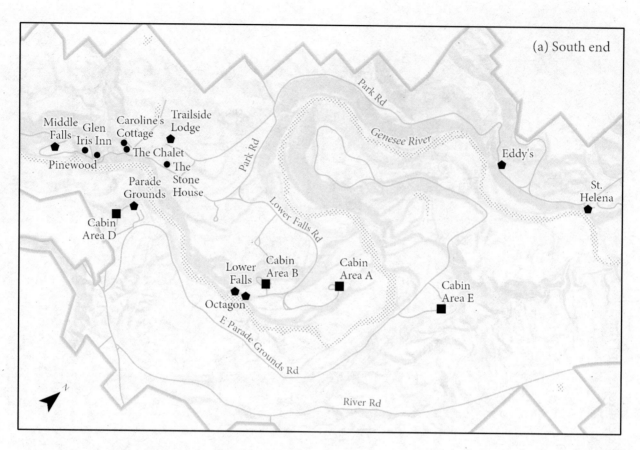

(a) South end

Middle Falls · Glen Iris Inn · Caroline's Cottage · Trailside Lodge

Pinewood · The Chalet · The Stone House

Parade Grounds

Cabin Area D

Park Rd · Genesee River · Eddy's · St. Helena

Park Rd

Lower Falls Rd

Lower Falls · Cabin Area B · Cabin Area A

Octagon · Cabin Area E

E Parade Grounds Rd

River Rd

Map 80. **Rentals in the park: campsites, cabins, inns, lodges, houses, and pavilions**

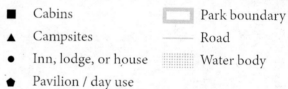

■ Cabins
▲ Campsites
● Inn, lodge, or house
⬠ Pavilion / day use

▭ Park boundary
— Road
░ Water body

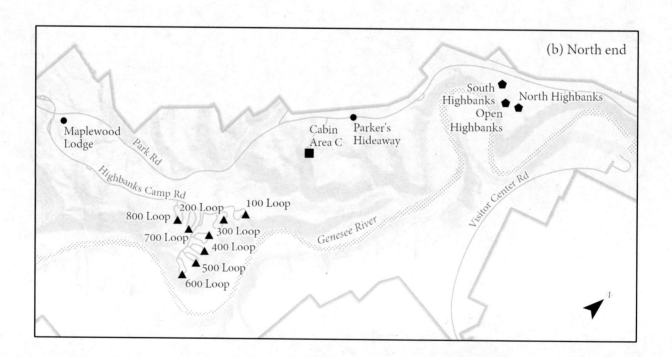

(b) North end

South Highbanks · North Highbanks · Open Highbanks

Maplewood Lodge

Park Rd

Cabin Area C · Parker's Hideaway

Highbanks Camp Rd

200 Loop · 100 Loop
800 Loop · 300 Loop
700 Loop · 400 Loop
500 Loop
600 Loop

Genesee River

Visitor Center Rd

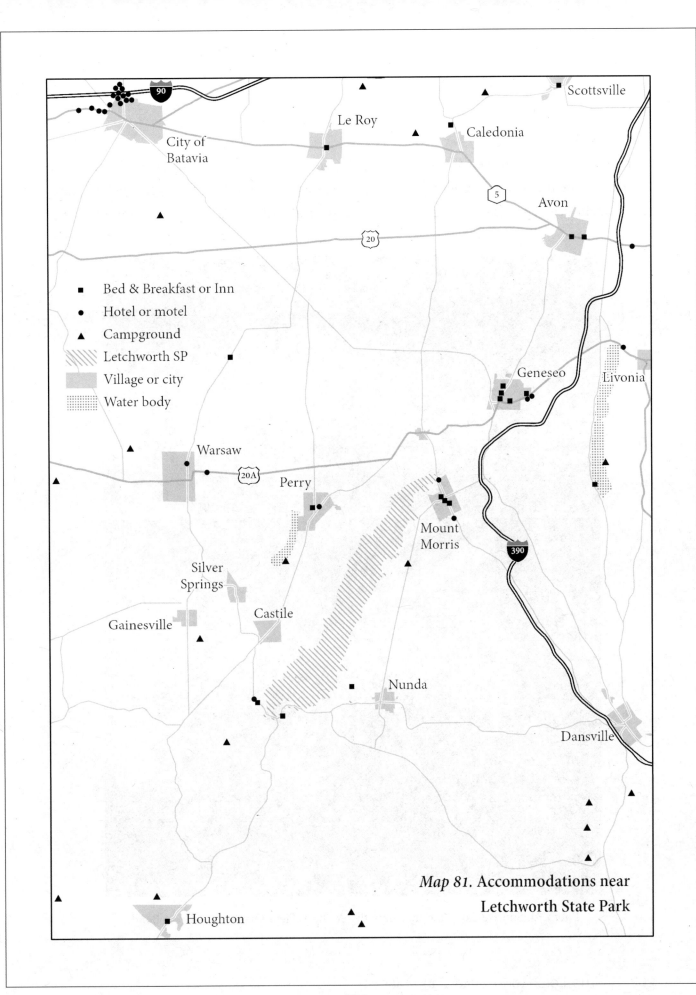

Bed & Breakfast or Inn

Hotel or motel

Campground

Letchworth SP

Village or city

Water body

Scottsville

Le Roy

Caledonia

City of
Batavia

Avon

Geneseo

Livonia

Warsaw

Perry

Mount
Morris

Silver
Springs

Castile

Gainesville

Nunda

Dansville

Houghton

Map 81. Accommodations near
Letchworth State Park

Activities

Perhaps the most common activities in the park today are sightseeing and photography. Map 82 shows the relative frequency of where visitors take photos, based on a sample of geotagged photos (those that contain geographic coordinates) on the photo-sharing website Flickr. Unsurprisingly, visitors

Photo 31. Sunrise along the trail near the Archery Field Overlook at Great Bend.

Photo 32. The Archery Field area viewed from the east side of the park.

take photographs at major scenic attractions. Map 83 presents another perspective on photography: park landmarks that most often appear in photos based on a sample of photos on a Google Images search. The most scenic destinations in the park are once again the most photographed according to this sample: Middle Falls (in 31% of all photos), Upper Falls (27%), the railroad bridge above Upper Falls (27%; currently the Genesee Arch Bridge), Great Bend (12%), and Lower Falls (10%).

This map suggests that the three most iconic photos of the park would be of Great Bend, the view from Inspiration Point, and an up-close shot of Upper Falls and Genesee Arch Bridge. Tourists and photographers often visit the park in mid-October during peak autumn foliage—recall that Map 23 shows peak foliage from space within the park.

The park presents many other recreational opportunities, and the geography of where these activities can occur varies. Its trail network totals nearly eighty miles, embracing trails of differing use, length (see Map 2), quality, and difficulty (see Map 12 to understand how steep some trail segments can be). Map 84 depicts whether five activities—hiking, mountain biking, skiing, horseback riding, and snowmobiling—are allowed or restricted along each trail. All trails are open to foot travel. Trails

Photo 33. A white-tailed deer (*Odocoileus virginianus*).

Photo 34. A bald eagle (*Haliaeetus leucocephalus*).

are open to mountain biking generally on the east side and south end, including a 24-mile (39 km) spur of the Finger Lakes Trail, a regional trail system. With a few exceptions, cross-country skiing is open on virtually all trails, although numerous segments can be steep. Both horseback riding and snowmobiling are generally restricted to the wider and gentler-sloped trails at the southern end. Snowmobilers can also ride the grass shoulder of Park Road, or the seasonally closed portion of Park Road itself from the Perry to Castile entrances in winter. Park trails have different origins: some were trails on the original Glen Iris Estate, some were laid out more recently as foot or bike trails, and some follow the former grade of roads of the mid–nineteenth century—compare Map 84 with Map 46. Some trails are even former bulldozer paths that provided access to clean up debris and remove vegetation along the valley bottom for flood and reservoir management purposes.

Other maps convey various aspects of recreational activities and outdoor sports in the park. An undoubtedly twenty-first-century activity is geocaching: a person hides a cache (typically an ammo box or plastic container) holding a logbook and small prizes, and then provides geographic coordinates and hints regarding the cache's location via a website that others use to find the cache and exchange prizes. Nearly fifty caches are hidden in the park as of 2020 (Map 85). Participants hiding geocaches within the park must fill out a renewable two-year permit to do so. One of the park's most iconic activities, but one that few visitors experience, is hot-air ballooning: local companies fly clients during calm weather before dusk for unique scenic views of the gorge and waterfalls.

The park hosts more traditional outdoor sports such as fishing and hunting: Map 86 shows fishing access points along the Genesee River and at Trout Pond, as well as deer hunting zones. Map 87 provides bear and deer harvest numbers for the years 2015–2019 in the four nearest counties. Hunters harvest several hundred deer in nearby towns, including within the park itself. Bears are a far rarer prize, but in 2017 a hunter made local news by killing a 350-pound, 5-foot-long (1.5 m) black bear in the park. Map 88 presents the number of fish stocked in the Genesee River watershed upstream from Mount Morris Dam, showing that the Department of Environmental Conservation

Photo 35. A turkey vulture (*Cathartes aura*) soaring above Inspiration Point in winter.

stocks mainly brown and rainbow trout in the river's southern reaches and its coldwater tributaries, which may occasionally end up in the park. In the Genesee River within the park, warmwater fish such as smallmouth bass and panfish are most common.

As an Audubon-designated Important Bird Area and State-designated Bird Conservation Area, the last two maps convey the value of the park as habitat for birds and as a prime location for birdwatchers. Map 89 shows the number of unique species observed and reported to the Cornell Lab of Ornithology's eBird.org, a citizen science website, from 2012 to 2019. Birdwatchers at three locations—Mount Morris Dam, Archery Field Overlook, and Dishmill Creek—have observed over 100 bird species: the first two locations provide wide vistas that afford observation, and the third is a location with diverse habitats featuring a stream through one of the most forested areas in the park. Note, however, that these data may manifest where birdwatchers are active rather than true bird diversity at each location. Map 90 shows the number of observations of six species reported on eBird.org that together represent birds found in different habitats: those found soaring in the gorge or perched on cliff outcrops such as the turkey vulture, bald eagle, or peregrine falcon; forest dwellers like the barred owl or hooded warbler; and those found on the Genesee River like the common merganser.

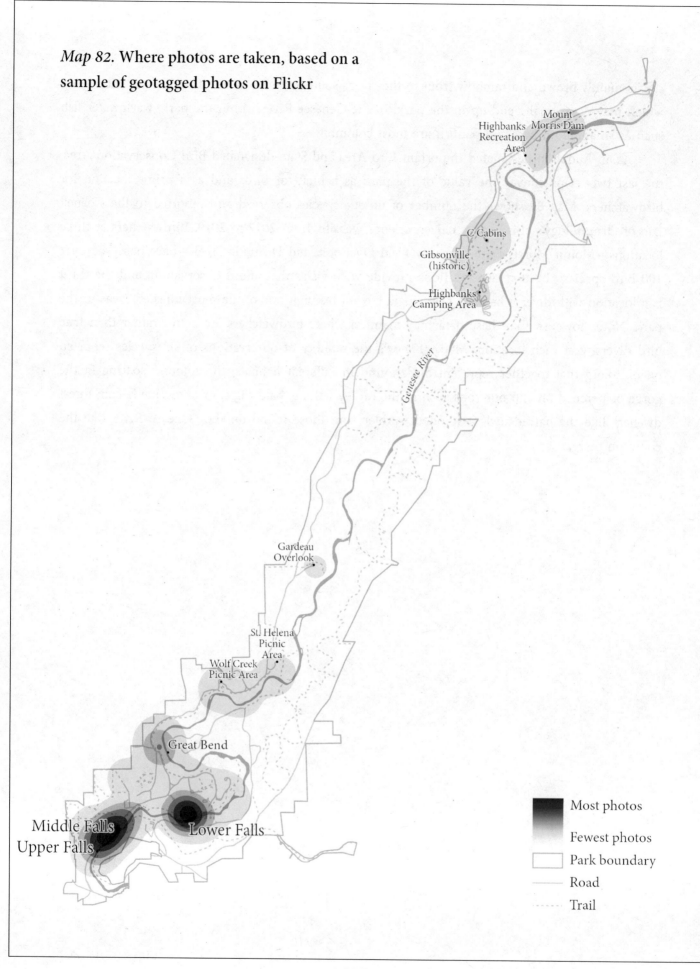

Map 82. Where photos are taken, based on a sample of geotagged photos on Flickr

Mount
Morris Dam
Highbanks
Recreation
Area

C Cabins

Gibsonville
(historic)

Highbanks
Camping Area

Genesee River

Gardeau
Overlook

St. Helena
Picnic
Area

Wolf Creek
Picnic Area

Great Bend

Middle Falls
Upper Falls

Lower Falls

Most photos

Fewest photos

Park boundary

Road

Trail

208

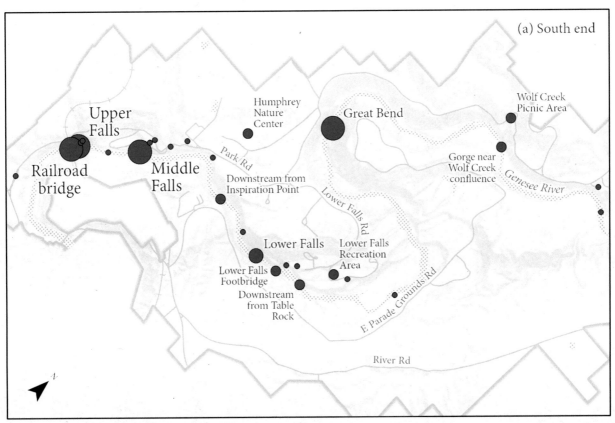

(a) South end

Wolf Creek
Picnic Area

Humphrey
Nature
Center

Great Bend

Upper
Falls

Gorge near
Wolf Creek
confluence

Park Rd

Railroad
bridge

Middle
Falls

Genesee River

Downstream from
Inspiration Point

Lower Falls Rd

Lower Falls

Lower Falls
Recreation
Area

Lower Falls
Footbridge

Downstream
from Table
Rock

E. Parade Grounds Rd

River Rd

Map 83. **Landmarks that appear most often in photos, based on a sample from a Google Images search for "Letchworth State Park" (circa 2020)**
Percentages do not sum to 100% since multiple landmarks can appear in a single photo

% of photos

- >0–1%
- >1–5%
- >5–10%
- >10–30%

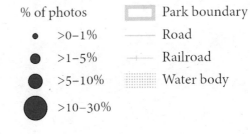

Park boundary
Road
Railroad
Water body

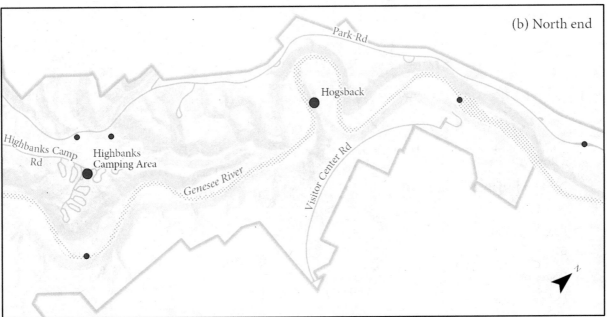

(b) North end

Park Rd

Hogsback

Highbanks Camp
Rd

Highbanks
Camping Area

Genesee River

Visitor Center Rd

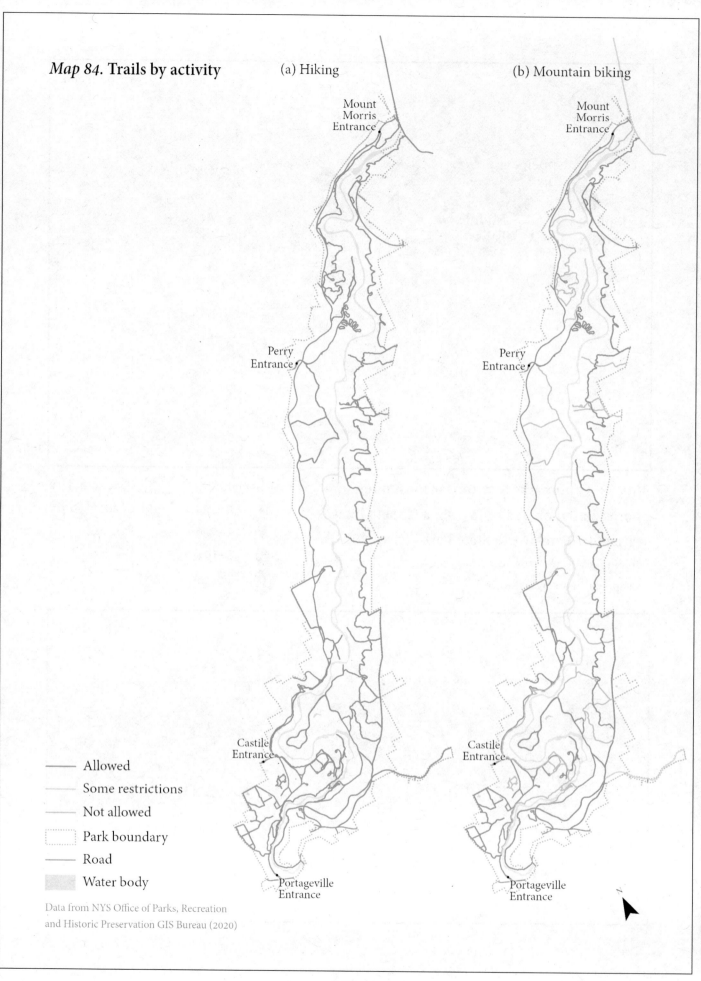

Map 84. **Trails by activity** (a) Hiking (b) Mountain biking

Mount Morris Entrance

Perry Entrance

Castile Entrance

Portageville Entrance

— Allowed
— Some restrictions
— Not allowed
⋯ Park boundary
— Road
▨ Water body

Data from NYS Office of Parks, Recreation
and Historic Preservation GIS Bureau (2020)

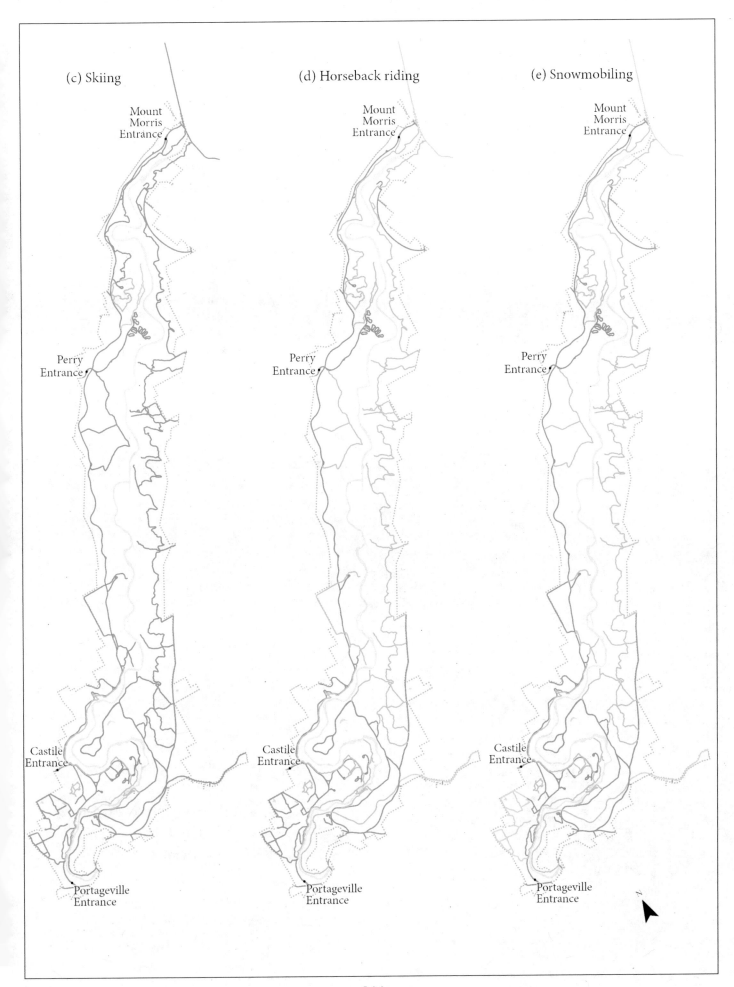

(c) Skiing   (d) Horseback riding   (e) Snowmobiling

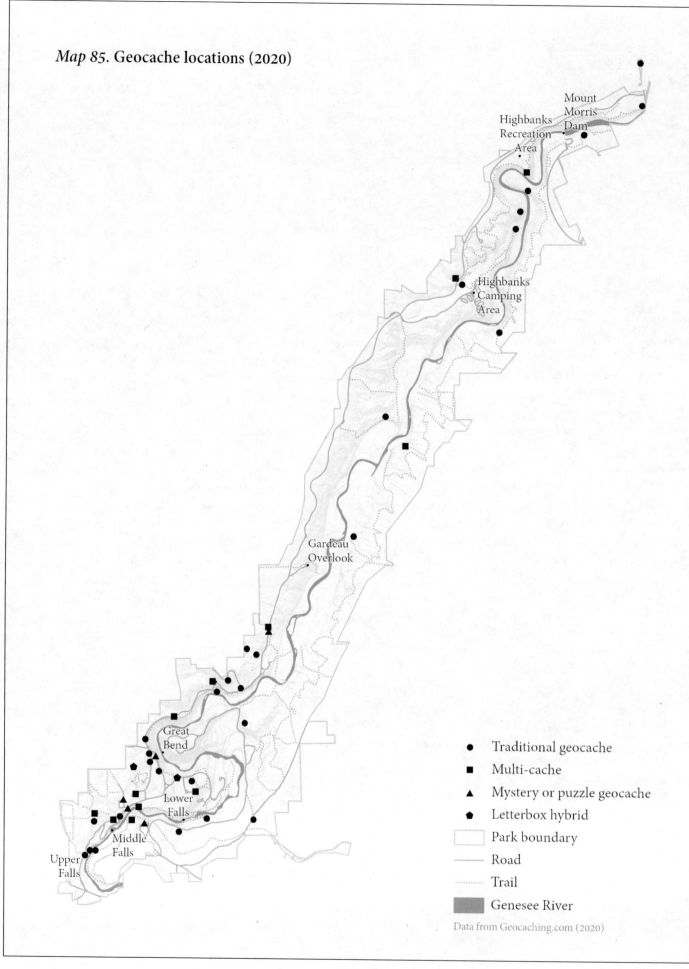

Map 85. Geocache locations (2020)

Mount
Morris
Dam

Highbanks
Recreation
Area

Highbanks
Camping
Area

Gardeau
Overlook

Great
Bend

Lower
Falls

Middle
Falls

Upper
Falls

●   Traditional geocache

■   Multi-cache

▲   Mystery or puzzle geocache

⬟   Letterbox hybrid

▭   Park boundary

—   Road

····   Trail

▬   Genesee River

Data from Geocaching.com (2020)

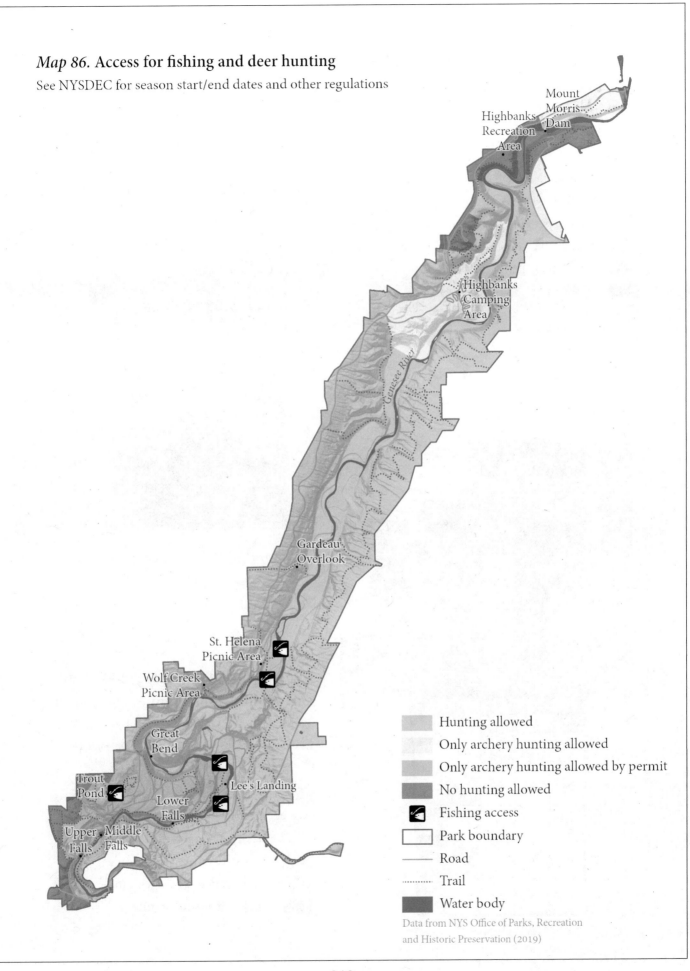

Map 86. **Access for fishing and deer hunting**
See NYSDEC for season start/end dates and other regulations

Mount
Morris
Dam

Highbanks
Recreation
Area

Highbanks
Camping
Area

Genesee River

Gardeau
Overlook

St. Helena
Picnic Area

Wolf Creek
Picnic Area

Great
Bend

Trout
Pond

Lee's Landing

Lower
Falls

Upper   Middle
Falls   Falls

Hunting allowed

Only archery hunting allowed

Only archery hunting allowed by permit

No hunting allowed

Fishing access

Park boundary

Road

Trail

Water body

Data from NYS Office of Parks, Recreation
and Historic Preservation (2019)

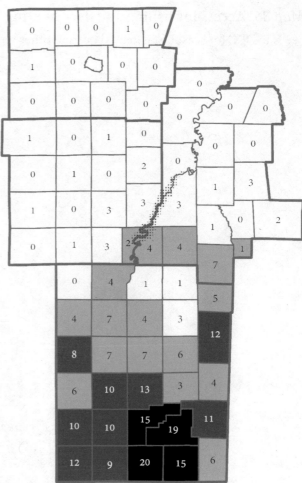

Map 87(a). Bear harvest per town in surrounding four counties, 2015 to 2019

Labels indicate TOTAL number of bear harvested per town during the five-year period

▦ Letchworth State Park

Average bear harvest density per year

☐ 0.5 bear per 25 square miles or fewer

▨ >0.5 to 1.0 bear per 25 square miles

▨ >1 to 2 bears per 25 square miles

■ >2 bears per 25 square miles

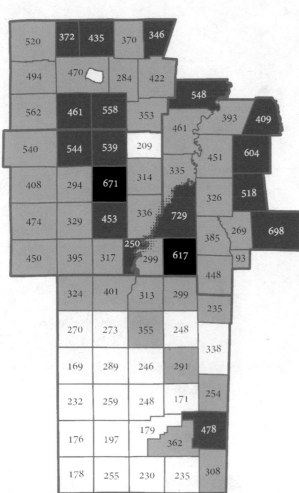

Map 87(b). Deer harvest per town in surrounding four counties, 2015 to 2019

Labels indicate AVERAGE number of deer harvested per town during the five-year period

▦ Letchworth State Park

Average deer harvest density per year

☐ 8 deer per square mile or fewer

▨ >8 to 12 deer per square mile

▨ >12 to 16 deer per square mile

■ >16 deer per square mile

Data from NYS DEC (2021)

214

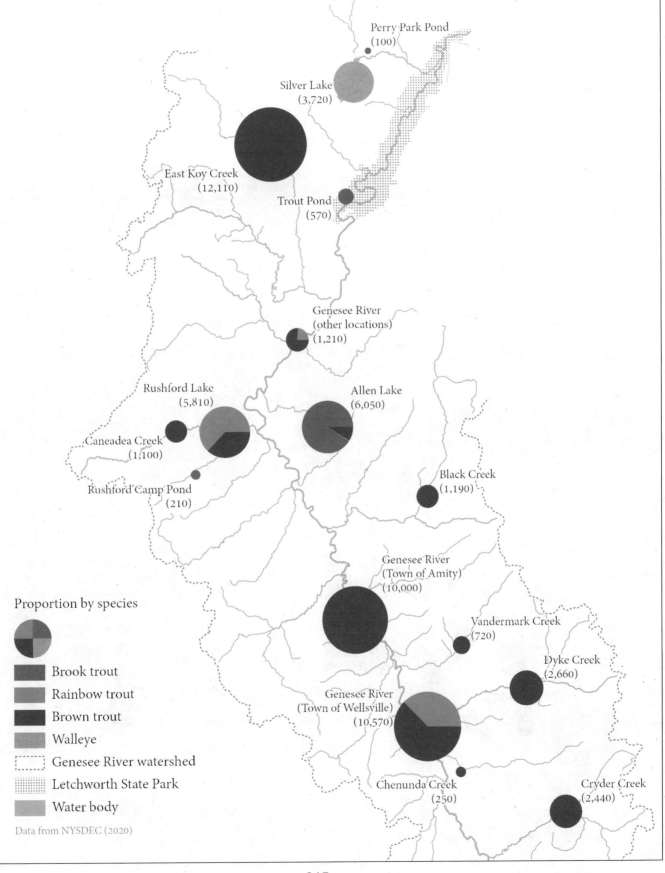

Map 88. Fish stocked in the Genesee River watershed upstream from Mount Morris Dam

Pie charts are proportional to the average annual number of fish stocked from 2011 to 2019 (labeled)

Perry Park Pond
(100)

Silver Lake
(3,720)

East Koy Creek
(12,110)

Trout Pond
(570)

Genesee River
(other locations)
(1,210)

Rushford Lake
(5,810)

Allen Lake
(6,050)

Caneadea Creek
(1,100)

Rushford Camp Pond
(210)

Black Creek
(1,190)

Genesee River
(Town of Amity)
(10,000)

Vandermark Creek
(720)

Dyke Creek
(2,660)

Genesee River
(Town of Wellsville)
(10,570)

Chenunda Creek
(250)

Cryder Creek
(2,440)

Proportion by species

Brook trout

Rainbow trout

Brown trout

Walleye

Genesee River watershed

Letchworth State Park

Water body

Data from NYSDEC (2020)

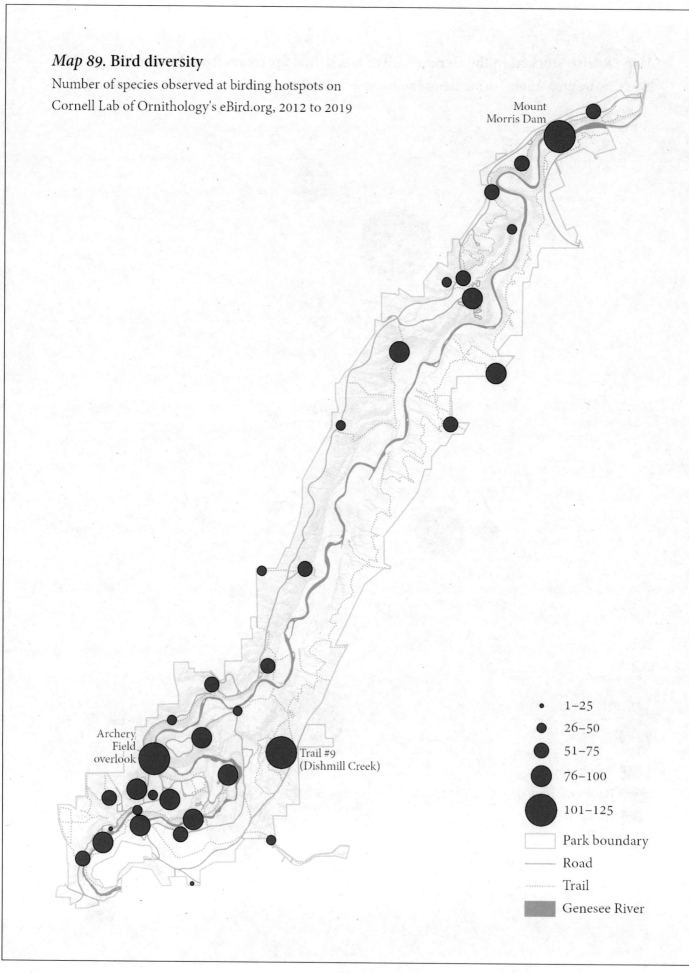

Map 89. **Bird diversity**

Number of species observed at birding hotspots on
Cornell Lab of Ornithology's eBird.org, 2012 to 2019

Mount
Morris Dam

Archery
Field
overlook

Trail #9
(Dishmill Creek)

- 1–25
- 26–50
- 51–75
- 76–100
- 101–125

☐ Park boundary

— Road

⋯ Trail

▬ Genesee River

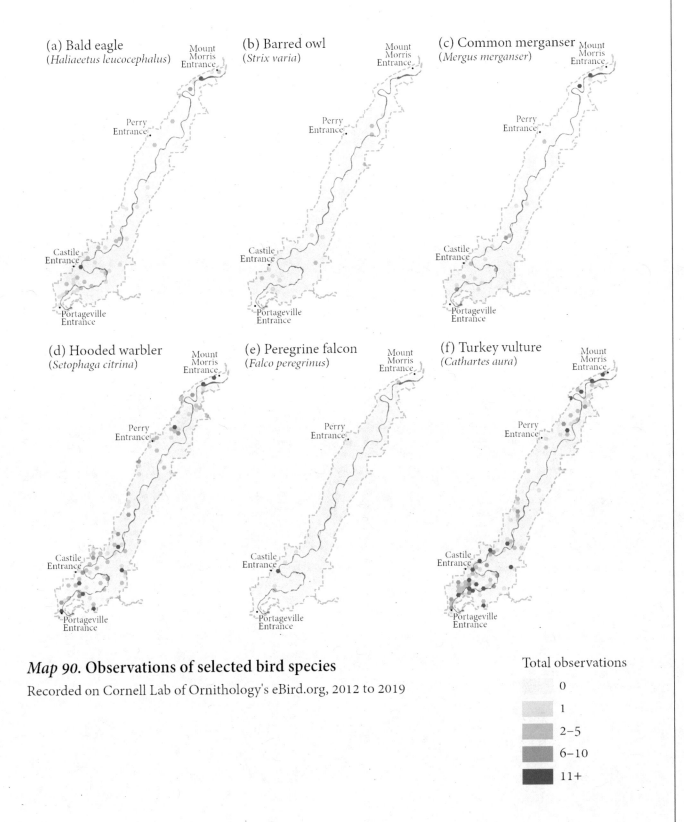

(a) Bald eagle
(*Haliaeetus leucocephalus*)

(b) Barred owl
(*Strix varia*)

(c) Common merganser
(*Mergus merganser*)

(d) Hooded warbler
(*Setophaga citrina*)

(e) Peregrine falcon
(*Falco peregrinus*)

(f) Turkey vulture
(*Cathartes aura*)

Mount Morris Entrance

Perry Entrance

Castile Entrance

Portageville Entrance

Map 90. Observations of selected bird species

Recorded on Cornell Lab of Ornithology's eBird.org, 2012 to 2019

Total observations

0
1
2–5
6–10
11+

Bibliography

Below are sources of data, information, and software used for creating this atlas. The bibliography first presents sources used commonly throughout the maps to provide base data layers, or other sources providing reference on the locations of features within and around Letchworth State Park past and present. It also references commonly used sources in the accompanying text. The bibliography then presents sources used for creating maps and writing each chapter's text, and is subdivided further by chapter section. Last, the bibliography lists the software used for managing data and creating maps. Note that many data files—both tabular and in GIS format—required processing and manipulation in the software listed below to create the maps in this atlas.

Note also that the maps and text benefitted from personal communication with the following individuals: Thomas Cook (author, former Letchworth State Park employee, and current President of Nunda Historical Society); Karen Russell (museum assistant, Interpretive Department, Letchworth State Park); Charles King (maintenance supervisor, Letchworth State Park); Dr. Richard Young (professor emeritus, Department of Geology, SUNY Geneseo); Dr. Michael Oberg (distinguished professor, Department of History, SUNY Geneseo); Dr. Paul Pacheco (professor, Department of Anthropology, SUNY Geneseo); Dr. D. Jeffrey Over (professor, Department of Geology, SUNY Geneseo); Cynthia Amrhein (Wyoming County Historian); Douglas Bassett (Letchworth State Park naturalist); Elijah Kruger (environmental educator at Letchworth State Park); Thomas Breslin (author and former Letchworth State Park manager); and Amanda Schultz (director of communications at Livingston County Sheriff's Office).

Frequently Used Data Sources

Atack, J. (2016). Historical Geographic Information Systems (GIS) database of U.S. Railroads [GIS data file]. https://my.vanderbilt.edu/jeremyatack/data-downloads

Bien, J. R. (1895). *Atlas of the State of New York*. New York: Julius Bien and Company. www.davidrumsey.com

Breslin, T. A., Cook, T. S., Judkins, R. A., and Richens, T. C. (2008). *Letchworth State Park: Images of America series*. Charleston, SC: Arcadia Publishing.

Burr, D. H. (1829). *An Atlas of the State of New York*. New York: David H. Burr. www.davidrumsey.com

Cook, T. S., and Breslin, T. A. (2000). Exploring Letchworth Park History. http://letchworthparkhistory.com/table.html

Doty, L. L. (1876). *A History of Livingston County, New York*. Geneseo, NY: Edward E. Doty.

Esri Data and Maps. (2019). USA Major Roads [GIS data file]. www.arcgis.com/home/item.html?id=871852b13b53426dabdf875f80c04261#

Esri Data and Maps. (2020). USA Census Populated Places [GIS data file]. https://hub.arcgis.com/datasets/esri::usa-census-populated-places/about

History of Wyoming County, NY. (1880). New York: F.W. Beers and Co.

Natural Earth. (2018). Admin 0—Countries, Version 4.1.0 [GIS data file]. 1:50,000,000. www.naturalearthdata.com/downloads/50m-cultural-vectors

Natural Earth. (2018). Admin 1—States, Provinces, Version 4.1.0 [GIS data file]. 1:10,000,000. www.naturalearthdata.com/downloads/10m-cultural-vectors

Natural Earth. (2018). Admin 1—States, Provinces, Version 4.1.0 [GIS data file]. 1:50,000,000. www.naturalearthdata.com/downloads/50m-cultural-vectors

Natural Earth. (2018). Populated Places, Version 4.1.0 [GIS data file]. 1:10,000,000. www.naturalearthdata.com/downloads/10m-cultural-vectors

NYS Office of Information Technology Services GIS Program Office. (2020). New York State Civil Boundaries [GIS data file]. http://gis.ny.gov/gisdata/inventories/details.cfm?DSID=927

NYS Office of Information Technology Services GIS Program Office. (2020). Street Segment Simplified GDB—National Geospatial Data Asset (NGDA) [GIS data file]. http://gis.ny.gov/gisdata/inventories/details.cfm?DSID=932

NYS Office of Parks, Recreation and Historic Preservation. (n.d.). [Interpretive signs throughout Letchworth State Park]. Castile, NY.

NYS Office of Parks, Recreation and Historic Preservation GIS Bureau. (2018). New York State Historic Sites and Park Boundary [GIS data file]. https://gis.ny.gov/gisdata/inventories/details.cfm?DSID=430

NYS Office of Parks, Recreation and Historic Preservation GIS Bureau. (2019). *Letchworth State Park (North Section)* [Map]. Albany, NY: NYS Office of Parks, Recreation and Historic Preservation GIS Bureau. https://parks.ny.gov/documents/parks/LetchworthTrailMapNorth.pdf

NYS Office of Parks, Recreation and Historic Preservation GIS Bureau. (2019). *Letchworth State Park (South Section)* [Map]. Albany, NY: NYS Office of Parks, Recreation and Historic Preservation GIS Bureau. https://parks.ny.gov/documents/parks/LetchworthTrailMapSouth.pdf

NYS Office of Parks, Recreation and Historic Preservation GIS Bureau. (2020). Infrastructure [GIS data file]. Obtained via a NYS Freedom of Information Law request at https://openfoil.ny.gov/#/newfoilrequest.

United States Department of Homeland Security. (2020). Homeland Infrastructure Foundation-Level Data (HIFLD): Railroads [GIS data file]. https://hifld-geoplatform.opendata.arcgis.com/datasets/geoplatform::railroads/about

USGS. (1905). *Nunda Quadrangle, New York* [Map]. 1:62,500. Reston, VA: USGS. https://ngmdb.usgs.gov/topoview

USGS. (1905). *Portage Quadrangle, New York* [Map]. 1:62,500. Reston, VA: USGS. https://ngmdb.usgs.gov/topoview

USGS. (1943). *Mount Morris Quadrangle, New York* [Map]. 1:24,000. Reston, VA: USGS. https://ngmdb.usgs.gov/topoview

USGS. (1944). *Castile Quadrangle, New York* [Map]. 1:31,680. Reston, VA: USGS. https://ngmdb.usgs.gov/topoview

USGS. (1944). *Nunda Quadrangle, New York* [Map]. 1:31,680. Reston, VA: USGS. https://ngmdb.usgs.gov/topoview

USGS. (1944). *Ossian Quadrangle, New York* [Map]. 1:31,680. Reston, VA: USGS. https://ngmdb.usgs.gov/topoview

USGS. (1944). *Portageville Quadrangle, New York* [Map]. 1:31,680. Reston, VA: USGS. https://ngmdb.usgs.gov/topoview

USGS. (1944). *Sonyea Quadrangle, New York* [Map]. 1:31,680. Reston, VA: USGS. https://ngmdb.usgs.gov/topoview

USGS. (1950). *Geneseo Quadrangle, New York* [Map]. 1:24,000. Reston, VA: USGS. https://ngmdb.usgs.gov/topoview

USGS. (1951). *Leicester Quadrangle, New York* [Map]. 1:24,000. Reston, VA: USGS. https://ngmdb.usgs.gov/topoview

USGS. (1951). *Wyoming Quadrangle, New York* [Map]. 1:24,000. Reston, VA: USGS. https://ngmdb.usgs.gov/topoview

USGS. (2019). USGS 3D Elevation Program 1/3rd arc-second digital elevation model [GIS data file]. https://apps.nationalmap.gov/downloader/#

USGS. (2019). USGS National Landcover—Woodland in New York 20190924 State or Territory FileGDB 10.1 [GIS data file]. https://apps.nationalmap.gov/downloader/#

USGS. (2020). National Hydrography Dataset 20200218 for New York State or Territory FileGDB 10.1 Model Version 2.2.1 [GIS data file]. https://apps.nationalmap.gov/downloader/#

Chapter 1: Overview of the Park

Adirondack Park Agency. (2018). Adirondack Park Boundary [GIS data file]. https://apa.ny.gov/gis

Adirondack Park Land Use Classification Statistics. (2018, March 20). Adirondack Park Agency. www.apa.ny.gov/gis/stats/colc201803.htm

Amish Studies. (2020). Amish Population in the United States by State and County, 2020. Young Center for Anabaptist and Pietist Studies at Elizabethtown College. http://groups.etown.edu/amishstudies/files/2020/10/Amish_Pop_by_state_and_county_2020.pdf

Anderson, M.L.H. (1956). *Genesee Echoes: The Upper Gorge and Falls Area from the Days of the Pioneers.* Dansville, NY: F.A. Owen Publishing Company.

Breslin, T. A. (2000). *"The Vernacular": Local Place Names in Letchworth Park*. Letchworth Park History. www.letchworthparkhistory.com/vernacular.html

Breslin, T. A., and Cook, T. S. (2000, May). *A Short History of Letchworth Park*. Letchworth Park History. www.letchworthparkhistory.com/history.html

Breslin, T. A., Cook, T. S., Judkins, R. A., and Richens, T. C. (2008). *Letchworth State Park: Images of America Series*. Charleston, SC: Arcadia Publishing.

Brown, P. J. (1853). *Map of Wyoming County, New York: From Actual Surveys* [Map]. Philadelphia, PA: Newel S. Brown. www.loc.gov/item/2008627968

Center for International Earth Science Information Network, Columbia University. (2018). Gridded Population of the World, Version 4 (GPWv4): Population Count, Revision 11 [GIS data file]. NASA Socioeconomic Data and Applications Center. https://sedac.ciesin.columbia.edu/data/set/gpw-v4-population-count-rev11

Center for International Earth Science Information Network, Columbia University. (2018). Gridded Population of the World, Version 4 (GPWv4): Population Density, Revision 11 [GIS data file]. NASA Socioeconomic Data and Applications Center. https://sedac.ciesin.columbia.edu/data/set/gpw-v4-population-density-rev11

Chao, M. (2015, April 1). Letchworth State Park No. 1 with USA Today readers. *Democrat and Chronicle / USA Today*. www.usatoday.com/story/news/local/2015/04/01/letchworth-state-park-no-1-with-usa-today-readers/70777950

Conheady, M., Lucero, K., and Champlin, M. (2021). *Letchworth Waterfall List*. NYFalls. https://nyfalls.com/waterfalls/letchworth/waterfall-locations

Ensminger, S. A. (2016). *Letchworth State Park Waterfall Locations With GPS Data*. Western New York Waterfall Survey. http://falzguy.com/letchworth-wf-tabel.html

Ensminger, S. A., and Bassett D. K. (2016). *A Waterfall Guide to Letchworth State Park*. Raleigh, NC: Lulu Press.

Google. (n.d.). Driving times between various cities and Letchworth State Park. www.google.com/maps

Google. (n.d.). Driving times between various places within Letchworth State Park. www.google.com/maps

Hall, E. H. (1907). *Letchworth Park* [Map]. 1:4,572. Scanned PDF file version provided by Letchworth State Park Engineering Department.

Land Information Ontario. (2019). Municipal Boundary—Lower and Single Tier [GIS data file]. https://data.ontario.ca/dataset/municipal-boundaries

Lohmann, P. (2019, January 30). Seward House Painting "Portage Falls on the Genesee" to Finally Be Sold. *Syracuse.com*. www.syracuse.com/news/2018/05/seward_house_painting_portage_falls_on_the_genesee_to_finally_be_sold.html

Minard, J. S. (1890). *Map of the Estate of Hon. William P. Letchworth* [Map]. Scanned PDF file version provided by Letchworth State Park Engineering Department.

National Park Service. (2021). *National Register Database and Research*. National Register of Historic Places. www.nps.gov/subjects/nationalregister/database-research.htm#table

National Park Service Land Resources Division. (2019). NPS—Land Resources Division Boundary and Tract Data Service [GIS data file]. www.arcgis.com/home/group.html?id=00f2977287f74c79aad558708e3b6649#overview

National Park Service Land Resources Division. (2020). *Summary of Acreage*. www.nps.gov/subjects/lwcf/upload/NPS-Acreage-9-30-2020.pdf

Natural Earth. (2018). Cross Blended Hypso with Shaded Relief, Version 3.2.0 [GIS data file]. www.naturalearthdata.com/downloads/10m-cross-blend-hypso/10m-cross-blended-hypso-with-shaded-relief-and-water

Nelson A. Rockefeller Institute of Government. (2014). *New York State Statistical Yearbook: 2014*. https:// rockinst.org/wp-content/uploads/2017/11/2015_Yearbook_Section_O_Environmental.pdf

New York City Department of City Planning. (2020). NYC Borough Boundaries [GIS data file]. https://data. cityofnewyork.us/City-Government/Borough-Boundaries/tqmj-j8zm

NYS Office of Parks, Recreation and Historic Preservation. (2020). *State Park Annual Attendance Figures by Facility: Beginning 2003* [Data file]. https://data.ny.gov/Recreation/State-Park-Annual-Attendance-Figures-by-Facility-B/8f3n-xj78/data

QuickFacts. (2019). United States Census Bureau. www.census.gov/programs-surveys/sis/resources/data-tools/quickfacts.html

Rea and Otley. (1852). *Map of Livingston County, New York: from actual surveys*. Philadelphia, PA: Smith and Gillett. www.loc.gov/item/2013593275

United States Census Bureau. (2019). American Community Survey 5-year estimates. https://censusreporter.org

United States Census Bureau. (2019). New York County (Manhattan Borough), New York. United States Census Bureau QuickFacts. www.census.gov/quickfacts/newyorkcountymanhattanboroughnewyork

Westgard, A. L., and Barthel, O. (1902). *New Century Atlas of Livingston County, New York*. Philadelphia, PA: Century Map Company.

Westgard, A. L., and McClure, J. O. (1902). *New Century Atlas of Wyoming County, New York*. Philadelphia, PA: Century Map Company.

Chapter 2: Physical Geography

Geology

Clarke, J. M., Luther, D. D., and Fairchild, H. L. (1908). Geologic map and descriptions of the Portage and Nunda quadrangles, including a map of Letchworth Park [Map]. Albany, NY: NYS Museum. https:// ngmdb.usgs.gov/Prodesc/proddesc_90906.htm

Cook, T. S., and Breslin, T. A. (2000). *Hall's Sketches of the Portage Falls, 1843*. Exploring Letchworth Park History. www.letchworthparkhistory.com/halls.html

Dyke, A. S., Moore, A., and Robertson, L. (2003). Deglaciation of North America, Open File 1574 [GIS data file]. Natural Resources Canada. https://github.com/awickert/North-American-Ice-Sheets

Fenneman, N. M. (1938). *Physiography of Eastern United States*. New York: McGraw-Hill Book Co.

Fisher, D.W., Isachsen, Y.W., and Richard, L.V. (1970). *Geologic Map of New York; Niagara Sheet*. 1:250,000. NYS Museum and Science Service Map and Chart Series No. 15. Albany, NY: SUNY Press.

Isachsen, Y. W., Landing, E., Lauber, J. M., Rickard, L. V., and Rogers, W. B. (eds.). (2000). *Geology of New York: A Simplified Account*. Albany, NY: The NYS Education Department.

Johnson, E. (1807). *The Survey Bill of a Tract of Land Granted to Garrett Cottringer by Robert Morris, Esquire* [Land survey notes]. Wyoming County Historian's Office, Warsaw, New York.

Kirchgasser, W. T., Over, D. J., and Woodrow, D. L. (1994). Frasnian (Upper Devonian) Strata of the Genesee River Valley, Western New York State. In C.E. Brett and J. Scatterday (eds.), *NYSGA Field Trip Guidebook*, 66th Annual Meeting (325–358). The University of Rochester, New York.

Letchworth Gorge: An Overview of "The Grand Canyon of the East" (n.d.). New York State Museum. www.nysm.nysed.gov/research-collections/geology/resources/letchworth-gorge

Muller, E. H., Braun, D. D., Young, R. A., and Wilson, M. P. (1988). Morphogenesis of the Genesee Valley. *Northeastern Geology* 10(2): 112–133.

NYS Museum. (2000). Bedrock Geology Shape Files: Niagara Bedrock Sheet [GIS data file]. 1:250,000. www.nysm.nysed.gov/research-collections/geology/gis

NYS Museum. (2000). Surficial Geology Shape Files: Niagara Surficial Shape [GIS data file]. 1:250,000. www.nysm.nysed.gov/research-collections/geology/gis

Ross, P. (2021, May 28). Magnitude 2.4 Earthquake Reported Near Letchworth State Park. *WKBW*. www.wkbw.com/news/local-news/magnitude-2-4-earthquake-reported-near-letchworth-state-park

Scotese, C. R., and Wright, N. (2018). PALEOMAP Paleodigital Elevation Models (PaleoDEMS) for the Phanerozoic PALEOMAP Project [GIS data file]. www.earthbyte.org/paleodem-resource-scotese-and-wright-2018

USDA Natural Resources Conservation Service. (n.d.). SSURGO database [GIS database]. 1:12,000. https://datagateway.nrcs.usda.gov/GDGOrder.aspx

Van Diver, B. B. (1985). *Roadside Geology of New York.* Missoula, MT: Mountain Press Publishing Company.

Whitbeck, R. H. (1902). The Pre-Glacial Course of the Middle Portion of the Genesee River. *Bulletin of the American Geographical Society* 34(1): 32–44.

Young, R. A., and Burr, G. S. (2006). Middle Wisconsin Glaciation in the Genesee Valley, New York: A Stratigraphic Record Contemporaneous with Heinrich Event, H4. *Geomorphology* 75: 226–247.

Young, R. A., Gordon, L. M., Owen, L. A., Huot, S., and Zerfas, T. D. (2021). Evidence for a Late Glacial Advance Near the Beginning of the Younger Dryas in Western New York State: An Event Postdating the Record for Local Laurentide Ice Sheet Recession. *Geosphere* 17(1): 271–305.

Land History and Ecological Communities

Clark, J. S., Royall, P. D., and Chumbley, C. (1996). The Role of Fire during Climate Change in an Eastern Deciduous Forest at Devil's Bathtub, New York. *Ecology* 77(7): 2148–2166.

Cornell Institute for Resource Information Sciences (Cornell IRIS) and NYS Department of Agriculture and Markets. (2016). Agricultural Districts, Livingston County NY, 2016 [GIS data file]. 1:24,000. https://cugir.library.cornell.edu/catalog/cugir-007970

Cornell Institute for Resource Information Sciences (Cornell IRIS) and NYS Department of Agriculture and Markets. (2019). Agricultural Districts, Wyoming County NY, 2019 [GIS data file]. 1:24,000. https://cugir.library.cornell.edu/catalog/cugir-007999

Doty, L. L. (1876). *A History of Livingston County, New York.* Geneseo, NY: Edward E. Doty.

Ellis, E. C., Goldewijk, K. K., Siebert, S., Lightman, D., and Ramankutty, N. (2010). Anthropogenic Transformation of the Biomes, 1700 to 2000. *Global Ecology and Biogeography* 19(5): 589–606.

Ellis, E. C., Goldewijk, K. K., Siebert, S., Lightman, D., and Ramankutty, N. (2014). Anthropogenic Biomes of the World, Version 2: 1700 [GIS data file]. NASA Socioeconomic Data and Applications Center. https://sedac.ciesin.columbia.edu/data/set/anthromes-anthropogenic-biomes-world-v2-1700

Ellis, E. C., Goldewijk, K. K., Siebert, S., Lightman, D., and Ramankutty, N. (2014). Anthropogenic Biomes of the World, Version 2: 1800 [GIS data file]. NASA Socioeconomic Data and Applications Center. https://sedac.ciesin.columbia.edu/data/set/anthromes-anthropogenic-biomes-world-v2-1800

Ellis, E. C., Goldewijk, K. K., Siebert, S., Lightman, D., and Ramankutty, N. (2014). *Anthropogenic Biomes of the World, Version 2: 1900* [GIS data file]. NASA Socioeconomic Data and Applications Center. https://sedac.ciesin.columbia.edu/data/set/anthromes-anthropogenic-biomes-world-v2-1900

Ellis, E. C., Goldewijk, K. K., Siebert, S., Lightman, D., and Ramankutty, N. (2014). *Anthropogenic Biomes of the World, Version 2: 2000* [GIS data file]. NASA Socioeconomic Data and Applications Center. https://sedac.ciesin.columbia.edu/data/set/anthromes-anthropogenic-biomes-world-v2-2000

Engelbrecht, W. (2005). *Iroquoia: The Development of a Native World*. Syracuse, NY: Syracuse University Press.

Evans, D. J., and VanLuven, D. E. (2007). *Biodiversity in New York's State Park System: Summary of Findings*. Albany, NY: New York Natural Heritage Program. https://parks.ny.gov/environment/biodiversity.aspx

Global Biodiversity Information Facility. (2021 August 9). GBIF Occurrence Download [Data file]. www.gbif.org/occurrence/search

Hall, E. H. (1907). *Letchworth Park* [Map]. 1:4,572. Scanned PDF file version provided by Letchworth State Park Engineering Department.

Hardenbergh, J. L., McKendry, W., Griffis, W. E., and Adler, S. L. (eds.). (2010). *Narratives of Sullivan's Expedition, 1779: Against the Four Nations of the Iroquois and Loyalists by the Continental Army*. Driffield, UK: Leonaur Ltd.

Johnson, E. (1807). *The Survey Bill of a Tract of Land Granted to Garrett Cottringer by Robert Morris, Esquire* [Land survey notes]. Wyoming County Historian's Office, Warsaw, NY.

Landsat 8. (2014, October 24). Landsat 8 image LC08_L2SP_016030_20141024_20200910_02_T1 [satellite imagery]. NASA/USGS. https://earthexplorer.usgs.gov

Minard, J. S. (1890). *Map of the Estate of Hon. William P. Letchworth* [Map]. Scanned PDF file version provided by Letchworth State Park Engineering Department.

New York Center for Forestry Research and Development. (n.d.). *Changes in New York's Forest Land Area*. New York State Department of Environmental Conservation. www.dec.ny.gov/lands/42065.html

NYS Office of Parks, Recreation and Historic Preservation GIS Bureau. (2004). Letchworth State Park Ecological Communities [GIS data file]. Obtained via a NYS Freedom of Information Law request at https://openfoil.ny.gov/#/newfoilrequest.

Paciorek, C. J., Goring, S. J., Thurman, A. L., Cogbill, C. V., Williams, J. W., Mladenoff, D. J., Peters, J. A., Zhu, J., and McLachlan, J. S. (2015). Settlement vegetation composition maps [GIS data file]. https://sites.nd.edu/paleonproject/maps

Paciorek, C. J., Goring, S. J., Thurman, A. L., Cogbill, C. V., Williams, J. W., Mladenoff, D. J., Peters, J. A., Zhu, J., and McLachlan, J. S. (2016). Statistically-Estimated Tree Composition for the Northeastern United States at Euro-American Settlement. *PLoS ONE 11*(2): e0150087.

Pease, S., and Stoddard, R. M. *Field books of Seth Pease and a Mr. Stoddard's 1799 survey of the 5,000,000 acre tract west of the Genesee River for the assignees of Robert Morris* [Land survey notes]. De Zeng Family (Geneva, NY) Papers, 1729–1925 (Manuscript Group 800, Box 2, Folders 8–12), The New Jersey Historical Society, Newark, New Jersey.

Porter, A. (1798). *Map of the Indian Reservation at Gardeau* [Map]. www.iroquoisgenealogysociety.org/map-gallery

Porter, A. (1799). *Indian Reservation at Squawky-hill* [sic] [Map]. www.iroquoisgenealogysociety.org/map-gallery

Short, F. W., and Dake, W. F. (1948). *Native and Exotic Trees, Shrubs, Vines and Ferns*. Castile, NY: Genesee State Park Commission.

Tulowiecki, S. J., Larsen, C.P.S., and Robertson, D. (2018). Tree-ring Records from Eight Trees in Letchworth State Park [Unpublished raw data]. Geneseo, NY: SUNY.

Tulowiecki, S. J., Robertson, D., and Larsen, C.P.S. (2020). Oak Savannas in Western New York State: Synthesizing Predictive Spatial Models and Historical Accounts to Understand Environmental and Native American Influences. *Annals of the American Association of Geographers 110*(1): 184–204.

USDA. (1938). [Aerial photographs]. Provided by the Livingston County Soil and Water Conservation District, Geneseo, NY.

USDA National Agricultural Statistics Service Cropland Data Layer. (2008). Published crop-specific data layer [GIS data file]. https://nassgeodata.gmu.edu/CropScape

USDA National Agricultural Statistics Service Cropland Data Layer. (2009). Published crop-specific data layer [GIS data file]. https://nassgeodata.gmu.edu/CropScape

USDA National Agricultural Statistics Service Cropland Data Layer. (2010). Published crop-specific data layer [GIS data file]. https://nassgeodata.gmu.edu/CropScape

USDA National Agricultural Statistics Service Cropland Data Layer. (2011). Published crop-specific data layer [GIS data file]. https://nassgeodata.gmu.edu/CropScape

USDA National Agricultural Statistics Service Cropland Data Layer. (2012). Published crop-specific data layer [GIS data file]. https://nassgeodata.gmu.edu/CropScape

USDA National Agricultural Statistics Service Cropland Data Layer. (2013). Published crop-specific data layer [GIS data file]. https://nassgeodata.gmu.edu/CropScape

USDA National Agricultural Statistics Service Cropland Data Layer. (2014). Published crop-specific data layer [GIS data file]. https://nassgeodata.gmu.edu/CropScape

USDA National Agricultural Statistics Service Cropland Data Layer. (2015). Published crop-specific data layer [GIS data file]. https://nassgeodata.gmu.edu/CropScape

USDA National Agricultural Statistics Service Cropland Data Layer. (2016). Published crop-specific data layer [GIS data file]. https://nassgeodata.gmu.edu/CropScape

USDA National Agricultural Statistics Service Cropland Data Layer. (2017). Published crop-specific data layer [GIS data file]. https://nassgeodata.gmu.edu/CropScape

USDA National Agricultural Statistics Service Cropland Data Layer. (2018). Published crop-specific data layer [GIS data file]. https://nassgeodata.gmu.edu/CropScape

USDA National Agricultural Statistics Service Cropland Data Layer. (2019). Published crop-specific data layer [GIS data file]. https://nassgeodata.gmu.edu/CropScape

USDA National Agricultural Statistics Service Cropland Data Layer. (2020). Published crop-specific data layer [GIS data file]. https://nassgeodata.gmu.edu/CropScape

USGS Gap Analysis Project. (2020). Protected Areas Database of the United States (PAD-US) 2.1: U.S. Geological Survey data release [GIS data file]. www.sciencebase.gov/catalog/item/602597f7d34eb12031138e15

Venter, O., Sanderson, E. W., Magrach, A., Allan, J. R., Beher, J., Jones, K. R., Possingham, H. P., Laurance, W. F., Wood, P., Fekete, B. M., Levy, M. A., and Watson, J. E. (2018). Last of the Wild Project, Version 3 (LWP-3): 2009 Human Footprint, 2018 Release [GIS data file]. NASA Socioeconomic Data and Applications Center. https://sedac.ciesin.columbia.edu/data/set/wildareas-v3-2009-human-footprint

Williams, J. W., Shuman, B. N., Webb III, T., Bartlein, P. J., and Leduc, P. L. (2004). Late-Quaternary Vegetation Dynamics in North America: Scaling from Taxa to Biomes. *Ecological Monographs 74*(2): 309–334.

Yu, Z. (2003). Land Quaternary Dynamics of Tundra and Forest Vegetation in the Southern Niagara Escarpment, Canada. *The New Phytologist 157*(2): 365–390.

Weather and Climate

Cook, T. (2000). *Centennial Tornado at Portageville.* Exploring Letchworth Park History. www.letchworthparkhistory.com/tornado.html

Federal Emergency Management Agency. (2021). OpenFEMA Dataset: Disaster Declarations Summaries—v1 [Data file]. www.fema.gov/openfema-data-page/disaster-declarations-summaries-v1

Kottek. M., Grieser, J., Beck, C., Rudolf, B., and Rubel, F. (2006). World Map of the Köppen-Geiger Climate Classification Updated. *Meteorologische Zeitschrift 15*(3): 259–263.

National Center for Atmospheric Research. (2021). NCAR Community Climate System Model (CCSM) projections in GIS formats [GIS data file]. https://gisclimatechange.ucar.edu/gis-climatedata

NOAA National Centers for Environmental Information. (2020). International Best Track Archive for Climate Stewardship (IBTrACS) [GIS data file]. www.ncdc.noaa.gov/ibtracs/index.php?name=ib-v4-access

NOAA National Centers for Environmental Information. (2021). *Storm Events Database* [Database]. www.ncdc.noaa.gov/stormevents

NOAA National Climatic Data Center. (2011). 1981–2010 Annual Climate Normals: Long-term Averages of Annual Snowfall Totals [Data file]. www.ncdc.noaa.gov/cdo-web

NOAA Storm Prediction Center. (2019). Hail (1955–2018) [GIS data file]. www.spc.noaa.gov/gis/svrgis

NOAA Storm Prediction Center. (2019). Tornadoes (1950–2018) [GIS data file]. www.spc.noaa.gov/gis/svrgis

NOAA Storm Prediction Center. (2019). Wind (1955–2018) [GIS data file]. www.spc.noaa.gov/gis/svrgis

PRISM Climate Group. (2012). 30-Year Normals, 1981–2010 [GIS data file]. Northwest Alliance for Computational Science and Engineering, Oregon State University. https://prism.oregonstate.edu/normals

Thompson, A. (2016, November 1). Drought and Climate Change Could Throw Fall Colors Off Schedule. *Climate Central / Scientific American.* www.scientificamerican.com/article/drought-and-climate-change-could-throw-fall-colors-off-schedule

Vanasse Hangen Brustlin, Inc., and Highland Planning. (2018). *Climate Vulnerability Assessment Report: City of Rochester, NY.* Prepared for the City of Rochester Office of Energy and Sustainability. http://cityofrochester.gov/WorkArea/DownloadAsset.aspx?id=21474839738

The Genesee River

Adamski, J. (2020). A River Runs through It—The Genesee. *Life in the Finger Lakes.* www.lifeinthefingerlakes.com/a-river-runs-through-it

Anderson, M.L.H. (1956). *Genesee Echoes: The Upper Gorge and Falls Area from the Days of the Pioneers.* Dansville, NY: F.A. Owen Publishing Company.

Multi-Resolution Land Characteristics Consortium. (2016). National Land Cover Database (NLCD) Land Cover (CONUS) [GIS data file]. www.mrlc.gov/viewer

Conheady, M., Lucero, K., and Champlin, M. (2021). *Letchworth Waterfall List.* NYFalls. https://nyfalls.com/waterfalls/letchworth/waterfall-locations

Ensminger, S. A. (2016). *Letchworth State Park Waterfall Locations with GPS Data*. Western New York Waterfall Survey. http://falzguy.com/letchworth-wf-tabel.html

Ensminger, S. A., and Bassett D. K. (2016). *A Waterfall Guide to Letchworth State Park*. Raleigh, NC: Lulu Press.

NYS Office of Parks, Recreation and Historic Preservation. (n.d.). [Interpretive Signs throughout Letchworth State Park]. Castile, New York.

Perham, R. E. (1988). *Elements of Floating-Debris Control Systems* (Technical Report REMR-HY-3). U.S. Department of the Army. https://apps.dtic.mil/sti/pdfs/ADA200454.pdf

USGS. (2020). National Hydrography Dataset 20200218 for New York State or Territory FileGDB 10.1 Model Version 2.2.1 [GIS data file]. https://apps.nationalmap.gov/downloader/#

USGS 04224000 Mount Morris Lake Near Mount Morris NY. (2021). USGS National Water Information System. https://waterdata.usgs.gov/nwis/dv?referred_module=sw&site_no=04224000

Vandas, S. J., Winter, T. C., and Battaglin, W. A. (2002). *Water and the Environment* (AGI Environmental Awareness Series, 5). American Geological Institute. www.agiweb.org/environment/publications/water.pdf

Chapter 3: Human History

Introduction

Allegany County Historical Society. (n.d.). Maps. Allegany County Historical Society. http://gallery.allegany-history.org/album/Maps/Timeline

Amrhein, C. (n.d.). Wyoming County Towns. Document provided by the Wyoming County Historian's Office.

Anderson, M.L.H. (1956). *Genesee Echoes: The Upper Gorge and Falls Area from the Days of the Pioneers*. Dansville, NY: F.A. Owen Publishing Company.

Bartlett, T. (2002). *The Glen Iris Inn: Walking Tour Companion*. Perry, NY: Perry Herald.

Breslin, T. A., Cook, T. S., Judkins, R. A., and Richens, T. C. (2008). *Letchworth State Park: Images of America series*. Charleston, SC: Arcadia Publishing.

Brown, P. J. (1853). *Map of Wyoming County, New York: From Actual Surveys* [Map]. Philadelphia, PA: Newel S. Brown. www.loc.gov/item/2008627968

Chao, M. (2015, April 1). Letchworth State Park No. 1 with *USA Today* readers. *Democrat and Chronicle / USA Today*. www.usatoday.com/story/news/local/2015/04/01/letchworth-state-park-no-1-with-usa-today-readers/70777950

Cook, T. S. (2015). *The Civilian Conservation Corps in Letchworth State Park: Images of America series*. Charleston, SC: Arcadia Publishing.

Cook, T. S., and Breslin, T. A. (2000). Exploring Letchworth Park History. http://letchworthparkhistory.com/table.html

Decennial Census of Population and Housing—By Decade. (2021). United States Census Bureau. www.census.gov/programs-surveys/decennial-census/decade.html

Doty, L. L. (1876). *A History of Livingston County, New York*. Geneseo, NY: Edward E. Doty.

Genesee Valley Flint Knappers Association, Inc. (n.d.) In *Facebook* [Group page]. www.facebook.com/ GeneseeValleyFlintKnappersAssociationInc

History of Mount Morris Dam. (n.d.) U.S. Army Corps of Engineers Buffalo District. www.lrb.usace.army.mil/ Missions/Recreation/Mount-Morris-Dam/Project-History

History of Wyoming County, NY. (1880). New York: F.W. Beers and Co.

Humphrey Nature Center at Letchworth. (n.d.). NYS Office of Parks, Recreation and Historic Preservation. https://parks.ny.gov/environment/nature-centers/19/details.aspx

Kim E. K. (2015, February 20). Arctic Weather Transforms New York Fountain into Growing "Ice Volcano." *NBC Today*. www.today.com/news/arctic-weather-transforms-new-york-fountain-growing-ice-volcano-t4341

Letchworth Arts and Crafts Show and Sale. (2021). Arts Council for Wyoming County. https://artswyco.org/ lacs/overview.html

Letchworth Red, White and Blue Balloon Festival. (n.d.). In *Facebook* [Group page]. www.facebook.com/ groups/167362823622622

McDermott, M. M. (2018, January 24). Letchworth State Park's Iconic Trestle Bridge over Genesee River Is Being Torn Down. *Democrat and Chronicle*. www.democratandchronicle.com/story/news/2018/01/24/ letchworth-state-park-bridge-being-dismantled/1047921001

National Park Service. (2021). *National Register Database and Research*. National Register of Historic Places. www.nps.gov/subjects/nationalregister/database-research.htm#table

NYS Office of Information Technology Services GIS Program Office. (2020). NYS Address Points [GIS data file]. http://gis.ny.gov/gisdata/inventories/details.cfm?DSID=921

NYS Office of Parks, Recreation and Historic Preservation. (n.d.). [Interpretive signs throughout Letchworth State Park]. Castile, New York.

NYS Office of Parks, Recreation and Historic Preservation GIS Bureau. (2020). Infrastructure [GIS data file]. Obtained via a NYS Freedom of Information Law request at https://openfoil.ny.gov/#/newfoilrequest.

NYS Office of Parks, Recreation and Historic Preservation. (2003). *Letchworth State Park National Register of Historic Places Registration Form*. NPS Form 10-900. www.nps.gov/subjects/nationalregister/database-research.htm#table

Rea and Otley. (1852). *Map of Livingston County, New York: From Actual Surveys* [Map]. Philadelphia, PA: Smith and Gillett. www.loc.gov/item/2013593275

Seaver, J. E. (1824). *A Narrative of the Life of Mrs. Mary Jemison*. Canandaigua, NY: J.D. Bemis and Co.

United States Census Bureau. (1820). *United States Census, 1820* [Database]. www.familysearch.org/search/ collection/1803955

United States Census Bureau. (1840). *United States Census, 1840* [Database]. www.familysearch.org/search/ collection/1786457

Westgard, A. L., and Barthel, O. (1902). *New Century Atlas of Livingston County, New York*. Philadelphia, PA: Century Map Company.

Westgard, A. L., and McClure, J. O. (1902). *New Century Atlas of Wyoming County, New York*. Philadelphia, PA: Century Map Company.

Whitford, N. E. (1906). *History of the Canal System of the State of New York: Together with Brief Histories of the Canals of the United States and Canada* (Volume 1). Albany, NY: Brandow Printing Company.

Arrowsmith, A., and Lewis, S. (1804). *A New and Elegant General Atlas*. Philadelphia, PA: John Conrad and Co. https://mapgeeks.org/newyork/#Arrowsmiths_1804_Atlas_Map_of_New_York

Bien, J. R. (1895). *Atlas of the State of New York*. New York: Julius Bien and Company. www.davidrumsey.com

Breslin, T. A., and Cook, T. S. (2000). *Mary Jemison's Timeline*. Exploring Letchworth Park History. www.letchworthparkhistory.com/mjtimeline.html

Burr, D. H. (1829). *An Atlas of the State of New York*. New York: David H. Burr. www.davidrumsey.com/

Canadian Archaeological Radiocarbon Database. (2021). *Samples* [Data file]. www.canadianarchaeology.ca/samples

Cook, T. S., and Breslin, T. A. (2000). Exploring Letchworth Park History. http://letchworthparkhistory.com/table.html

Doty, L. L. (1876). *A History of Livingston County, New York*. Geneseo, NY: Edward E. Doty.

Engelbrecht, W. (2005). *Iroquoia: The Development of a Native World*. Syracuse, NY: Syracuse University Press.

Granger, Jr., J. E. (1978). *Anthropological Papers, Museum of Anthropology, University of Michigan: 65. Meadowood Phase Settlement Pattern in the Niagara Frontier Region of Western New York State*. Ann Arbor: University of Michigan.

Hasenstab, R. J. (1987). Canoes, Caches, and Carrying Places: Territorial Boundaries and Tribalization in Late Woodland Western New York. *The Bulletin: Journal of the New York State Archaeological Association 95*: 39–49.

Hauptmann, L. M. (2001). *Conspiracy of Interests: Iroquois Dispossession and the Rise of New York State*. Syracuse, NY: Syracuse University Press.

Howard, S. P. (2010). *Northeastern Middle Woodland, from the Perspective of the Upper Allegheny Valley*. Doctoral dissertation, The Ohio State University, Columbus, Ohio. OhioLINK Electronic Theses and Dissertations Center.

Johnson, E. (1807). *The Survey Bill of a Tract of Land Granted to Garrett Cottringer by Robert Morris, Esquire* [Land survey notes]. Wyoming County Historian's Office, Warsaw, New York.

Jordan, K. A. (2004). Seneca Iroquois Settlement Pattern, Community Structure, and Housing, 1677–1779. *Northeast Anthropology 67*: 23–60.

Jordan, K. A. (2008). *The Seneca Restoration, 1715–1754: An Iroquois Local Political Economy*. Gainesville: University Press of Florida.

Kirkland, S. (1791, October 15). Census of the Six Nations [Government record]. Hamilton College Library Digital Collections, Samuel Kirkland Collection (Kirkland 140a), Hamilton, NY. https://sparc.hamilton.edu/islandora/object/hamLibSparc%3A12354282#page/1/mode/1up

Kocik, C. A. (2017). The Edges of Wood: Dendrochronological Analysis of Three Seneca Iroquois Log Structures at Letchworth State Park, New York. *Historical Archaeology 51*: 194–217.

Laub, R. S. (2012). A Hiscock Primer. *Proceedings of the Rochester Academy of Science 20*(1): 2–9. www.rasny.org/Publications/Laub.Online%20version1.7.12-2.pdf

Morgan, L. H. (1851). *Map of Ho-De-No-Sau-Nee-Ga: Or the Territories of the People of the Long House in 1720* [Map]. www.loc.gov/item/2019585091

NYS Office of Parks, Recreation and Historic Preservation. (2003). *Letchworth State Park National Register of Historic Places Registration Form.* NPS Form 10-900. www.nps.gov/subjects/nationalregister/database-research.htm#table

NYS Office of Parks, Recreation and Historic Preservation GIS Bureau. (2020). Archaeological Sites in New York State [GIS data file]. Obtained via email request from the NYS Office of Parks, Recreation and Historic Preservation.

Parker, A. C. (1920). *The Archeological History of New York.* Albany, NY: SUNY Press.

Parker, A. C. (1926). *Skunny Wundy and Other Indian Tales.* New York: George H. Doran Company.

Pendergast, J. F. (1994). The Kakouagoga or Kahkwas: An Iroquoian nation destroyed in the Niagara Region. *Proceedings of the American Philosophical Society 138*(1): 96–144.

Porter, A. (1798). *Map of the Indian Reservation at Gardeau* [Map]. www.iroquoisgenealogysociety.org/map-gallery

Porter, A. (1799). *Indian Reservation at Squawky-hill* [sic] [Map]. www.iroquoisgenealogysociety.org/map-gallery

Ritchie, W. A. (1938). *Research Records of the Rochester Museum of Arts and Sciences Division of Anthropology: 4. Certain Recently Explored New York Mounds and Their Probable Relation to the Hopewell Culture.* Rochester, NY: Rochester Museum of Arts and Sciences.

Ritchie, W. A. (1965). *The Archaeology of New York State.* Garden City, NY: The Natural History Press.

Ryan, B. (2017). *Crowding the Banks: The Historical Archaeology of Ohagi and the Post-Revolutionary Haudenosaunee Confederacy, Ca. 1780–1826.* Doctoral dissertation, Cornell University, Ithaca, New York. Cornell University Library eCommons.

Turner, O. (1852). *History of the Pioneer Settlement of Phelps and Gorham's Purchase, and Morris Reserve.* Rochester, NY: William Alling.

Settlement before Park Creation (circa 1790 to 1910)

Atack, J. (2016). Historical Geographic Information Systems (GIS) database of U.S. Railroads [GIS data file]. https://my.vanderbilt.edu/jeremyatack/data-downloads

Bien, J. R. (1895). *Atlas of the State of New York.* New York: Julius Bien and Company. www.davidrumsey.com

Brackney, W. H. (2000). *Letchworth, William Pryor.* American National Biography. www.anb.org/view/10.1093/anb/9780198606697.001.0001/anb-9780198606697-e-1500408

Breslin, T. A. (2000). *Gibsonville: An Early Village on Silver Lake Outlet.* Exploring Letchworth Park History. www.letchworthparkhistory.com/gibson.html

Breslin, T. A. (2000). *St. Helena: 1797–1954.* Exploring Letchworth Park History. www.letchworthparkhistory.com/sthe.html

Breslin, T. A., Cook, T. S., Judkins, R. A., and Richens, T. C. (2008). *Letchworth State Park: Images of America series.* Charleston, SC: Arcadia Publishing.

Brown, P. J. (1853). *Map of Wyoming County, New York: From Actual Surveys* [Map]. Philadelphia, PA: Newel S. Brown. www.loc.gov/item/2008627968

Cook, T. S., and Breslin, T. A. (2000). Exploring Letchworth Park History. http://letchworthparkhistory.com/table.html

Hough, F. B. (1857). *Census of the State of New-York, for 1855*. Albany, NY: Charles Van Benthuysen. www.nysl.nysed.gov/scandocs/nyscensus.htm

Kipp, D. L. (1999). *Locking the Heights: The Rise and Demise of the Genesee Valley Canal.*

Larned, J. N. (1912). *The Life and Work of William Pryor Letchworth: Student and Minister of Public Benevolence*. Boston: Houghton Mifflin Company. https://archive.org/details/lifeworkofwillia00larn

Lenski, L. (1941). Forward. In L. Lenski, *Indian Captive: The Story of Mary Jemison* (xi–xvii). Philadelphia, PA: J. B. Lippincott Co.

Manson, S., Schroeder, J., Van Riper, D., Kugler, T., and Ruggles, S. (2020). IPUMS National Historical Geographic Information System: Version 15.0 [GIS data file]. IPUMS. https://data2.nhgis.org/main

NYS Office of Parks, Recreation and Historic Preservation. (2003). *Letchworth State Park National Register of Historic Places Registration Form*. NPS Form 10-900. www.nps.gov/subjects/nationalregister/database-research.htm#table

Palmer, R. (1999). Remembering the Genesee Valley Canal. *The Crooked Lake Review*. www.crookedlakereview.com/articles/101_135/111spring1999/111palmer.html

Rea and Otley. (1852). *Map of Livingston County, New York: From Actual Surveys* [Map]. Philadelphia, PA: Smith and Gillett. www.loc.gov/item/2013593275

Seaver, J. E. (1824). *A Narrative of the Life of Mrs. Mary Jemison*. Canandaigua, NY: J.D. Bemis and Co.

United States Department of Homeland Security. (2020). Homeland Infrastructure Foundation-Level Data (HIFLD): Railroads [GIS data file]. https://hifld-geoplatform.opendata.arcgis.com/datasets/geoplatform::railroads/about

Westgard, A. L., and Barthel, O. (1902). *New Century Atlas of Livingston County, New York*. Philadelphia, PA: Century Map Company.

Westgard, A. L., and McClure, J. O. (1902). *New Century Atlas of Wyoming County, New York*. Philadelphia, PA: Century Map Company.

Whitford, N. E. (1906). *History of the Canal System of the State of New York: Together with Brief Histories of the Canals of the United States and Canada* (Volume 1). Albany, NY: Brandow Printing Company.

The William P. Letchworth Era (circa 1860 to 1910)

Anderson, M.L.H. (1956). *Genesee Echoes: The Upper Gorge and Falls Area from the Days of the Pioneers*. Dansville, NY: F.A. Owen Publishing Company.

Breslin, T. A. (2015). *Building the Glen Iris Estate*. Exploring Letchworth Park History. www.letchworthparkhistory.com/landacquisitiontab.html

Breslin, T. A., Cook, T. S., Judkins, R. A., and Richens, T. C. (2008). *Letchworth State Park: Images of America series*. Charleston, SC: Arcadia Publishing.

Cook, T. S. (2000). *The Council Grounds*. Exploring Letchworth Park History.

Cook, T. S., and Breslin, T. A. (2000). Exploring Letchworth Park History. http://letchworthparkhistory.com/table.html

Documents of the Assembly of the State of New York, One Hundred and Thirty-Fifth Session, Volume 26, no. 41 (1912). Albany, NY: The Argus Company.

Hall, E. H. (1907). *Letchworth Park* [Map]. 1:4,572. Scanned PDF file version provided by Letchworth State Park Engineering Department.

Larned, J. N. (1912). *The Life and Work of William Pryor Letchworth: Student and Minister of Public Benevolence*. Boston: Houghton Mifflin Company. https://archive.org/details/lifeworkofwillia00larn

NYS Office of Parks, Recreation and Historic Preservation. (2003). *Letchworth State Park National Register of Historic Places Registration Form*. NPS Form 10-900. www.nps.gov/subjects/nationalregister/database-research.htm#table

After Park Creation (circa 1910 until present)

Bailey, J. F., Patterson, J. L., and Paulhus, J.L.H. (1975). *Hurricane Agnes Rainfall and Floods, June–July 1972 (Geological Survey Professional Paper 924)*. USGS and NOAA. Washington, DC: United States Government Printing Office. https://pubs.usgs.gov/pp/0924/report.pdf

Breslin, T. A., Cook, T. S., Judkins, R. A., and Richens, T. C. (2008). *Letchworth State Park: Images of America series*. Charleston, SC: Arcadia Publishing.

Breslin, T. A., and Cook, T. S. (2004). *The Glen Iris Threatened: The Portageville Dam Project*. Exploring Letchworth Park History. http://letchworthparkhistory.com/portagedam.html

Cook, T. S. (2001). *The St. Helena Cemetery*. Exploring Letchworth Park History. www.letchworthparkhistory.com/StHelenacem.html

Cook, T. S. (2015). *The Civilian Conservation Corps in Letchworth State Park: Images of America Series*. Charleston, SC: Arcadia Publishing.

Cook, T. S., and Breslin, T. A. (2000). Exploring Letchworth Park History. http://letchworthparkhistory.com/table.html

Genesee River Protection Act of 1989, 16 U.S.C. § 1276 (November 27, 1989). https://uscode.house.gov/statutes/pl/101/175.pdf

Genesee State Park Commission. (1976). *Letchworth State Park Master Property Map* [Map]. 1:12,000. Castile, NY: Genesee State Park Commission. Scanned PDF file version provided by Letchworth State Park Engineering Department.

History of Mount Morris Dam. (n.d.) U.S. Army Corps of Engineers Buffalo District. www.lrb.usace.army.mil/Missions/Recreation/Mount-Morris-Dam/Project-History

Levenson, J. (2019, December 22). Innovative thinking at Mount Morris Dam saves taxpayers' time and money. *U.S. Army*. www.army.mil/article/231293/innovative_thinking_at_mount_morris_dam_saves_taxpayers_time_and_money

Mount Morris Dam and Recreational Area, Livingston County, New York (2011, February 28). U.S. Army Corps of Engineers. https://web.archive.org/web/20110807135412/www.lrb.usace.army.mil/WhoWeAre/MMD/MMD.html

NOAA National Centers for Environmental Information. (2020). Climate Data Online daily summaries by year, 1972 [Data file]. https://www1.ncdc.noaa.gov/pub/data/ghcn/daily/by_year

NOAA National Centers for Environmental Information. (2020). International Best Track Archive for Climate Stewardship (IBTrACS) [GIS data file]. www.ncdc.noaa.gov/ibtracs/index.php?name=ib-v4-access

NYS Office of Parks, Recreation and Historic Preservation. (2003). *Letchworth State Park National Register of Historic Places Registration Form*. NPS Form 10-900. www.nps.gov/subjects/nationalregister/database-research.htm#table

NYS Office of Parks, Recreation and Historic Preservation. (2011). OPRHP—Genesee Region—Land Acquisition [Data file]. Provided by Letchworth State Park Engineering Department.

U.S. Department of the Interior National Park Service and State of New York Genesee State Park Commission. (1937). Letchworth State Park Base Map [Map]. Provided by Letchworth State Park Engineering Department.

USDA. (1938). [Aerial photographs]. Provided by the Livingston County Soil and Water Conservation District, Geneseo, New York.

USDA Farm Service Agency Aerial Photography Field Office. (2019). National Agricultural Imagery Program Ortho County Mosaic [GIS data file]. https://datagateway.nrcs.usda.gov/GDGHome_DirectDownLoad.aspx

USGS 04224000 Mount Morris Lake Near Mount Morris NY. (2021). USGS National Water Information System. https://waterdata.usgs.gov/nwis/dv?referred_module=sw&site_no=04224000

Whitney-Graham Co., Inc. (1935). *Guide Map of Letchworth Park, State of New York* [Map]. Buffalo, NY: Whitney-Graham Co., Inc. www.letchworthparkhistory.com/1935map.html

Chapter 4: Tourism

Introduction

Manapol, N., and Archie, M. (2017). 2017 Visitor Survey [Data file]. Letchworth Gateway Villages Initiative. Obtained via email request.

Manapol, N., and Archie M. (2018). *2017 Visitor Survey: Summary of Findings and Strategic Directions*. Letchworth Gateway Villages Initiative. www.letchworthgatewayvillages.org/insights

National Park Visitor Spending Generates Economic Impact of More Than $41 Billion. (2020, June 11). *Interior Press* (United States Department of Interior). www.doi.gov/pressreleases/national-park-visitor-spending-generates-economic-impact-more-41-billion

Visitation

About the Adirondack Park. (2021). Adirondack Council. www.adirondackcouncil.org/page/the-adirondack-park-19.html

American Scenic and Historic Preservation Society. (1918). *Twenty-Third Annual Report of the American Scenic and Historic Preservation Society*. Albany, NY: J.B. Lyon Company. www.google.com/books/edition/Annual_Report_of_the_American_Scenic_and/P3kIAQAAMAAJ?hl=en&gbpv=0

Arthur, Andy. (2018). Catskill Park Boundaries [GIS data file]. https://andyarthur.org/kml-maps-catskill-park-boundaries.html

Best State Park: Letchworth State Park Wins Readers' Choice. (2015). *USA Today*. www.10best.com/awards/travel/best-state-park

Bnbfinder.com (2021). www.bnbfinder.com/s/New-York-State--USA-Bed-And-Breakfast

Canedo, C. (2019, May 21). The Tragic History of Letchworth State Park: Fatal Accidents, Disasters, More. *New York Upstate*. www.newyorkupstate.com/western-ny/2016/06/letchworth_state_park_deaths_fatal_accidents_tragic_history.html

Cascade House. (1886–1904). Guestbook, June 1886–July 1904 (Volumes 1 and 2) [Data file]. Portage, New York. Provided by Livingston County Historian's Office, Mount Morris, New York.

Chao, M. (2015, April 1). Letchworth State Park No. 1 with *USA Today* readers. *Democrat and Chronicle / USA Today*. www.usatoday.com/story/news/local/2015/04/01/letchworth-state-park-no-1-with-usa-today-readers/70777950

Curran, E. J. (2019, February 14). 20 Wild and Beautiful U.S. State Parks. *National Geographic*. www.nationalgeographic.com/travel/article/state-parks-worth-the-trip

Gentile, J. (2021, February 4). The 30 Best State Parks in America. *Thrillist*. www.thrillist.com/travel/nation/best-us-state-parks-to-visit-na-pali-coast-state-park

Google. (n.d.). [Searches for accommodations near Letchworth State Park]. www.google.com/maps

Google. (n.d.). Letchworth State Park (State Park in New York State) Interest by Subregion, 1/1/2004 to 12/31/2019 [Data file]. https://trends.google.com/trends/?geo=US

Hotels.com (2019). www.hotels.com

Humphrey Nature Center. (2018). Guestbook. Letchworth State Park, Castile, New York.

Kim E. K. (2015, February 20). Arctic Weather Transforms New York Fountain into Growing "Ice Volcano." *NBC Today*. www.today.com/news/arctic-weather-transforms-new-york-fountain-growing-ice-volcano-t4341

Letchworth State Park. (2020). TripAdvisor. www.tripadvisor.com/Attraction_Review-g47421-d123127-Reviews-Letchworth_State_Park-Castile_New_York.html

Letchworth State Park, New York—Camping and Reservations. (2019). Reserve America. www.reserveamerica.com/explore/letchworth-state-park/NY/375/overview

Manapol, N., and Archie, M. (2017). 2017 Visitor Survey [Data file]. Letchworth Gateway Villages Initiative. Obtained via email request.

Manapol, N., and Archie M. (2018). *2017 Visitor Survey: Summary of Findings and Strategic Directions*. Letchworth Gateway Villages Initiative. www.letchworthgatewayvillages.org/insights

Natural Earth. (2018). Lakes + Reservoirs, Version 3.2.0 [GIS data file]. 1:10,000,000. www.naturalearthdata.com/downloads/10m-physical-vectors/10m-lakes

National Park Service. (2021). Annual Visitation Report by Years: 2010 to 2020 [Data file]. National Park Service Integrated Resource Management Applications (IRMA) Portal. https://irma.nps.gov/STATS

National Park Service. (2021). *National Register Database and Research*. National Register of Historic Places. www.nps.gov/subjects/nationalregister/database-research.htm#table

National Park Service Land Resources Division. (2019). NPS—Land Resources Division Boundary and Tract Data Service [GIS data file]. www.arcgis.com/home/group.html?id=00f2977287f74c79aad558708e3b6649#overview

NYS Office of Parks, Recreation and Historic Preservation. (2003). *Letchworth State Park National Register of Historic Places Registration Form*. NPS Form 10-900. www.nps.gov/subjects/nationalregister/database-research.htm#table

NYS Office of Parks, Recreation and Historic Preservation. (2020). *State Park Annual Attendance Figures by Facility: Beginning 2003* [Data file]. https://data.ny.gov/Recreation/State-Park-Annual-Attendance-Figures-by-Facility-B/8f3n-xj78/data

Peglar, T. (2019, November 5). How Many People Fall in the Grand Canyon? *Outside*. www.mygrandcanyonpark.com/park/faqs/falling-to-death-grand-canyon

Poisson, J. (2011, August 15). Student Swept over Niagara Falls. *The Toronto Star*. www.thestar.com/news/gta/2011/08/15/student_swept_over_niagara_falls.html

Reserve America (2019). www.reserveamerica.com

Rielly, K., Collier, J., and Masle, L. (2014). *Adirondacks, USA*. Regional Office of Sustainable Tourism/Lake Placid CVB. www.roostadk.com/wp-content/uploads/2014/08/AdksusaMediaKit1.pdf

Tampone, K. (2020, March 16). Cuomo Briefing: Park Fees Waived, News for Local Government Workers. Syracuse.com. www.syracuse.com/coronavirus/2020/03/cuomo-briefing-park-fees-waived-news-for-local-government-workers.html

Tulowiecki, S. J. (2021). *Letchworth State Park Usage Survey* [Unpublished raw data]. SUNY Geneseo, New York.

WBFO Staff. (2018, February 19). State Park Police Rescue Couple and Two Dogs from Letchworth Gorge. *WBFO*. https://news.wbfo.org/post/state-park-police-rescue-couple-and-two-dogs-letchworth-gorge

WGRZ Staff. (2020, February 24). Body Found in Letchworth State Park. *WGRZ*. www.wgrz.com/article/news/local/body-found-in-letchworth-state-park/71-b253d58c-e88c-4744-9c17-f902dca2e7fd

William P. Letchworth Museum. (2018). Guestbook. Letchworth State Park, Castile, New York.

Activities

Bird Conservation Areas. (n.d.). NYS Office of Parks, Recreation and Historic Preservation. https://parks.ny.gov/environment/bird-conservation-areas.aspx

Deer and Bear Harvests. (2021). NYS Department of Environmental Conservation. www.dec.ny.gov/outdoor/42232.html

eBird. (2020). eBird Basic Dataset. Version: EBD_relOct-2020 [Data file]. Cornell Lab of Ornithology, Ithaca, New York. https://ebird.org/data/download/ebd

Fishing Warmwaters in Western New York. (n.d.). NYS Department of Environmental Conservation. www.dec.ny.gov/outdoor/26987.html

Geocaching.com. (2020). www.geocaching.com/play/search

Google. (n.d.). [Search for "Letchworth State Park" in Google Images.] https://images.google.com

Important Bird Areas: Letchworth State Park. (n.d.). Audubon. www.audubon.org/important-bird-areas/letchworth-state-park

Livingston County Sheriff. (2020). Cleared Search Call Results [Data file]. Obtained via Livingston County, NY FOIL Request at www.livingstoncounty.us/FormCenter/Administration-4/FOIL-Freedom-of-Information-Law-REQUEST-121

NYS Department of Environmental Conservation. (2020). Fish Stocking Lists (Actual): Beginning 2011 [Data file]. https://data.ny.gov/Recreation/Fish-Stocking-Lists-Actual-Beginning-2011/e52k-ymww/data

NYS Office of Parks, Recreation and Historic Preservation. (2019). *Deer Hunting Map: Letchworth State Park (North Section)* [Map]. Castile, NY: NYS Office of Parks, Recreation and Historic Preservation Genesee State Park Region. https://parks.ny.gov/documents/parks/LetchworthDeerHuntingMap-North.pdf

NYS Office of Parks, Recreation and Historic Preservation. (2019). *Deer Hunting Map: Letchworth State Park (South Section)* [Map]. Castile, NY: NYS Office of Parks, Recreation and Historic Preservation Genesee State Park Region. https://parks.ny.gov/documents/parks/LetchworthDeerHuntingMap-South.pdf

NYS Office of Parks, Recreation and Historic Preservation GIS Bureau. (2019). *Letchworth State Park (North Section)* [Map]. Albany, NY: NYS Office of Parks, Recreation and Historic Preservation GIS Bureau. https://parks.ny.gov/documents/parks/LetchworthTrailMapNorth.pdf

NYS Office of Parks, Recreation and Historic Preservation GIS Bureau. (2019). *Letchworth State Park (South Section)* [Map]. Albany, NY: NYS Office of Parks, Recreation and Historic Preservation GIS Bureau. https://parks.ny.gov/documents/parks/LetchworthTrailMapSouth.pdf

NYS Office of Parks, Recreation and Historic Preservation GIS Bureau. (2020). Infrastructure [GIS data file]. Obtained via a NYS Freedom of Information Law request at https://openfoil.ny.gov/#/newfoilrequest.

Quackenstein Graphic Design Co. (2019). *Letchworth State Park* [Map]. Castile, NY: NYS Office of Parks, Recreation and Historic Preservation. https://issuu.com/quackenstein/docs/letchworth_map

Smith, K. (2017, December 22). Hunter Gets Massive Black Bear in Letchworth State Park. *WHAM.* https://13wham.com/news/local/hunter-gets-massive-black-bear-in-letchworth-state-park

Thomee, B., Shamma, D. A., Friedland, G., Elizalde, B., Ni, K., Poland, D., Borth, D., and Li, L.-J. (2016). YFCC100M: The New Data in Multimedia Research. *Communications of the ACM 59*(2): 64–73.

Wyoming County Sheriff. (2020). 911 incidents [Data file]. Obtained via email request to Sheriff Gregory Rudolph, Wyoming County, New York.

Yahoo! Flickr. (2015). Yahoo Flickr Creative Commons 100 Million (YFCC100m) dataset [Data file]. http://projects.dfki.uni-kl.de/yfcc100m

Software Used for Creating Maps and Processing Sata

Esri Inc. (2019). *ArcMap* (Version 10.7.1). https://desktop.arcgis.com/en/arcmap

Esri Inc. (2020). *ArcGIS Pro* (Version 2.6.0). www.esri.com/en-us/arcgis/products/arcgis-pro/overview

Microsoft Corporation. (2016). *Microsoft Excel.* https://office.microsoft.com/excel

QGIS Development Team. (2019). QGIS Geographic Information System (Version 3.10.0). QGIS Association. https://qgis.org/en/site

R Core Team (2020). *R: A language and environment for statistical computing.* R Foundation for Statistical Computing, Vienna, Austria. www.R-project.org

RStudio Team (2020). RStudio: Integrated Development for R. RStudio, PBC, Boston, Massachusetts. www.rstudio.com

About the Author

Stephen J. Tulowiecki is an associate professor of geography and sustainability studies at the State University of New York at Geneseo. He teaches courses in geographic information systems, and his research studies forests of the eastern United States. An avid hiker, he currently resides in Caledonia, New York (twenty-five minutes from Letchworth State Park), with his wife Grace and son Jonah.